C000127242

THE PEOPLE'S VICTORY

THE
PEOPLE'S
VICTORY

HOW **MALAYSIANS** **SAVED** THEIR **COUNTRY**

Kee Thuan Chye

Marshall Cavendish
Editions

© 2019 Kee Thuan Chye

Published by Marshall Cavendish Editions
An imprint of Marshall Cavendish International

A member of the
Times Publishing Group

All rights reserved

No part of this publication may be reproduced, stored in a retrieval system or
transmitted, in any form or by any means, electronic, mechanical, photocopying,
recording or otherwise, without the prior permission of the copyright owner.
Requests for permission should be addressed to the Publisher, Marshall Cavendish
International (Asia) Private Limited, 1 New Industrial Road, Singapore 536196.
Tel: (65) 6213 9300. E-mail: genref@sg.marshallcavendish.com
Website: www.marshallcavendish.com/genref

The publisher makes no representation or warranties with respect to the contents of this
book, and specifically disclaims any implied warranties or merchantability or fitness for
any particular purpose, and shall in no event be liable for any loss of profit or any other
commercial damage, including but not limited to special, incidental, consequential, or
other damages. The publisher states that the printer was engaged solely to provide
full printing, binding and delivery services for the book and is not responsible for the
contents of the book.

Other Marshall Cavendish Offices
Marshall Cavendish Corporation. 99 White Plains Road, Tarrytown NY 10591-9001,
USA • Marshall Cavendish International (Thailand) Co Ltd. 253 Asoke, 12th Flr,
Sukhumvit 21 Road, Klongtoey Nua, Wattana, Bangkok 10110, Thailand • Marshall
Cavendish (Malaysia) Sdn Bhd, Times Subang, Lot 46, Subang Hi-Tech Industrial Park,
Batu Tiga, 40000 Shah Alam, Selangor Darul Ehsan, Malaysia

Marshall Cavendish is a registered trademark of Times Publishing Limited

National Library Board, Singapore Cataloguing-in-Publication Data

Name(s): Kee, Thuan Chye, 1954-
Title: The people's victory : how Malaysians saved their country / Kee Thuan Chye.
Description: First edition. | Singapore : Marshall Cavendish, [2018]
Identifier(s): OCN 1056702101 | ISBN 978-981-48-2884-0 (paperback)
Subject(s): LCSH: Elections--Malaysia--21st century. | Malaysia--Politics and
government--21st century. | Government accountability--Malaysia. | Political
corruption--Malaysia.
Classification: DDC 320.9595--dc23

Printed in Malaysia

This book is dedicated to my wife,
Lim Choy Wan,

and my children,
Soraya Sunitra Kee Xiang Yin
and
Jebat Arjuna Kee Jia Liang,

Lim Jack Kin
and all those of his generation
who represent the hope and future of Malaysia

the comrades for change who protested in the sun and rain,
stood up to tear gas and water cannons,
were harassed by the police and even arrested,
helped out in any way they could,

and, above all,
the Malaysian people who voted for change
for without them, there would not have been
a people's victory.

CONTENTS

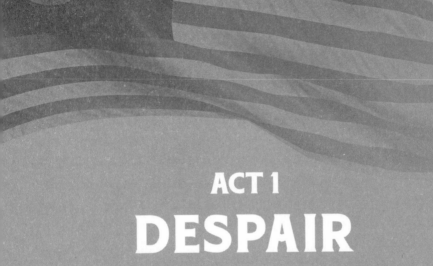

ACT 1
DESPAIR

THIS IS THE TIME!

On May 5, 2013, hopes ran high that by the end of the day Malaysia would have a change of government. Even before polling stations opened at 8am, throngs of voters were already queuing up, many of them eager to make that happen.

This was the day they had been waiting for, five years after the watershed 12th general election (GE12) in 2008 when the Opposition pact stunned Barisan Nasional (BN) by denying the incumbent ruling coalition its customary two-thirds majority in Parliament and capturing five of the 11 state governments in Peninsular Malaysia.

Now, with the Opposition having exposed the once-mighty BN's vulnerability and also unified itself as an entity going by the name of Pakatan Rakyat (PR), or The People's Pact, it looked ready to take over the federal government at this 13th general election (GE13). Malaysians disgruntled with the ruling coalition felt cheered.

BN had ruled for 56 years since the country attained independence from the British in 1957. Its brand of politics had come to be dictated more strongly than ever before by its dominant party, the United Malays National Organisation (Umno), which had become self-serving, arrogant, divisive and corrupt. This had compromised the ability of the other component parties in the coalition to function as effectively as they should.

With Umno firmly in command, BN had turned out to be indecisive in its administration, lavish in its spending, indifferent to racial harmony, oppressive in its exercise of power, and more. If the coalition were to be allowed to stay in government, the outlook for the next five years could be unbearably bleak. It was time to vote the whole lot out.

"*Ini kalilah!*" roared the change-seekers at PR's campaign stumps, asserting that this was the time to do it. They would turn up by the thousands at many of these *ceramahs* (rallies) to show solidarity, listen to the speeches and feel uplifted, convinced that the Opposition could win.

At Gelang Patah, one of the constituencies in the southern state of Johor, as many as 70,000 people swarmed the car park of a shopping mall on May 1, blowing vuvuzelas and cheering the PR leaders who spoke. Two nights later, an unprecedented 100,000 people filled up the Esplanade in Penang, shouting "*ubah!*" (change), breaking all records of rally attendances.

When a PR politician on stage shouted, "*Ini kalilah!*", the supporters yelled back, "Change the government!" The camaraderie was powerful; campaigners and supporters were in sync.

Outside of the hustings, calls for change resounded on social media, but it was not all just talk. Individuals and groups reinforced it by taking action.

They organised events to help PR parties raise funds, influenced fence-sitters to attend PR rallies, mobilised friends to sign up and be trained to be polling agents for PR candidates for election day. They helped to indirectly campaign against BN by circulating e-mails exposing BN's excesses, corruption and abuse of power, or by posting comments on media websites condemning in strong language the incompetence and the lies of government ministers.

On Facebook, like-minded ones adopted as their profile photos the *ubah* hornbill mascot (launched by one of PR's component parties), as if giving themselves a group identity as comrades for the same cause. Those with more resources created and produced short videos to spread the message of change in a more direct and effective way.

'Remember to *ubah*, ya?'
The comrades for change were frank about the side they would vote for and

had no qualms about declaring it openly. They rebuffed the maxim about keeping their vote secret and proudly stated their stand to get others to join their cause or engage in communion with fellow Opposition supporters, even if they were strangers.

Once, I was in a taxi going home from the airport when the driver and I started talking about politics. As the elections were coming up, it seemed the natural thing to do. I was not surprised that the driver complained about the Government. Actually, he did most of the talking as he spoke out against the cash handouts the Government was dispensing, obviously to buy votes; the bias the Election Commission (EC) was showing towards BN although it was supposed to be neutral and independent; the awarding of lucrative government projects to Umno's cronies; and so on.

I was impressed by his articulate analysis of the issues, his candour and his disregard for the fact that I was a total stranger to him. I happily listened till I got to my destination. Then when I was getting out of his taxi, he said something that got me smiling delightedly. He said, "Remember to *ubah*, ya?"

The wave for change was almost a movement, but not one that was formally created or organised. It had its beginnings in the aftermath of GE12, which sensitised Malaysians to the possibility of a better future for themselves and their children. It grew in presence as campaigns and rallies organised by Opposition parties and civil society bodies raised greater public awareness of the Government's unfair policies and practices.

Soon it burgeoned into a loose fraternity that was not represented only by Malaysians resident at home. Those working and residing overseas, from Singapore to China to Australia to the United States of America, felt united by the same purpose and joined in. When the Coalition for Clean and Fair Elections (Bersih) organised street rallies in 2011 and 2012, overseas Malaysians in more than 30 international cities held simultaneous ones in solidarity with the NGO.

These rallies called on the EC to clean up the electoral roll which was alleged to contain phantom voters; reform postal voting; introduce the use of indelible ink; allow all political parties free access to the media; and put an end to electoral fraud.

Tens of thousands of concerned Malaysians spilled onto the streets of Kuala Lumpur's city centre to support Bersih's calls. Many more overseas came up with initiatives to support the cause, and when Bersih appealed for a large turnout of voters at GE13 because this would be the only way to defeat cheating or fraudulent manipulation, they made plans to fly home and vote. Even from as far as the U.S.

Weeks before election day, those resident in Singapore encouraged one another to return to vote and even organised the logistics for group travel. They chartered buses and coordinated carpooling. They were as excited as their compatriots in Malaysia about the prospect of *ubah*.

On polling day, however, all that excitement was quite contained. No campaigning was allowed in the polling centre and within 50 metres of it. Anyone caught sporting a party's logo or emblem or the candidate's name could face a fine of RM5,000 or one year's jail, or both.

When the gates opened, voters headed for the officials' desk to check which *saluran* (stream) they should join and proceeded there accordingly. Despite the numbers present, there was no loud chatter. Most of the voters were generally reticent, perhaps relishing a moment that comes only once every five years and appreciating the significance of the task at hand.

They did not complain that the lines were long or that they had to stand in the sun at times. They waited patiently, some for as long as over an hour, for their turn to enter the voting room, have their identity card verified and their index finger painted with indelible ink, receive their ballot paper, mark that all-important cross on it against the candidate of their choice, and drop the precious ballot paper into the box.

That done, they stepped out of the polling station feeling satisfied and valued for having performed a worthy deed. They had made their preference known. They had spoken. Now the anxiety would start.

The rise, fall and rise of Anwar

PR was led by the charismatic Anwar Ibrahim, the *de facto* head of Parti Keadilan Rakyat (PKR), or National Justice Party, one of the parties in the Opposition pact.

He was courted to join Umno in 1982 by then prime minister Mahathir Mohamad and made a minister the very next year. By 1993, he had risen to become deputy prime minister and was widely seen to be Mahathir's designated successor.

But he fell from grace in 1998, when he was sacked and charged with sodomy and abuse of power and subsequently jailed.

It was sparked by his fallout with Mahathir over the 1997 Asian Financial Crisis when as finance minister, Anwar adopted an austerity plan recommended by the International Monetary Fund without his boss's prior knowledge. The plan would cut public spending by 18% and halt infrastructure projects initiated by Mahathir. It also insisted that the Government would not bail out companies affected by the crisis.

An angry Mahathir retaliated. He brought in his old friend, businessman Daim Zainuddin, to head the newly formed National Economic Action Council, undercutting Anwar's position as finance minister.

Three months later, in March 1998, state-owned oil company Petronas was co-opted to bail out Mahathir's son Mirzan's troubled company to the tune of RM2 billion.

In June, Umno Youth chief Ahmad Zahid Hamidi spoke out against Mahathir at the Umno general assembly when he called for an end to cronyism and nepotism in the Government. He was punished in September with detention without trial under the Internal Security Act (ISA), and was released when he agreed to step down as Umno Youth chief.

The following year, he admitted that Anwar was the one who instructed him to raise the issues of cronyism and nepotism in return for business opportunities. He sought forgiveness from Mahathir and was welcomed back to the Umno fold.

It looked like he had no qualms about telling on his friend or ally in order to save his own skin. This same Ahmad Zahid Hamidi would later bounce back from being an outcast to become Najib's deputy prime minister in 2015.

The man who would not be forgiven was Anwar. At the same Umno general assembly, a book titled *50 Dalil Kenapa Anwar Tidak Boleh Menjadi Perdana Menteri* (50 Reasons Why Anwar Cannot Become Prime Minister) was circulated to undermine him. The book contained graphic sexual allegations as well as accusations of corruption against him.

Mahathir, who had earlier publicly declared that sexual allegations made against Anwar in poison-pen letters that emerged in June 1997 were false, now ordered police investigations into the allegations. He also appointed Daim special functions minister in charge of economic development, further undermining Anwar's position.

On September 2, Mahathir sacked Anwar after the latter refused an ultimatum to step down. The next day, Anwar claimed he was the victim of a conspiracy. He led a series of mass protests calling for *reformasi* (political reform).

Police then submitted affidavits alleging sexual misconduct and other crimes committed by Anwar. He was arrested, and his arrest sparked the *reformasi* movement that eventually culminated in the formation of PKR while he was in prison.

Evidently, Mahathir was one person you did not want to fight against. When Zahid accused the Government of practising nepotism and cronyism, Mahathir hit back by revealing the names of others who had benefited from government contracts and low-priced share allocations. They included Zahid himself and Anwar's friends and family.

To address the financial crisis, Mahathir eventually imposed capital controls, pegging the ringgit at RM3.80 to the U.S. dollar, to curb currency speculation that he blamed on the West, calling the speculators "neo-colonialists", "racists", "international criminals" and "wild beasts". To his credit, he was later widely applauded for making the right move.

On his release in 2004, Anwar bounced back with fervour to lead the Opposition to GE12 in 2008. Although his jail sentence disqualified him from standing in the elections, he proved to be a powerhouse in galvanising PKR and its partners – the Democratic Action Party (DAP) and Parti Islam Se-Malaysia (PAS), or Malaysian Islamic Party – to achieve a stunning electoral performance on March 8.

On July 31, 2008, by which time Anwar's disqualification from standing for public office had lapsed, his wife, Wan Azizah Wan Ismail, who had been holding the PKR fort while he was in prison, vacated her parliamentary seat of Permatang Pauh. It allowed Anwar to contest in that constituency, an Anwar family stronghold, in the subsequent by-election. As expected, he won it by a landslide, and was sworn in as a member of Parliament after an absence of 10 years.

Pact of strange bedfellows

Now at GE13, PR was, among other things, banking on its track record of running the state governments of Penang, Kedah, Selangor and Kelantan to sell the idea that it was ready for federal government.

It proposed an affirmative action policy based on needs so that all races would benefit, in contrast to the one practised by BN, which was based on race.

It promised to abolish highway tolls and repeal laws that restricted media freedom and academic freedom. It also declared war against corruption.

Clearly for many voters PR would bring much-needed reform if it took over the seat of federal government in Putrajaya, the country's administrative capital.

They were prepared to accept the mix of strange bedfellows in the pact – a Malay-led multi-racial party founded on *reformasi* and social justice and the idea that Anwar must be prime minister; a Chinese-dominated multi-racial party that championed democracy and advocated equality for all; and an Islamist party bent on establishing a theocratic state and occasionally on fostering Malay-Muslim unity.

These three were disparate groups with differences in political dreams. In time, problems might arise out of these differences, but so far, the three parties had remained united and focused on their goal of conquering Putrajaya.

More importantly, Anwar was holding them together, and the DAP looked well-organised and solid, while PAS was currently taking a politically pragmatic approach of broaching the idea of a Benevolent or Welfare State instead of an Islamic State. The mixed bunch appeared a better bet than BN.

BN thrives on old tricks

The ruling regime, on the other hand, seemed more concerned with playing its old tricks of cajoling, bribing and threatening the electorate instead of attending to its own flaws.

Just a month before the elections, Prime Minister Najib Abdul Razak, who was also BN chairman, announced bigger cash handouts for the people in the form of the 1Malaysia People's Aid (BR1M), increasing it from RM500 to RM1,200 a year for households earning less than RM3,000 a month, and from RM250 to RM600 for singles earning less than RM2,000 a month. BN of course denied that it was a tactic to buy votes.

Umno leaders threatened that if Malaysians did not vote BN back to power, they could face another outbreak of racial violence, like that of May 13, 1969.

Former prime minister Mahathir, still an Umno stalwart, also warned of racial confrontation in the event of DAP candidate Lim Kit Siang winning Gelang Patah in Johor.

BN was really worried by PR's bold strategy to take the fight to Umno's fortress, Johor, long considered to be impregnable, with the veteran Kit Siang leading the charge. When it started looking like PR might have a good chance of breaking down at least parts of the fortress, Umno leaders resorted to racial threats.

But these virulent threats were not based on reality, they were merely meant to frighten the voters. Naturally, they did not succeed. In fact, they made the voters more angry.

Acid test for Najib

For Najib, GE13 was an acid test. He had become the nation's 6th prime minister in 2009 and this was his first general election as top leader. He needed a good showing to consolidate his position.

He knew only too well that the man he succeeded, Abdullah Ahmad Badawi, had been pressured to step down by his own party for being accountable for the GE12 debacle. If he himself failed to perform well at GE13, he could face the same consequences.

So over the years since ascending to the premiership, Najib had gone all out to work on increasing his popularity ratings. He tried to project a "cool" and "hip" image of himself to the young, extensively made use of social media to show he was "with it", turned himself into a personal brand that often polled higher than that of Umno, and even had numerous public relations events staged that demonstrated how people "loved" the PM!

Unfortunately, however, his job ratings were far from satisfactory. Despite promising "transformation" through projects called Economic Transformation Programme (ETP), Government Transformation Programme (GTP), Political Transformation Programme (PTP) and Rural Transformation Programme (RTP), he could not reach out to the layman for whom such fancy project names were too abstract to comprehend. Neither could they feel the effects of the so-called "transformation".

Money makes Umno go round

Indeed if there was anything that needed transformation, it had to be Najib's own party, Umno. As the biggest partner in the BN coalition of 13 parties and the one that called the shots, it was accountable for having corrupted the system through its abuse of power and promotion of cronyism and rent-seeking.

The party itself was infested with greed. It became a talking point that joining the party was not so much about serving the nation or fighting for the Malay cause anymore but about getting government projects and amassing personal wealth.

It all started in the 1980s, when money politics set in. This was during the time when Mahathir was Umno president and also prime minister. It was alleged that any Umno member who wanted to contest for just the position of divisional head had to spend hundreds of thousands of ringgit to feed and provide for supporters who would vote for them in divisional polls. By the 1990s, the amount had gone up to a million ringgit. But it was worth it. The huge pickings would come during national party elections when each division would send 14 delegates to the annual general assembly to vote for the top positions from party president to Supreme Council members.

These delegates, numbering about 2,500, were actually the people who would pick the country's prime minister and most of his Cabinet members, not the 3 million Umno members, not the many million more Malaysian voters who go to the polling booths whenever a general election is called. Only 2,500 or so individuals, and they had the biggest say in determining the personnel of the country's top administration. Incredible!

However, in 2009, the Umno constitution was changed to increase the number of delegates voting for the top positions to nearly 150,000, and this was to be implemented for the first time at the 2013 national party elections to be held in November that year.

The divisional chief would of course be among the delegates at the general assembly. He or she would also control how the division would vote. As such, their goodwill had to be sought by the candidates vying for the top positions. They were offered not only money but special perks as well, like positions on the board of government agencies or lucrative housing development projects.

A 2013 interview that the online news website *Free Malaysia Today* did with Abdul Kadir Sheikh Fadzir was most revealing. Kadir was a former Umno Supreme Council member and government minister and therefore someone who had first-hand knowledge of the party's culture and practices. What he disclosed corroborated the allegations.

"You can get top positions in Umno by buying votes," he said. "You don't have to bother going down to the divisions, to the branches, work hard, be popular with the *rakyat* (people), no, no, not necessary anymore. If you have the money and you are prepared to spend it, you can get elected to be a Supreme Council member or even a vice-president or deputy president and so on. So it works in Umno. Money really can buy things. So much so that Najib in his closing speech (at the 2009 general assembly) joked, *'Inilah kita ini Umno dalam dilema. Beri, salah. Tak beri, kalah.'* (Umno is in a dilemma. Giving money is wrong. But not giving means losing.) And everybody down there, the delegates, started clapping and laughing. Because they'd been receiving. And those on the stage, the Supreme Council members, also clapped because they'd been giving."

However, Kadir conceded that not all delegates sold their votes and not all Supreme Council candidates gave money. "Most use money, but some are very reluctant. They do not like it. But as Najib joked, if you don't give, you lose, so when you lose, you lose your ministerial post or your *menteri besar* (chief minister) post, you lose your Supreme Council position, etc. So since that is the culture, you also join in and start giving. … I've heard that now you have to have a few million ringgit just to get a position in the Supreme Council. And even if you're a nobody who's not gone down to the divisions to work hard at the grassroots level, if you are prepared to spend this money, you can get a position in the Supreme Council quite easily. Just spend money."

'Coffee money' at midnight

Veteran journalist A. Kathirasen touched on the subject in a commentary article published by *Free Malaysia Today* on June 26, 2018.

He wrote about a friend attending an Umno general assembly years before that. The friend, who came from a northern state, was put up in a luxury hotel in the Malaysian capital of Kuala Lumpur and had all his expenses paid.

Around midnight, he and his roommate, another delegate, heard a knock on the door. He opened it to find "a man smiling from ear to ear". The man stepped into the room and asked if everything was all right. The two delegates said yes. The man looked around, smiled and pushed some notes into their shirt pockets. He said, "*Tan Sri kata minum kopi.*" (Tan Sri says this is for coffee). Then the man left.

"Tan Sri" is the second highest federal title bestowed to someone who is regarded to have provided distinguished service to the nation. When someone is given such a title, their actual name usually becomes secondary and they are publicly referred to mostly by the honorific. In this case, the delegates would know who "Tan Sri" referred to as there would have been only one such title-holder among the candidates for the top positions they would be voting for the next day.

As for *minum kopi*, literally "drink coffee", that is commonly acknowledged as a euphemism for taking a bribe.

After the Tan Sri's man had left, the two delegates reached into their pockets and took out the notes. They counted them. Their hearts leapt when they realised they had been gifted RM4,000 each.

When money politics became the culture of Umno, it appeared all the more evident that the party was not about public service but self-service. It also appeared to have deviated far from the principles of its founders who, if they were alive, would not have recognised the Umno of 2013 as the party they had formed in 1946.

Then, it was to fight for the Malays under British rule. But later it worked with Chinese and Indian parties to achieve independence and thereafter govern the multi-racial nation on the principle of power-sharing.

Under the leadership of Tunku Abdul Rahman, who was the country's first prime minister from 1957 to 1970, Umno largely showed fairness to the other races. It managed to forge with its partners in the coalition called the Alliance Party, the forerunner of BN, a reasonably harmonious multi-racial, multi-religious, multi-lingual nation.

But on May 10, 1969, the Alliance Party fared badly at the 3rd general election. It was returned to power but lost its two-thirds majority in

Parliament and four state governments (nearly comparable to the 2008 general election results).

Then on May 13, racial riots broke out. Now acknowledged to have been orchestrated by Umno right-wingers, the riots forever changed the race narrative.

And so Malaysia became divided

The New Economic Policy (NEP) was introduced in 1970. It was a social re-engineering and affirmative action policy that was aimed at aiding *Bumiputeras* (sons of the soil) – comprising the majority race of Malays as well as the natives of Sabah and Sarawak – and ensuring that they attained 30% participation in the economy by 1990.

From the look of it, the NEP was racially discriminatory. This made the non-*Bumiputeras* feel disenfranchised. Fewer of them could get into public universities, fewer get employed in the civil service. Many were bypassed for promotion in the public sector on account of race.

Being *Bumiputera* also meant getting the special privilege of a 7 to 10% discount on property purchases, irrespective of the value of the property, which the non-*Bumiputera* did not enjoy. This is still applicable today, even for multi-million-ringgit properties which only the rich can afford.

Yet even so, if the NEP were to be well implemented and to achieve its aims by the allotted period of 20 years, and if it would truly help the Malays feel confident of themselves in due course, it would have to be accepted as a necessary measure. Care, however, needed to be taken to prevent the disruption of the harmonious racial co-existence that the Federal Constitution was designed to protect and preserve.

As it turned out, the policy did help to expand the Malay middle class and provide opportunities for many Malays to improve their well-being in education, business and other areas. But it also aroused the greed of what came to be disparagingly called Umnoputeras, the Umno elite who used their connections to benefit from the policy more easily and more bountifully than others.

The spirit and letter of the policy came to be abused in practice. One of its aims, the eradication of poverty, was not concertedly addressed, so that a large proportion of the people it was meant to benefit, particularly the poor, remained deprived.

When 1990 came around, the NEP was terminated in name but replacement policies maintained the affirmative action for *Bumiputeras*. Even so, as late as 2007, the Government shockingly declared that the 30% *Bumiputera* equity target had not yet been achieved. This was greeted with incredulity. Something must have gone dreadfully amiss in the last 37 years, or the figures were wrong!

However, Lim Teck Ghee, who had done a study of *Bumiputera* corporate equity ownership up till 2004, disagreed. His report on it for the Asian Strategy and Leadership Institute's Centre for Public Policy Studies showed that the *Bumiputera* corporate share could be as high as 45%, rather than the official 2004 estimate of 18.9%.

Meanwhile, Malaysian society became divided. The non-Malays felt more than just being marginalised because of the abuse of the NEP; they also felt that their rights were being challenged, although these rights were guaranteed by the Federal Constitution.

Chinese and Indians were derogatorily called *pendatang* (immigrant), even by Umno leaders, thus depriving them of a sense of belonging in the land of their birth and citizenship. Sometimes they were rudely told to go back to where their ancestors came from. There were even calls to strip them of their citizenship.

The idea of *Ketuanan Melayu* (Malay Supremacy) was summarily invoked in the 1980s, and over the years it was ingrained in the national psyche, ever ready to be exploited now and again for political purposes. It was also concretised in government policies and practices.

Almost all the highest positions in public office came to be reserved for Malays. Not a single vice-chancellor in the country's public universities was non-Malay. The most important positions in the prime minister's Cabinet went to Malays, unlike during the time of Tunku Abdul Rahman.

In the civil service, Malay staffing increased from 64.5% in 1969 (before the NEP) to 76.2% in 2009, while the Chinese and Indian proportions declined from 18.8% and 15.7%, respectively, in 1969 to 6% and 4.3% in 2009. By 2010, out of 1.2 million civil service employees, only about 10% were non-Malays.

Race was just one of the divisive factors. The other significant one was religion. Umno leaders would politicise both to consolidate their power.

Article 3 of the Federal Constitution states that "Islam is the religion of the Federation" and Article 160 defines a Malay as a person who professes the religion of Islam. This means that all Malays are officially worshippers of the country's premier religion. It gave Umno the moral authority to play both the *Ketuanan Melayu* and *Ketuanan Islam* (Islamic Supremacy) cards to its advantage. Which of course it did.

Malaysia an Islamic state?

When he was prime minister, Mahathir added fuel to the religious fire by declaring in 2001 that Malaysia was an Islamic state, much to many people's dismay and distress, because Malaysia had been widely considered to be secular since independence. It was inconceivable that the British and Tunku Abdul Rahman would have agreed to anything other than that.

The Tunku himself said in Parliament in 1958, "I would like to make clear that this country is not an Islamic state as is generally understood, we merely provide that Islam shall be the official religion of the State." On February 9, 1983, he reiterated this stand in a report published by the English daily *The Star* under the headline 'Don't make Malaysia an Islamic state: Tunku'.

Four days later, he was supported by Hussein Onn, the country's 3rd prime minister, in a report by the same newspaper headlined 'Hussein says no to Islamic state too'.

But Mahathir was obviously not receptive of their position. And in 2007, Najib reinforced Mahathir's line by saying, "Islam is the official religion and Malaysia is an Islamic state ... we have never been secular because being secular by Western definition means separation of the Islamic principles in the way we govern a country." He was deputy prime minister at the time, but when he later took the higher office, he maintained the same line.

Clearly, what Mahathir and Najib declared was rhetoric designed to win the support of Muslims which they feared losing to PAS, which had been advocating the establishment of an Islamic state since the 1980s after it was inspired by the Iranian Revolution of 1979.

This was the period when Mahathir began his premiership, and the course he then chose to counter PAS's influence on the Malay-Muslim electorate was to out-PAS PAS by making the Government appear more Muslim than the Islamic party. It served Umno and BN's cause, but in doing so, Mahathir turned religion into a monstrous issue that was to have a serious impact on the future of Malaysian politics and the lives of Muslims and non-Muslims alike.

Islam's ascendancy affected the development of the other religions. Although the Federal Constitution protects freedom of religion and guarantees that religions other than Islam may be practised in peace and harmony, restrictions came to be imposed on the building of new churches and temples.

Apart from that, it could take years to get an application for the building of a church approved. For example, the Latter Rain Church in the state of Selangor had to wait 20 years for its approval. Conditions were also made that churches must not look like churches, forcing some to operate out of shophouses and looking nondescript like ordinary businesses.

Hinduism was not spared. Temples built many decades before got demolished by the authorities on the grounds that they were built illegally. Many were relocated because they were too near Malay-Muslim neighbourhoods.

Instances of Islamic extremism also arose, in the form of protests against elements of other religions that were considered objectionable, like a cross on a church too prominently displayed, or something more violent like the desecration of Hindu temples.

Then there was the cow-head incident in 2009 in which protestors stomped on the head of a cow, considered a sacred animal by the Hindus, and spat on it, to show their disapproval of a proposed relocation of a Hindu temple to a Muslim-majority area.

Instead of quelling such religious persecution and tempering extremist sentiments in order to foster public harmony and inter-faith understanding, Umno actually exploited the situation and drummed it in that the Malays and Islam occupied a special place in the country, therefore anyone who questioned, let alone challenged, this established fact would be disrupting the peace, even committing sedition.

Sometimes it got ridiculous, as when Umno would illogically warn from time to time that Islam in Malaysia was under threat, therefore followers of the faith should beware their enemies. But who were the enemies? And how could Islam be under any threat when it is enshrined in the Federal Constitution as the religion of the Federation?

Convention of rednecks

But that was what Umno had become. A party that operated on no real ideology and depended for its survival on engendering insecurities among Malays and Muslims and exploiting these insecurities for the longest time.

At its general assembly every year, the party harped on the issues of race and religion without fail. Anyone who reads reports of the things said during the proceedings would be forgiven for feeling shocked by the racism and bigotry gushing from the assembly, and mistaking it for an annual convention of rednecks.

It is to Umno's utter discredit that its members have exhibited crude ethnocentric sentiments like brandishing a *keris* to warn other races against questioning *Ketuanan Melayu*; blaming the non-Malays for not helping the Malays to achieve their 30% equity target; proposing that there should not be open tenders for government projects because contracts should instead be given to Umno members.

Incredible, isn't it? A party of supremacists or at least of leaders and followers with a supremacist attitude calling the shots in the governing of a nation made up of many different races? How did this central contradiction arising from race-based politics survive for so long?

No wonder non-Malays increasingly felt that they were being short-changed not only for being citizens with unequal standing but also for being treated like bogeymen or punching bags whenever Umno needed to target them to unite the Malays.

They also felt betrayed by the Malaysian Chinese Association (MCA) and the Malaysian Indian Congress (MIC), the oldest and original partners of Umno going back to before independence. While in the past, these similarly race-based parties had exerted stronger influence in government in accordance with the power-sharing principle, from the 1980s onwards they began to be eclipsed by Umno's shadow.

Despite this, they continued insisting that they stood up for their respective communities and demanded support because their participation in the BN government was essential. But when it came to matters of great import, even those affecting their communities, they were invariably shouted down by the bigger voices of Umno.

Even someone like Najib's own aide, carrying the designation of special officer to the prime minister, could insult the Chinese and the Indians with impunity to the faces of MCA and MIC representatives attending a seminar in 2010.

Nasir Safar called them by the derogatory term of *pendatang*, said Chinese women immigrated to *jual tubuh* (sell their bodies), dismissed the contributions of the non-Malays in the country's effort to attain independence, and threatened to revoke the citizenships of some MIC members. All the MCA and MIC representatives could do in response was walk out of the seminar.

Later, their leaders complained to the media. The MIC president called

Nasir "a racist of the highest order" and demanded that he be punished under the Sedition Act. His demand came to nothing, of course, because Nasir was from Umno and protected, so the MIC chief looked glaringly ineffectual.

But by then Chinese and Indian voters had already wised up to the lame claims of the MCA and the MIC and written them off as "running dogs" and "lapdogs", and they had punished these flunkeys severely at the ballot box in 2008. Come GE13, these voters were expected to inflict more punishment.

Condos for cows?

Leading up to GE13, Malaysia was more divided than ever, and Najib's premiership was characterised by weak governance, gross mismanagement of public funds, leakages and wastage in the civil service, corruption and scandals.

The hardest-hitting scandal that broke out under his watch was what came to be called the 'Cowgate' scandal.

In 2006, the Ministry of Finance had allocated a grant of RM13 million to the National Feedlot Corporation and also approved a soft loan amounting to RM250 million with a 2% interest rate for it to run the National Feedlot Centre (NFC), which was aimed at increasing the country's self-reliance in the production of beef.

However, instead of investing the money in rearing cows, the company used it to pay for the purchases of luxury condominiums in Malaysia and Singapore, land in Putrajaya and a Mercedes, and for expensive overseas trips. It therefore failed to meet the beef production target set by the Government. The Auditor-General's Report of 2010 discovered this and called the project "a mess".

What was equally shocking is the fact that the people running the project were the husband and children of Cabinet minister Shahrizat Abdul Jalil. She disavowed any involvement in the awarding of the project to her family, and claimed she had nothing to do with her husband's company or business. But this did not stop Malaysians from cackling over jokes about how pampered the cows must have been with luxury condos provided for them to live in.

Roti Najib without eggs

Scandals aside, Najib had to battle the public's perception of him as prime minister. A little more than a week before GE13, a survey by Universiti Malaya's Democratic and Election Centre (Umcedel) revealed that only 39% of voters believed that Najib was qualified to be prime minister whereas 43% preferred Anwar.

The same survey showed that more than 60% favoured PR's manifesto, compared to 50% for BN's.

Najib of course disagreed with the survey findings. "We have our own poll," he said. "My poll indicates that we are ahead." He also said he was confident that BN would win with a two-thirds majority in Parliament, unless there was internal sabotage.

Winning two-thirds majority would set him on a pedestal and secure his position as Umno president. But was he realistic in thinking that he could attain it?

His four years as prime minister had so far shown that he was nothing if not a weak leader, famous for his numerous flip-flops on government decisions, over matters ranging from toll hikes to civil servants' remuneration to electoral reform.

He also appeared indecisive when it came to calling for the elections. People waited anxiously for him to dissolve Parliament but he kept delaying his decision. He even considered it apposite to quip that guessing of the election date could turn out to be a "favourite national pastime".

Annoyed by this, netizens derisively christened him the prime minister with no balls. A meme that went viral on the social media circuit had a picture of Najib giving what appeared to be a fiery speech accompanied by a caption in Malay that cheekily named a popular Indian *roti* (flatbread) dish after him: "*Sekarang ada Roti Najib – roti tanpa telur!*" (And now there is Roti Najib, *roti* without eggs!)

Najib had more eggs on him, however, when, as finance minister as well, he allocated billions of ringgit to his own Prime Minister's Office (PMO) from where expenditure could be made without transparency or accountability because it was not subject to the scrutiny of the Auditor-General. There were allegations that he charged expenses incurred for private events to the PMO, like his daughter's expensive engagement party and his own extravagant birthday bash in 2011.

The liability named Rosmah

Having a wife known to enjoy a lavish lifestyle was also a liability for Najib. Rosmah Mansor was reported going on shopping sprees overseas, and amassing a collection of super-expensive Hermes Birkin bags. Allegations were made, fake or otherwise, that public funds were utilised for some of her purchases.

In 2010, when she visited New York with Najib, a two-page colour advertisement appeared in *The New York Times* to welcome Rosmah as "First Lady of Malaysia" and congratulate her for being conferred a little-known International Peace and Harmony Award. It carried a huge picture of her and a few smaller group photos in which she also appeared.

The online news portal *The Nut Graph* did some checking with *NYT* and was told that the advertisement was placed by an advertising agency on behalf of the Malaysian Government.

The Nut Graph estimated from research that the cost of a full-page advertisement in *NYT* would range "between RM580,000 and RM740,000". As Rosmah's advertisement was a two-page spread, it would have cost much more. If indeed the Malaysian Government paid for that expensive advertisement, was it justified in doing so?

Then there was that matter of a US$24 million (RM73 million) diamond ring that the NGO Solidariti Anak Muda Malaysia (SAMM) reported to the Malaysian Anti-Corruption Commission (MACC) as having been purchased by Rosmah in April 2011.

"US$24 million is a lot of money, so the question is, where did she get the money to buy such an expensive ring?" asked SAMM's president, Badrul Hisham Shaharin.

Nothing came of it, however. A few months later, a government minister declared that there was no case to pursue. The MACC had checked with the Customs Department and confirmed that there was "no such purchase of the ring" because after a few days, it was returned to the jeweller in New York.

Did this quell public suspicion? No, because the matter was still talked about for a long time to come. In fact, the people made fun of Rosmah all the more, and a joke went around that she started saving from when she was a child so she could finally have enough money to buy that ring!

1Malaysia sham and shambles

In March 2010, Najib unveiled the first part of his New Economic Model (NEM), which was supposed to be one of the reformist moves of his early days as prime minister.

It was indeed full of promise. Aimed at achieving "high income, sustainability and inclusiveness", it advocated opening the economy to anyone, including international fund managers, who could help stimulate the country's economic growth.

It gave indication of replacing the NEP and even admitted that the implementation of the NEP had engendered rent-seeking, patronage and rampant corruption. It proposed the setting-up of an Equal Opportunities Commission (EOC) "to ensure fairness and address undue discrimination".

These positive measures were welcomed by the business community but not by Malay right-wing groups like Pertubuhan Pribumi Perkasa (Perkasa), or Powerful Indigenous Organisation.

When Perkasa exerted pressure by lobbying against the more inclusive, race-blind provisions in the model, reportedly threatened to burn the document and insisted that the *Bumiputera* agenda should be the national agenda to determine the economic future of the country, Najib exposed his egglessness.

THE PEOPLE'S VICTORY

In the second part of the NEM, launched nine months later, the EOC proposal was removed. So were other recommendations aimed at boosting competitiveness by reducing *Bumiputera* quotas.

The late Zainal Aznam Mohd Yusof, who was a highly respected economist and member of the National Economic Advisory Council which drafted the NEM, expressed his ire. "I am not very happy with the final version of the NEM," he spoke out frankly. "The Cabinet did not really want the EOC ... This was the Government's litmus test and at this time, I have to say that there is no political will." This was a slap on Najib's face.

But then Najib was not one noted for conviction and substance. In 2009, he came up with the '1Malaysia' concept, coined to connote inclusivity and promote national unity, but two years after it came into being, race relations had actually worsened, with BN politicians and civil servants making racist remarks publicly and behind closed doors, and social media abuzz with comments spewing racial hatred.

Anwar Ibrahim questioned the sincerity behind 1Malaysia by pointing out that the government agency Biro Tata Negara (BTN), or the National Civics Bureau, was still continuing to promote *Ketuanan Melayu*.

It was still indoctrinating Malay civil servants, employees of state subsidiaries and students at State-owned institutions to beware the Chinese and the Indians. How could that be in line with 1Malaysia's stated goal of making "a nation where, it is hoped, every Malaysian perceives himself or herself as Malaysian first, and by race, religion, geographical region or socio-economic background second, and where the principles of 1Malaysia are woven into the economic, political and social fabric of society"?

On top of that, in 2010, no less than the deputy director of BTN, Hamim Husin, used derogatory terms to refer to the Chinese and the Indians: "The *Si Mata Sepet* (slant-eyed Chinese) who has never gone to a mosque or *surau* only has one vote. The *Si Botol* (alcoholic Indian) who only knows how to go up and down Batu Caves only has one vote." Why had Najib not put a stop to the racist tendencies and practices of BTN?

Perhaps the answer lay in the fact that his 1Malaysia concept was not widely accepted. Not by civil servants. Not even by his own party. Or the then deputy prime minister, Muhyiddin Yassin.

Challenged in 2010 by Kit Siang to prove his commitment to 1Malaysia by answering if he considered himself "Malaysian first", Muhyiddin replied, "I am Malay first, but being Malay doesn't mean I am not Malaysian. How can I say I'm Malaysian first and Malay second? All the Malays will shun me... and it's not proper." What a cop-out!

A bigger cop-out came about the following year when Najib himself was asked by a student what he thought of his deputy's stance and whether he himself was prepared to state that he was Malaysian first.

Najib replied, "I don't want to respond in a way that will divide me from my deputy. 1Malaysia is our guiding philosophy. It does not matter what you say, just as long as you follow it."

He didn't answer the question. He was not man enough, or leader enough, to stand up for his "guiding philosophy". He probably didn't have the guts either to take his deputy aside and impress upon him the need to show commitment not only to the boss but more importantly to the philosophy as well.

It all became clear that 1Malaysia was a sham, and a shambles. It also boded negatively for Najib that Malay pressure groups were against it because they feared that 1Malaysia was an initiative to bring about racial equality and allow all races to share the nation's wealth with no particular race being given special treatment.

The highest turnout ever

At GE13, most voters saw the larger picture. They knew that Umno-BN would not change, would not reform the corrupt system. If it got another mandate to rule, they would have to suffer another five years of poor governance, mismanagement, corruption, racial strife, political bullying and violence, and the arrogance of Umno. They could not bear the thought of putting up with that.

THE PEOPLE'S VICTORY

So they went out to vote to change the government. In huge numbers. When voting closed, the EC recorded a voter turnout of 84.8%, the highest ever in Malaysian electoral history.

That night, they waited anxiously for the result.

DO WE HAVE A WINNER?

On election day, I cast my votes for the state and parliamentary seats in my suburb in Petaling Jaya in the state of Selangor.

The state was the richest and most developed in the country, often alluded to as "the jewel in the crown". In 2013, it accounted for about 22% of Malaysia's gross domestic product (GDP). PR captured it in GE12 to almost everyone's surprise, and since then, BN had been pulling all the stops to try and win Selangor back.

When BN lost it in 2008, the coalition was traumatised. Its leaders couldn't believe how it could have happened. They blamed the then *menteri besar*, Mohamad Khir bin Toyo, for a few mistakes he had made close to the elections, but the reasons for the defeat were probably more deep-seated. A large part of Selangor was already urbanised by then, with easy access to information, so many Selangorians were clued-in to the excesses of BN.

One example was the palatial mansion of Zakaria Mat Deros, an Umno state assemblyman. It had a swimming pool, several gazebos, an orchard, a two-hole golf lawn, 16 bedrooms, 21 bathrooms, a VIP room, three living rooms, a dining hall and a prayer room. There was even a bowling room inside. Photographs of the "*istana*" (palace) were widely circulated via e-mail.

Adding to the controversy was the discovery by the law that Zakaria did not submit building plans for his mansion. He had also not paid assessment tax for a few properties for 10 years or more, and was operating a *satay* restaurant which he had built illegally on government reserve land – without a business licence, to boot. Zakaria's *istana* and his arrogant attitude of not following the law came to symbolise the decadence of Umno and BN.

Now at GE13, Selangorians were determined not to let the decadent Umno-BN get back into power. Nonetheless, they felt apprehensive that Najib and his cohorts might pull something off to win back the state by hook or by crook. After all, Najib had made himself BN Selangor election chief to increase his side's chances, and it had spent a lot of money conducting an aggressive campaign to court the voters. People wondered if the money came out of public coffers.

Selangor BN coordinator Mohd Zin Mohamed reached out to voters by sending them letters and SMSes on festive occasions or national holidays to wish them well, but the catch came at the end where they were invariably reminded to vote for BN. Some of these letters were signed by Najib and carried a picture of him.

Mohd Zin's campaign backfired when he also sent out birthday greetings. This peeved the recipients. They didn't appreciate having had their personal information accessed. They felt it was an invasion of privacy and gave Mohd Zin hell for that. Social media was full of curses and invective directed at him.

The upshot of it was that BN was desperate to win. And as election chief, Najib would have a lot to answer for if Selangor slipped through his net. This prompted Selangorians to be vigilant, fearful that BN might stoop to cheating at the polls. More signed up to be polling agents this time than in 2008, to keep close watch on election proceedings.

I signed up too, as I had done the previous general election, and was posted to the state seat of Kota Damansara to help out Nasir Hashim of Parti Sosialis Malaysia (PSM) who was standing under the PKR banner. He was the incumbent and would have been expected to win against his BN opponent in a straight fight but PAS had broken from the agreement made by all three PR parties not to contest against each other by fielding its own candidate. This made it tough for Nasir.

When I got to the polling centre, I expressed my annoyance at this disappointing development to the PAS candidate's polling agent. I didn't mince my words, I said it was a stupid move because it would only split the votes for the Opposition and help BN win the seat. The agent knew damn well what I meant, but he had no counter-argument to offer. All he could say was, "*Sabar*" (Calm down).

Anwar tweets victory

After I had done my polling agent bit, I joined a couple of hundred comrades-for-change at a post-vote gathering organised by DAP candidate Tony Pua Kiam Wee. He was defending his Petaling Jaya Utara parliamentary seat which he had won on his maiden election outing in 2008. He was expected to win it again hands down.

A large screen mounted in the open-air square of a suburban commercial enclave in the SS2 area of Petaling Jaya showed the polls results as they were gradually announced by the EC on state television. But relying on this alone was not enough, because the official announcements took time to come on. Most people turned to the online news website *Malaysiakini* for much faster updates.

Malaysiakini also kept followers enthralled by providing them the latest vote tallies for some of the contests. The crowd cheered whenever a PR victory was proclaimed. Or when the latest update showed that a particular PR candidate was leading in his or her constituency.

In the first couple of hours, it looked like the DAP in particular was doing well. Lim Kit Siang, who was initially trailing in the vote count for the Gelang Patah constituency, was now in the lead.

The DAP strategy of taking the fight to BN's fortress, Johor, was working out well, with another candidate holding a steady lead in Kulai while Liew Chin Tong, the DAP master strategist who dreamed up the idea to attack Johor, was slightly ahead in Kluang.

PKR was also doing well, it had won the Bayan Baru parliamentary seat in Penang and was leading in the contests for the parliamentary seat of Miri in Sarawak and the state seat of Indera Kayangan in Perlis.

One of the party's leading lights, Nurul Izzah Anwar, who was facing a tough fight for the parliamentary seat of Lembah Pantai in Kuala Lumpur, had just broken into a narrow lead against Raja Nong Chik of BN. Much interest was focused on this battle not only because Izzah was Anwar's daughter but also because she was considered a potential future leader.

PAS was winning in its stronghold of Kelantan, the state in the northeast that it had ruled since 1990, and Khalid Samad was leading in the parliamentary seat of Shah Alam in Selangor while Mohd Shukri Ramli looked like retaining the state seat of Sanglang in Perlis for the party.

The mood at the SS2 gathering was buoyant and optimistic. My friend Eng Keong, a retired engineer, was confident the BN government would fall.

Then at 7.28pm, Anwar Ibrahim tweeted, "PR has won. We urge Umno and the EC to not attempt to hijack the results." The word spread through the crowd. Shouts of elation pierced the night sky. I was, however, sceptical. It was still too early to call, how could Anwar be sure?

Malaysiakini contacted PKR's social media strategist for comment. He assured that Anwar's social media accounts had not been hacked, which meant that the tweet did come from the man himself. But he also said, "The results are still coming in and are being counted. The tweet just reflects Anwar's confidence, it is more of a statement of confidence than of fact."

That was unbecoming of Anwar, I thought. If it were truly not based on fact, then he was not acting responsibly by sending out the claim.

By 9.30pm, though, the prospects were still good for PR. It had managed to deprive the Sarawak United Peoples' Party (SUPP) of five out of its six parliamentary seats, which was quite a feat. It had also won Indera Kayangan, which had never fallen to the Opposition before.

The DAP was winning all the seats it contested in Perak, Negeri Sembilan and Selangor. And in Penang, incumbent chief minister Lim Guan Eng announced that PR had retained the state and held on to its two-thirds majority in the state assembly. The BN parties Parti Gerakan Rakyat Malaysia (Gerakan), or Malaysian People's Movement Party, and the MCA were totally wiped out there.

However, these were mostly based on unofficial results. The EC had made no move yet to announce those PR victories. In fact, about an hour or so after Anwar's tweet went viral, the EC appeared to be concentrating mainly on announcing BN victories. PR's triumphs seemed to be held back, even long after the unofficial results had been known.

Some of us felt an ominous foreboding. The official tally was not keeping up with unofficial results. Officially, BN's score of victories kept rising while that of PR improved only bit by bit. Why was the EC holding back the results of seats won by PR?

At 11.30pm, the DAP's Charles Santiago told supporters that PR had retained Selangor and won two seats more than in GE12. It was not official of course, but still cause for celebration.

Also uplifting was the unofficial news that the Opposition had wrested many more seats from BN in Sabah than it did in 2008, when the DAP won the sole Opposition seat. As Sabah had long been considered BN's electoral "safe deposit", this was a good sign for PR.

It came upon a midnight dreary

By midnight, the crowd at SS2 was thinning out. There was still no official announcement yet on the winner of Putrajaya. Many were still hopeful that Anwar had been right in his tweet, including Eng Keong who went home after telling me that the next day would be a great day for Malaysia. I wasn't so sure, partly because I felt the tweet claiming victory was just another display of bravado from Anwar, and partly because the unofficial results hadn't indicated that either. I decided to go home too, to watch the rest of the EC's announcements on my own TV set.

It got dismal after 12.30am. The EC confirmed that BN had been returned to power in five states, namely, Terengganu, Pahang, Perlis, Negeri Sembilan and Melaka. Analysts had expected PR to capture Negeri Sembilan and Perlis from BN, but this was not to be.

In Labis, Johor, BN's incumbent MP who had looked in danger of losing his seat at 10pm was now declared winner, with a razor-thin majority of 353 votes.

THE PEOPLE'S VICTORY

At 12.45am, the EC confirmed that BN had won 108 parliamentary seats, only four short of forming the federal government with a simple majority. Meanwhile, PR was trailing significantly with only half of BN's haul because official news of its victories was being held back.

I hoped against hope that each new result that came in thenceforth would herald a PR victory, but nine minutes later, at 12.54am, it was all over. The EC announced that BN had attained its simple majority, with 112 seats. PR had secured only 58 then.

More dismal news followed. PR failed to win back Perak, which we had thought it had a good chance of recapturing after having won the state in 2008 only to lose it deplorably soon after when three of its assemblymen were induced to defect. But unfortunately, there was no poetic justice for PR this time.

Even worse, it lost the state of Kedah. That was not unexpected because the state government headed by PAS had been suffering internal friction, but the blow was still hard to take.

The final tally for Parliament was 133 seats for BN and 89 for PR. Najib failed to get the two-thirds majority he was desperately seeking. In fact, BN won seven seats fewer than it did in 2008. PR managed to improve on the 82 it won that time.

Umno, however, won nine seats more. But its Chinese partner, the MCA, turned out to be the biggest loser in BN. Out of the 37 parliamentary seats the MCA contested, it managed to win only seven, down from the 15 it had held before GE13. Its score of state seats was a miserable 11 out of the 90 it contested. This clearly showed that Chinese voters had largely rejected the race-based party.

Najib blames 'Chinese tsunami'

At around 1.20am, the TV cameras zoomed in on the BN camp. Its leaders looked dejected despite having won. Najib in particular appeared shell-shocked, as if he could not believe the result. He blamed BN's debacle on a "Chinese tsunami".

He said he had not expected the Chinese community to reject BN in such a big way. "I expected it but I did not expect it to this extent. None of us did. But despite the extent of the swing against us, BN did not fall."

He accused PR of playing on the racial sentiments of the Chinese to woo their support. "I think they were taken in by some of the undertakings given by the Opposition … and that's why there was that swing … and a lot of sentiments were being played up in this election, some of them racial in nature, which is not very healthy for this country," he said.

What about Anwar's camp? They looked dejected, too. And what was Anwar going to say about the victory he had claimed in his tweet but didn't achieve? He blamed it on fraud. "As of now, we are not accepting the results … until the EC responds and issues an official statement to the allegations of irregularities and fraud," he said.

PR won the vote but still lost

The next day, the full official results went up on the EC's website. The most eye-catching piece of information was the popular vote. PR had actually won it, having scored 50.87% compared to BN's 47.38%. But because of Malaysia's first-past-the-post electoral system and the way the electoral boundaries had been drawn, BN's percentage of the popular vote allowed it to win a disproportionately high share of the parliamentary seats (60%) and, with that, the general election.

It was the same with Perak. The newspaper *theSun* reported that PR won an overwhelming 54.8% of the popular vote there, nearly 9% more than BN's 44.4%, but still failed to win the state. PR's 54.8% translated into only 28 seats compared to BN's 31.

PR retained the state governments of Penang, Kelantan and Selangor – each with a two-thirds majority. It did particularly well in Selangor by winning eight seats more. That proved a major setback for its director of elections, Najib.

I was glad to see public nuisance Mohd Zin Mohamed lose to Mohamed

Hanipa Maidin of PAS in his bid for the state seat of Sepang, a loss described by pundits as a surprise.

But I was sad to be proven right that Nasir Hashim's candidacy in Kota Damansara would suffer from a split in the Opposition's votes. If PAS had stayed out, he would probably have won. The combined votes he and the PAS candidate got were higher than the votes of the eventual winner from BN. Stupid!

Mahathir slams Chinese and 'greedy' Malays

Mahathir was most unhappy about the GE13 result. Despite having stepped down as prime minister and Umno president in 2003, he was still a major influence on the party and was actively involved in GE13 behind the scenes.

Like Najib, he blamed it on a "Chinese tsunami", but he also fired his guns at those Malays who he said were greedy for power to the extent that they had forgotten the basic struggle for race, religion and country. "Even if they have to sell their own race to get what they want, they will do it," he asserted.

By this, Mahathir was obviously referring to the Malays in the Opposition parties, but then there had always been Malays in Opposition parties in every general election and they had stood against Umno candidates all the while, so what difference was there this time to warrant their being called traitors to their race? This was democracy. Surely Mahathir understood that.

He was clearly throwing out a racially charged statement for an ulterior purpose, like he had done to discourage the Gelang Patah constituents from voting for Kit Siang. He warned that racial violence would break out if Kit Siang won, but when the latter did win the contest, nothing of the sort happened. Mahathir, as expected, was just playing the role of race baiter.

Other Umno leaders slammed the Chinese, too. Mohd Ali bin Mohd Rustam's tone was particularly bitter. He had just lost in his contest for the Bukit Katil parliamentary seat to a virtual unknown from PKR. The surprise defeat caused him embarrassment as someone who was Melaka BN chairman and also incumbent chief minister of the state. So he scapegoated the convenient target.

"The results have proven that the Chinese do not appreciate the Government, they just want to change without considering the consequences and what we have done for them all this while," he lamented.

Wild racist claims

Two days after GE13, on May 7, *Utusan Malaysia*, a Malay-language newspaper largely owned by Umno, picked up the cue from Najib's "Chinese tsunami" remark and ran a front-page article with the headline '*Apa Lagi Cina Mahu?*' (What More Do the Chinese Want?).

It said the Chinese had failed to bring down the BN government which was, at its core, Malay. But if they had succeeded, it would have resulted in Kit Siang being appointed deputy prime minister, and this would have allowed the Chinese to make certain demands, like removing the Malay privileges guaranteed in the Federal Constitution.

This was not only hogwash, it was a lie wildly told. It was racist fabrication designed to appeal to the tribal emotions of the newspaper's largely Malay readership, to whip up hatred against the Chinese and stir up insecurity among the Malays.

First, it was wrong and mischievous to spin BN as being fundamentally Malay in order to make a racial issue of it. What about the 1999 general election when the Malays deserted Umno because of Mahathir's mistreatment of Anwar and the Chinese were the ones who actually came to BN's rescue?

Second, there was never any talk of Kit Siang becoming deputy prime minister if PR were to win.

Third, removing the Malay privileges was the last thing the Chinese would have dared to even propose, and it certainly was not something the PR pact would have ever entertained considering that PKR was a Malay-led multi-racial party and PAS was almost 100% Malay-Muslim. In fact, PR's manifesto very clearly affirmed the position of Islam as the country's official religion.

By publishing that article, *Utusan Malaysia* committed the worst sin of journalism. It published untruths. And it sought to create racial antagonism. This was not even a news report, it was an editorial. And it was placed on the newspaper's front page. No self-respecting newspaper does that.

But then publishing untruths was not something *Utusan Malaysia* was doing for the first time. It had been publishing reports without substantiation numerous times before targeting the DAP, a party with a strong Chinese base although it had a good number of Indian members and a small proportion of Malay ones as well.

One was about church leaders conspiring with the party to Christianise the country. As if that were possible! Another was about the DAP planning to dismantle the Malay royalty – protector of Malay rights and sovereignty – and turn the constitutional monarchy into a republic. And throw out all the nine rulers of what used to be known as the Malay States, including the Yang di-Pertuan Agong (the King)! Indeed! The DAP would have to secure a two-thirds majority vote to amend the Federal Constitution to do that. Before they could get that far, there would be an uprising on the streets.

It was not a 'Chinese tsunami'

To be sure, a huge majority of the Chinese did vote for PR. But this did not mean that BN suffered because of a "Chinese tsunami". The Chinese alone could not have made up the numbers to deny BN a more comfortable victory. They constituted at most only 23% of the electorate.

Someone did the mathematics on the voting and found that with the voter turnout at 84.4%, if as high as 80% of the Chinese voters had given their support to PR, this would have amounted to only 2.5 million votes. It was less than half of the 5.62 million votes that PR secured. The remaining number must have therefore come from non-Chinese.

According to independent pollster Merdeka Centre, the GE13 results showed a major swing among the multi-racial urban and middle-class electorate against BN.

"There were differences between the low-income and the middle-income areas, as well as between the urban and rural areas," its executive director, Ibrahim Suffian, said, adding that Najib's reading was inaccurate because urban Malays had also voted for PR.

Shamsul Amri Baharuddin, a political analyst and academic, told the online news website *The Malaysian Insider* that PR received Malay middle-class support, especially in urban areas. "So the DAP majority increased because of disgruntled Malay young voters' support. ... To label racial polarisation is too easy. Two other factors operate simultaneously with race: class (rich-poor, middle class) and spatial (urban and rural)," he said.

Another political analyst, Lim Teck Ghee, said the results in Selangor, "which has the highest percentage of urban population, as well as in the other west coast states", indicated the urban middle-class trend to vote for PR. He noted that large numbers of Malays formed part of this middle class, "perhaps as many as non-Malays".

In a paper analysing the GE13 results, Lee Kam Hing of Universiti Malaya and Thock Ker Pong of Universiti Sains Malaysia revealed that the urban and middle-class support for the Opposition was over "issues such as crime, the economy, and corruption that cut across ethnic lines", which the voters felt BN had failed to address.

In Johor, PR unprecedentedly won five parliamentary seats and 18 state seats, improving greatly on its 2008 score of only one and six, respectively.

Of these, the DAP won four parliamentary seats and 13 state seats; PKR got one parliamentary seat and one state seat, which signified a breakthrough for the party in the state; and PAS scored its best record with four state seat victories.

In Gelang Patah, Kit Siang defeated no less than the Johor BN chief Abdul Ghani Othman, who was also the incumbent *menteri besar*, with a convincing majority of 14,762 votes.

Umno lost two parliamentary seats and two state seats. All this would not have been possible without a significant contribution of Malay votes.

Even Shahrir Samad, an Umno stalwart who was re-elected MP for

Johor Bahru for the sixth time, agreed that voter support should not be seen from merely a racial perspective.

"Umno won 88 federal seats in this general election; most of them came from rural constituencies in states such as Sabah, Kedah, Kelantan. From the above results, instead of saying that there was a shift in Chinese voters' support, it should actually be analysed from the differences in area, from the urban-rural divide," he said.

Another Umno man, Saifuddin Abdullah, said he had seen the signs of change coming a few years before. "At GE12, for the first time, I saw a non-Malay carrying a PAS flag. At that moment, as an Umno candidate, I smelled trouble. This time, I saw a DAP flag in a Malay village. Coming from Umno, I felt this was even more trouble. ... I'd strongly say that if you really care to look at the GE13 campaign, there was strong evidence that more and more Malaysians have become colour blind, and I stand by this argument."

Despite these many assertions that were contrary to his belief, Najib still appeared to be in denial. He refused to accept what the polls data indicated about the rural-urban divide. He said BN's own study showed that in the urban areas, the coalition received increased Malay support. Oh, well.

The power of the young

What Najib also failed or refused to acknowledge was the pivotal role played by young voters.

More than five million of the 13.3 million registered voters were under the age of 40, and over two million were first-time voters. They were tech-savvy and adept at networking through social media. They could easily access on Facebook and Twitter the allegations of dirty BN practices that the mainstream media blacked out, and follow debates on political issues that mattered to them.

Najib knew that the Internet would be the battleground for GE13. After having seen how the Opposition had used the Internet to rewarding effect at the 2008 general election, he urged BN to catch up. He himself led the way by blogging, tweeting and Facebooking like crazy. He also got his lackeys to unleash thousands of cybertroopers to counter the Opposition online.

But at the end of the day, it was still up to the information consumer to decide what they would believe. The younger ones in Malaysia were to mostly believe that the old regime could no longer be trusted.

A survey conducted by Merdeka Centre in February 2013 showed that those aged between 21 and 30 were the most dissatisfied with Najib's performance.

The Bersih rallies of 2011 and 2012 which drew tens of thousands of participants also showed the commitment of the young to pressing national issues. So did the protest against the opening of a rare earth plant in 2012.

"I know what young people want," said Mohamed Bukhairy Mohamed Sofian, a 23-year-old political science student who headed a student group advocating academic freedom. "They want a voice and that means change. They have opened their eyes to see that they can change Malaysia for the better."

Ong Kian Ming, an election strategist for the DAP who was elected MP for Serdang on his first time out at GE13, saw the great potential in the young being kingmakers, and got his party to engage with them. "BN still has the advantage in terms of resources, media, money, and machinery," he said. "The X-factor we are relying on is the newly registered voters."

Arise student activism!
Another X-factor was the revival of student activism in public universities. After decades of oppression under the Universities and University Colleges Act (UUCA), which deprived them of their right to engage in not just political activities but also social activities that were not approved by the Vice-Chancellor, public university students started to break out in 2008.

They were no doubt encouraged by the political landscape that had emerged from the election result of March 8, and by what they saw of the more politically aware *rakyat* demanding real democracy. Some were influenced even earlier by the *reformasi* movement started in 1998 by Anwar before he went to prison.

From August 2008, students started to make their presence felt in public by staging protests and supporting political parties. They protested not only against the UUCA but also took up public causes like the rising prices of essential goods.

They were not afraid to use strong language to slam government leaders who cared more for their own "coffers and stomachs" or to warn that the Government would be "overthrown in the next general election" if it did not change its attitude.

In December 2011, in anticipation of GE13 being called, a few students like Shazni Munir bin Mohd Ithnin offered themselves as candidates to pro-*rakyat* political parties. This was open defiance of the UUCA.

Writing in an article that was published by the online news website *MalaysianDigest.com*, I called it "an act of courage". I was elated that students had come to realise that they had "more power now" than they had ever had in the last four decades.

'Cool' Najib failed to swing the young

At GE13, the young came out to reject BN. Statistics showed a common pattern of young voters swinging closer to the Opposition. Among young Chinese, as high as 90% of those aged 30 and below voted for PR.

PR also made large gains from Malay youths in urban seats, and on the whole obtained 5% more support from them while BN lost 3% of their support.

Of the PR parties, PAS garnered the highest support from Malay youths in Peninsular Malaysia, with 73% voting for it averaged from all the seats it contested. This amounted to an 8% swing.

It looked like Najib's efforts to reach out to the young by projecting a 'cool' image, gathering nearly 1.5 million followers on Twitter, organising free music concerts featuring international acts, inviting fans to watch televised football matches together with him, and offering BR1M cash handouts to those earning less that RM2,000 a month … all these failed to persuade more of them to vote for his coalition.

In fact, in the early hours of May 6, 2013, after the EC had declared BN the election victor, it was the young who felt the most disappointed. The utmost question that came to their minds was whether it was really true, as Anwar had claimed, that the elections were marred by fraud.

They became almost convinced when Bersih came out after Anwar did to announce that it, too, would withhold recognition of BN's victory, until it had verified reports of electoral fraud, phantom voters and other irregularities in the voting and vote-counting processes.

With Bersih and Anwar declining to accept the election result, the young felt hopeful that GE13 might somehow still be saved. Like Anwar, they were not willing to give up yet.

But was there fraud, really? And if there was, did it warrant denying BN its precious victory?

BLACKOUTS AND BANGLADESHIS

BN did have an unfair headstart.

For one, it heavily controlled the mainstream media. The Printing Presses and Publications Act kept newspapers in thrall with the restrictive requirement that they must have a permit in order to publish.

The Home Ministry monitored these publications to make sure they behaved. Its minister was given the authority to grant and revoke the permits. This meant that he could suspend or ban a publication if he thought it was justified.

For the sake of preserving their permits, newspapers toed the line. Editors would not jeopardise their positions by running reports that were controversial or detrimental to the ruling party. Or even slightly critical of it.

In any case, most of them did not have a free hand to perform their jobs also because most of the large-circulation newspapers like *Utusan Malaysia*, *Berita Harian*, *New Straits Times* and *The Star* were owned by BN component parties. They naturally harkened to their masters' voices and gave little or no positive coverage to the Opposition.

BN parties also owned the private television stations TV3, 8TV, ntv7 and TV9, which of course extended the reach of the coalition's propaganda.

The media control became complete with the BN government lording over state-funded media agencies as well. These included the radio and TV platforms of Radio Televisyen Malaysia (RTM) and the national news agency, Bernama.

With no access to any of these and facing hostility from the BN-owned media organisations, the Opposition was very much disadvantaged.

A 10-minute offer for 'beggars'

One of Bersih's demands for ensuring a free and fair general election was the allocation of proportionate and objective media coverage for all political parties, especially by media agencies paid for with the *rakyat's* money which should, by right, be open to all parties. But this was not to be so.

The BN government was willing to allow the Opposition some airtime on RTM to broadcast its election manifesto, but the amount of time it would allow was only 10 minutes. On top of that, the programme would have to be pre-recorded.

Feeling insulted, Opposition leaders rejected the ridiculously paltry offer and called it a mockery of free speech. They felt they were being treated like "beggars".

In response, the minister in charge of information and communications, Rais Yatim, called PR "arrogant". He of course would not acknowledge that the Government's offer was unfair in a democratic election.

But Bersih did. The day after GE13, after having observed the shameless partisanship shown by the print media in the run-up to election day, its co-chairperson Ambiga Sreenevasan called for a month-long boycott of several newspapers.

"The stance of the newspapers during the campaign was wholly unacceptable in a democratic society. I think we need to express our disgust," said Ambiga, an articulate and highly intelligent lawyer who was also noted for her brave and dynamic leadership as an activist, having led the impactful Bersih 2 and Bersih 3 rallies that captured the imagination of the Malaysian public.

Problem of 'phantom voters'

Another unfair advantage BN had over PR was the EC showing bias towards it instead of maintaining a neutral stand and conducting the elections fairly and equitably as it was mandated to do.

It also gerrymandered electoral boundaries, like hugely increasing the electorate sizes of Opposition strongholds and thereby diluting the worth of their votes, and turned a blind eye to blatant offences committed by BN during the campaign period.

Bersih and the Opposition were most unhappy with the electoral roll that the EC maintained and consistently pointed out irregularities in it, such as the continued existence of dead persons and multiple persons registered under a single address or non-existent addresses. They called for the electoral roll to be cleaned up to wipe out these "phantom voters". But the EC repeatedly ignored them.

The Government was pressured to do something about the conduct of free and fair elections only after the Bersih 2 rally of 2011 created a strong national impact. Faced with public opinion expressing scepticism over the integrity of the electoral system, Najib called for the establishment of a parliamentary select committee to examine the system and propose reforms.

Born in 1890 and still in voting roll

The committee proposed 22 recommendations on how to improve the electoral process. One of the things it highlighted was the discovery of 938 addresses that had 51 to 100 registered voters in each of them, and 324 with more than 100 registered voters.

The Malaysian Electoral Roll Analysis Project (Merap), a research effort headed by the DAP's Ong Kian Ming, identified several questionable categories of voter registrations.

One category related to voters with the same name and some with the same date of birth. For example, 369 voters named 'Fatimah binti Ismail' were found in the Terengganu electoral roll. Out of the 369 mentioned, 10 pairs of voters had the same date of birth. This seemed like too much of a coincidence.

Merap also discovered that more than 1,000 voters were listed as being 100 years old and above. Nineteen were born before 1900. One was registered as being born in 1890, which would make her 123 years old at GE13. Merap was concerned that the identity cards of dead voters could be used by unscrupulous elements to vote on their behalf.

Despite all these discoveries, EC chairman Abdul Aziz Mohd Yusof maintained that "I am happy with our electoral roll although it can never be 100% perfect. But for the Opposition, whatever we do, they are not happy. For them, we are like a punching bag. Whatever we do, they say we are wrong, we are not clean and cannot be trusted."

EC turned a blind eye

Actually, the EC did prove that it could not be trusted when it turned a blind eye to the election offences BN committed during the campaign period. As it was just a caretaker government at the time, BN was not allowed to make use of state machinery for campaigning, but it continued to do so regardless.

Merdeka Centre recorded in its 'GE13: Election Watch Report' that "there was plenty of campaigning at government venues, including schools and army camps".

It observed that at ground-breaking ceremonies and events addressing civil servants, "officials of the caretaker government consistently wore BN shirts and urged those in attendance to vote for the party".

At the Lumut naval base, Mahathir was allowed to campaign inside with BN's candidate for Lumut, Kong Cho Ha, but PR's candidate, a former navy officer with more than 30 years of service, was not even allowed into the camp "to perform his prayers at the mosque".

Merdeka Centre also recorded that "the federal caretaker government grossly violated its powers, especially in repeatedly making pledges offering financial grants and projects".

'If you love me, help me ...'

The most prominent transgressor was Najib. Once he dissolved Parliament to call for elections and became only caretaker prime minister, he was not supposed to make long-term policy decisions, enter into contracts involving public funds or give away money from the public purse.

But he abandoned propriety. He announced an allocation of RM3.8 million to 10 Sikh NGOs. He signed a memorandum of understanding with the Hindu Rights Action Force (Hindraf) to improve the welfare of the Indian community. He announced that the Federal Government would build 9,999 low-medium-cost and affordable houses in Penang.

Transparency International Malaysia (TI-M) was prompted to condemn Najib for violating the Election Integrity pledge he had signed with the organisation in February. It said Najib's actions "do not contribute to raising public trust that the 13th general election will be clean, free and fair".

TI-M quoted as examples his announcements of extending a 1Malaysia discount card to 725,000 civil service retirees, a RM400 million complex to be constructed in Perak, and affordable homes to be built in Putrajaya for civil servants.

When he launched the housing project, he appealed to civil servants to vote for BN. This was bad enough as it meant he was blatantly campaigning. But what he said to them was goosebumps-raising: "If you love me, help me …"

Love the PM, indeed. "What's love got to do, got to do with it? What's love when it's second-placed to *duit* (money)?" Ha ha ha!

'You help me, I help you'

This appeal for help was a variant of his famous "you help me, I help you" line that surfaced at the Sibu by-election in 2010. While campaigning for the BN candidate Robert Lau, he told residents of a housing estate that if they voted for BN and it won, he would sign a cheque for RM5 million to resolve their flood problems.

"I want to make a deal with you. *Boleh tidak?* (Can or not?) Can we have a deal? Can we have an understanding or not? The understanding is quite simple – you help me, I help you," he said to an audience of about a thousand. "If you deliver me Robert Lau on Sunday, on Monday I will ask for the cheque to be prepared."

This deal offer was recorded on video. It of course went viral. The late Karpal Singh, a lawyer and one of the DAP's highly revered leaders, called on the EC and the MACC to take action against Najib for this blatant attempt at vote-buying. But nothing came of it.

EC chief Abdul Aziz refused to take a stand on the matter, conveniently saying, "I am not an expert. I can't say this is definitely corruption. I don't know." The MACC said it was investigating the matter. Then a year later, Parliament said Najib did not commit any offence, and that was that.

No one left behind in vote-buying spree

The way Najib threw money and offered goodies, it appeared as if that was the only way he knew to win the people's hearts and votes.

He came up with the idea of giving the 1Malaysia People's Aid (BR1M) cash handouts in 2012, possibly timed to influence the voting at the impending GE13. It began as a single payment of RM500 to low-income households earning less than RM3,000 a month, a one-time bribe.

A substantial total of 4.2 million households benefitted from it. That made up an astonishing 80% of Malaysian households. This ironically showed that the Government must have fared pretty badly over the decades in raising household incomes.

But few people cared about that point, most were happy to get the money. And when Najib saw how much gratitude the Government got in return for that first handout, he decided to give it again.

In January 2013, the same amount was distributed to households that met the income criterion, but this time something else was added. Those who were single and aged 21 and above and earning not more than RM2,000 a month would also be entitled. They would get RM250. Najib was also targeting the younger voters.

Altogether, 4.3 million households and 2.7 million individuals benefitted from it. As a result, a lot of people felt beholden to the Government. Cheered by their response, Najib announced that the Government would give out more BR1M handouts if BN won the elections.

He also made sure he took good care of the 1.3 million civil servants of whom the majority were traditionally considered BN's vote bank. In 2012, he increased their salaries and awarded them an extra bonus.

In 2013, two months before GE13, he unveiled a new remuneration scheme that offered them more pay increments. And those who had reached the maximum level of their salary scale would be given three increments in the next 10 months to relieve them of their otherwise static salary.

Najib also catered for the staff of statutory bodies, announcing extensive benefits for them. And then he turned to taxi drivers and promised to award 10,000 individual permits to free them from their bondage to taxi companies, which had all this while been the ones issued the permits.

The way he was going, did he leave anyone out at all in his pork barrelling spree?

RoS scare for DAP

If all that vote-buying was still not enough, BN also had the Registrar of Societies (RoS) playing to its tune. Attached as it was to the Home Ministry, the RoS unsurprisingly did not treat all political parties equally, especially non-BN ones. It sat for a long time on PR's application to be registered as a coalition so that by the time GE13 came around, it was still not registered. This posed an electoral disadvantage for PR.

Three weeks before the elections, the RoS gave the DAP a big scare when it decided not to recognise the party's office bearers because of irregularities in its election process the previous December.

Thrown into disarray and worried that it might be disqualified from standing in GE13, the DAP scrambled to find another option for participation. Fortunately, PAS came forward and offered the party the use of its logo.

But, to everyone's relief, the contingency measure was eventually not needed. Just two weeks before the elections, the RoS as well as the EC said the DAP could contest under its own logo as per usual as the party had not been deregistered

The indelible ink that wasn't indelible

From all that, anyone could see that even before election day, BN was well-equipped to bulldoze to victory. If you're familiar with 'Sink the Bismarck', a 1960 song by Johnny Horton, you could think of BN as the Bismarck, which was "the biggest ship that had the biggest guns". How was PR going to "send the Bismark to the bottom of the sea"?

PR, however, had going for it the spirit of the people who wanted to "hit the decks a-runnin' and spin those guns around" and "then cut BN down". On election day, these eager beavers for a change of government kept a sharp lookout for any incidents of electoral hanky-panky that might arise. All over the country, they went all out to make sure that BN could not employ further means to win through foul play.

Myriads of reports surfaced of the unreliability of the indelible ink that was being used as a mechanism to prevent multiple voting. Many complained after voting that they were able to wash off the indelible ink easily with a hand sanitiser or soap although it was supposed to remain on the finger for seven days.

When the deputy EC chairman, Wan Ahmad Wan Omar, was straight away asked by the media about the ink being so delible, he dismissed the matter arrogantly, "I'm not worried about the indelible ink, I tell you very frankly. I'm not worried about it because tomorrow there is no voting anymore."

What a laugh! Because there's no more voting tomorrow, it's okay if there's a problem today? Where's the logic? So the EC was not going to do anything while the voting was still going on and fraud could happen?

It shouldn't have been an issue

In the first place, indelible ink should not have been an issue anymore on May 6. Because a week earlier, on April 30, when early voting was held for the country's armed forces personnel and their spouses, many of them found to their surprise that the ink washed off a few hours after they had voted.

This prompted Major Zaidi Ahmad of the Royal Malaysian Air Force, his wife and Sergeant Jamal bin Ibrahim to make a police report about it the next day.

They were the only ones who did that out of the more than 235,000 who cast their votes that day.

Major Zaidi thought it was his responsibility as a citizen to make the report to prevent unscrupulous people from voting multiple times. But at first he was not aware of the condition of the ink.

As he recalled, "After voting, I logged on to the Internet and found that my other friends from the army were complaining about the ease with which the ink could be removed from their fingers – but no one would dare speak up and reveal their identities. I tried washing the ink off my fingers with a handwash and dish soap and found that it went off in just a couple of hours!

"Then that night, the EC chairman proudly announced that the initial voting was carried out smoothly without a single complaint that the ink used could be removed or washed off. He went on to say that the ink would last up to seven days! I could not let this go – Malaysians were being blatantly lied to."

He decided to do something about it, partly because his army colleagues were not willing to stick their necks out for fear of the authorities. "I felt I would have betrayed the *rakyat* if I let it go, because I was being paid by the *rakyat* to do my job. ... As a Muslim, I had to be honest to the *rakyat* who place their faith in the army who are supposed to guard them from threats, whether foreign or domestic."

Punished for telling the public the truth

Two days after Zaidi made the police report and spoke to the media to warn people about the ink, he was transferred out from active duty to a desk job. The pilot who had been with the air force for more than 20 years was grounded from flying.

Nine months later, in February 2014, he was called to face seven charges in a military court. The nation was shocked. Zaidi was being punished for telling the truth.

Political commentator Mariam Mokhtar wrote an article in her blog saluting Major Zaidi and also warning that Malaysia was entering "the latest phase of a new reign of terror". She viewed the move against Zaidi as an attempt by Umno "to solidify its stranglehold on the nation" by vilifying a member of the armed forces.

She slammed Zaidi's superiors for keeping silent "despite being aware of voting irregularities" and called them "traitors" for having broken their oath of allegiance.

"Malaysians salute Zaidi for making a stand for the *rakyat*. Now in his hour of need, we too must make a stand and show our undivided support for him," she exhorted.

The *rakyat* did make a stand for Zaidi. At least 40 NGOs urged the Malaysian Armed Forces Council to drop all seven charges against him. Pahlawan, an NGO representing retired army veterans, said it was wrong to prosecute Zaidi because he had committed no offence in carrying out his duty of lodging the police report.

Bersih launched its 'Support Major Zaidi Campaign' calling for the charges against him to be dropped. "Why is action taken against Zaidi when he was merely speaking the truth for the sake of public interest?" the NGO asked.

Malaysians spoke out on social media against the injustice. They hailed Zaidi as a hero. Someone posted on an online forum: "His freedom to speak has won him support from ordinary citizens but not freedom from the Government. When the Government is wrong, nobody is right."

Zaidi's fellow servicemen, however, did not show him public support. Online current issues website *cilisos.my* wondered why and interviewed Zaidi about it.

He said, "Initially, some supported me, especially on Facebook. But as you know, Facebook accounts – especially those of government workers – are monitored, so fewer and fewer armed forces personnel became active on my Facebook page. My relations with my colleagues are still normal, but they just avoid talking about my case. Most military personnel are inculcated with the belief that the Government is the provider of their income, so don't go against the Government or else you're being ungrateful."

Five of the charges against Zaidi were eventually dropped because they were found to be defective. After more than a year, in January 2015, the military court found him guilty of the remaining two charges of making statements about the indelible ink to the media without approval and sharing confidential information with the media on his transfer order. He was discharged from the armed forces.

After the court pronounced his sentence, Zaidi caused a stir when he told his judges, "We will meet in Allah's court in the afterlife."

RM7.1 million spent on something useless

Meanwhile, what happened with the EC, the organisation that should have taken the bullet instead? Was it held accountable for the indelible ink fiasco? Did anyone's head roll? You guessed it, no.

In June, one-and-a-half months after the general election, the EC explained that the ink came off easily because the amount of silver nitrate in it was only 1% instead of the standard 4%. It said the higher amount would have been detrimental to health. So it supplemented the ink with food colouring instead.

Those who knew their chemistry contradicted the EC's claim about the danger posed to health by silver nitrate. They said a little exposure to it would cause no harmful side effects whatsoever. And 1% was way, way too low for indelible ink used in elections, as the industry standard for such ink was at least 10%.

This made the EC a laughing stock, but the whole fiasco was no laughing matter. Government minister Shahidan Kassim disclosed in Parliament that the ink had been purchased for RM7.1 million, which was a lot of money spent on something that turned out to be useless! More than that, its inefficacy compromised the integrity of the electoral process and intensified the people's suspicion that the EC could not be trusted.

Watch out for foreign voters!

Other reports of fraud on election day concerned alleged power outages (or "blackouts") occurring at polling stations during the vote-counting process. It was suspected that this allowed for extra ballot boxes filled with votes for BN to be brought in surreptitiously. In such instances, Opposition candidates who had been leading in the vote count eventually ended up losing.

Prior to the elections, there was also the alarming allegation that the BN government would be flying in 40,000 Bangladeshis to vote for the coalition. This spread like wildfire on social media and many people came to believe it.

No one knows who started that, but there was also a claim by PKR that it had sighted e-mails showing that the Prime Minister's Office was chartering dozens of flights to bring thousands of foreigners from Borneo to Peninsular Malaysia. Anwar's party feared that these people were going to be brought in to vote in marginal constituencies under phantom ballots. BN responded to that claim by affirming that the chartered flights were going to take place but that they were sponsored by supporters of the Government to bring registered voters home.

On election day itself, people in scattered parts of the country tweeted about spotting foreign-looking people entering polling stations; about citizens taking it upon themselves to bar Myanmar, Indonesian and Bangladeshi nationals from voting; about police finding foreigners voting in a list of stations nationwide ranging from Klang to Taman Tun Dr Ismail to Kuantan to Penang; even about Bangladeshis giving up their identity cards because they felt guilty!

Several witnesses also reported that they encountered busloads of voters who did not look Malaysian arriving at polling stations. When the passengers were confronted to show proof that they were Malaysian, many of them could not perform basic tasks like sing the national anthem or recite the address on their identity card.

In Bangsar, a precinct that fell under the constituency of Lembah Pantai, constituents turned up in hordes to guard against fraudulent activities at the final tallying centre where all the votes from the polling stations were being brought to be added up. As the race for Lembah Pantai was neck-and-neck, its constituents were particularly anxious to prevent any hanky-panky that could cause the candidate of their choice to lose unfairly.

The more anxious ones were the PR supporters. When they saw vehicles approaching the centre and suspected them, rightly or wrongly, of carrying ballot boxes that might help the BN candidate, they swarmed round these vehicles to prevent the occupants from getting out and going into the centre.

SMSes were subsequently sent, tweets posted, charging that the Federal Reserve Unit (FRU) was called in to intervene, and that it even threatened to use tear gas on the recalcitrant constituents. This caused distress to PR supporters in other parts of the country anxious to find out if it would all end well. They would find relief only hours later when it was confirmed that the PR candidate, Nurul Izzah, had won. By a fairly tight majority of 1,847 votes.

No tear gas, no fear of extra ballot boxes

I didn't believe all the allegations surrounding electoral fraud, particularly those regarding the blackouts at polling stations during the counting process and the 40,000 Bangladeshis. I thought they were too far-fetched. Besides, there was no evidence to back them up.

However, the power of rumour can be seductive and infectious. And once an alarming claim goes viral, it tends to get accepted even when it has not been verified. The acceptance is even easier when the claim coheres with our emotion. So if we are angry at the prospect of electoral fraud, as soon as we are presented with a report of an alleged fraudulent activity, we are inclined to believe that it's true, no matter what. Verifying it first becomes secondary.

For instance, the fracas in Bangsar to protect Nurul Izzah from losing through fraud was not like how it was sensationalised in the tweets and text messages. Polling agent Johann Sze's eyewitness account bears that out.

"Yes, there were many stories about extra ballot boxes, unauthorised recounting, firing of tear gas and fights with the FRU," he wrote on Facebook. "No teargas was fired nor was there any confrontation with the FRU. Hence, please, do not spread stories which have not been verified, find out more and understand the election process and do not cause unnecessary distress among the people!"

He also wrote, "I received countless SMSes asking about the extra mysterious boxes. Nothing of such at Lembah Pantai, at least."

He explained that it did not matter how many ballot boxes were in the final tallying centre, because the final count was derived by compiling the Form 14 from each *saluran*. Form 14 contained the crucial information about how many votes each candidate received in that *saluran*. It had to be signed by the polling agents of all the candidates as well as the EC official and brought to the tallying centre.

Form 14 was the all-important thing, not the ballot boxes. These were also brought to the tallying centre but only as a formality. They would not be opened up for any purpose, and certainly not for re-counting of votes.

"Re-counting is only allowed in the respective *saluran* in the polling centre, not at the final tallying centres. If we were actually required to re-count in the tallying centre, it would have been crazy, as we would need to recount up to 60,000 votes!"

So, no need to have feared extra ballot boxes going into a tallying centre. But what about reports of blackouts? And the photograph that was posted on the Internet showing an EC official using a torchlight to conduct the vote count because the lights were allegedly out?

No blackouts either

After an investigation and close scrutiny, it was found to portray a fake situation, set up before GE13. The official was not wearing an EC shirt, and reporters and photographers were present in the background. In reality, only EC officials and polling agents are allowed at the counting of votes. So this was a clear piece of disinformation.

Apart from this, the deputy EC chief reinforced the idea that there could not have been any blackouts anywhere because no police reports were ever lodged in that regard. "If there had been a blackout, certainly the polling agents would have lodged police reports. They represented the candidates, they were present at the counting venues. If there had been a blackout, they would have been the first to lodge police reports, but there was none," he said. That made sense.

Furthermore, Tenaga Nasional Berhad, Malaysia's electricity provider, confirmed that there were no power disruptions during vote-counting at GE13.

As for the 40,000 Bangladeshis, I had served as a polling agent twice and realised that using so many of them to cheat could only be a myth. It's not easy to masquerade as someone else in order to vote under that person's name and identity card. Such an impostor would have to get past the levels of monitoring before receiving their ballot.

The monitoring is stringently done also by polling agents of the candidates. If they noticed anything untoward, like the name and/or identity card number not tallying or if the appearance of the would-be voter not matching the ethnicity suggested by the name, they could raise a protest to the EC official supervising the process.

Four months after the elections, my doubts were confirmed by Bersih's election monitoring group Pemantau. It reported that it did not find evidence of blackouts and foreign voters in the 87 parliamentary seats it had kept watch on. However, it could not vouch for the remaining 135 seats that were not part of its monitoring.

Ong Kian Ming agreed with the findings. He also said there were reports floating around of the Bentong parliamentary constituency having suffered a blackout during vote-counting, but when he checked with his colleagues, he was told there was no blackout.

Where were the Bangladeshis?

Unfortunately for the Opposition, the '40,000 Bangladeshis' hoax was to turn around and bite it. Najib used it gleefully to hit out at PR's lack of credibility whenever he found the opportunity to do so.

The month after GE13, he told Malaysian students in Indonesia, "Until today, there is no proof of the Opposition's claim that we brought in 40,000 Bangladeshis to vote for BN. This was slander and a very big lie ... That's why I ask, are people not able to think?"

Despite Anwar protesting that while PR spoke of suspicious voters, "we never said anything about 40,000 Bangladeshis", Najib brought it up again, in his Budget speech in October, and laughed his head off over it. He also told those who made the allegation to repent.

Soon afterwards, he was able to gloat to an international audience in an interview with Christiane Amanpour of CNN that "they alleged that we brought in 40,000 people from Bangladesh to vote in the last election, but they've not been able to produce any evidence of that".

Unfair election but results are credible

The issue of the 40,000 Bangladeshis aside, it was nonetheless obvious that GE13 was not fought on a level playing field. The Institute for Democracy and Economic Affairs (IDEAS) and the Centre for Public Policy Studies (CPPS) cited the same factors mentioned above and concluded that GE13 was an "unfair election".

However, the two NGOs, which were among 16 appointed by the EC to be independent observers at the elections, believed that although the election was unfair, its results remained "credible".

As for Pemantau, its preliminary observation report sent out on May 6 remarked that GE13 was "marred by violations of the election laws".

It cited a case of the EC showing preferential treatment when it allowed a BN candidate to submit their nomination form in absentia while a PR candidate was not allowed to do the same.

It also pointed out that during the campaign period, BN set up booths to woo voters by offering lucky draws with cash rewards. Its members also distributed goodies and money directly to voters. And BN politicians made speeches that were racially and religiously charged.

Following up on the preliminary reports, Ambiga said, "The extent of these reports has led us to question the legitimacy of some of the results. We have no doubt that the election was not clean and fair."

She announced that the NGO would set up a people's tribunal to investigate the extent of the electoral fraud, and until it had studied the findings of this tribunal, "Bersih is withholding recognition of the new government".

This declaration did nothing, however, to stop BN from claiming victory, as was its right. On May 6, 2013, Najib was sworn in as prime minister for his second term. The *ubah* supporters felt supremely despondent. This meant another five years of suffering under BN rule, another five years of struggle. They had come so close to winning, and lost. Many wept.

The more deeply affected ones felt dissatisfied. Like Anwar, they would not accept the election result. All the more so because the declarations of BN's unfair practices and the allegations of fraud intensified their feeling of having been cheated. They strongly felt that GE13 had been stolen from them.

They waited for Anwar's cue to take the next step. They harboured hope that action would be taken to delegitimise BN's victory. They looked to the leader to take that action.

As it turned out, they didn't have to wait long. It wasn't all over yet.

RALLYING IS THE NEW BLACK

The call for action came on May 6. Anwar Ibrahim reiterated that he did not accept the election result. He told *Malaysiakini*, "This election has been stolen from us by Umno-BN. As far as I am concerned, we won it."

He said "the true aspirations of Malaysians wanting reform" had been thwarted, and accused the EC of having been "complicit in the crime" of pulling off the "worst electoral fraud in our history".

He asserted that there was evidence for it and that PR would not accept the results of "about 30 to 40" constituencies. He and the leaders of the DAP and PAS would decide on the next course of action, which would probably involve making petitions to the courts to re-examine the results of these disputed seats.

That was just the preamble. The real Anwar came out when he next announced that a mass rally would be held on May 8 at a stadium in Kelana Jaya in Selangor. He said the rally would be "the beginning of a fierce movement to clean this country of election malpractices and fraud, for there is no opportunity for renewal without a clean and fair election".

News agency Reuters was to report the next day that by May 7 afternoon, "about 20,000 people had confirmed on a Facebook page that they would attend the rally".

The colour of the moment

Anwar called on the public to wear black as a sign of protest. "I shall address fellow Malaysians at the Kelana Jaya stadium at 8.30pm fully dressed in black."

The wearing of black was apparently prompted by an Internet campaign calling on people to mourn what the proponents termed "the death of democracy" in Malaysia.

In fact, news agency AP had reported soon after BN was declared winner of GE13, "Within minutes of the result being announced, thousands of Opposition supporters replaced their Facebook profile pictures with black boxes."

This not only underscored the extent of the negative reaction towards BN's victory, it also showed that black was the colour of the moment. Anwar recognised that. "I leave it to the Malaysian people, they are just enraged, you can't imagine the amount of anger," he told Australia Network's *Newsline*. "Hundreds of thousands are saying, wear black."

Grand Master's smart move

The mood changed after he called for the rally. From despondency to optimism. It struck me that the call seemed so apt, so necessary. Because a rally would bring the angered, the dejected, the disappointed together in an act of communion. They could find group healing through participating in it. They could at the very least *lepas geram* (release their frustrations). More importantly, they could unite and regroup, and rekindle their spirits for the future.

It was a smart move by Anwar. Suddenly, there was hope again, no matter how slender. And he was being seen as a harbinger of that hope. At the rally, he would be the Grand Master galvanising all the forces of 'good' against the 'evil' BN empire.

The rally was also an opportunity for him to gauge how much public support he could actually garner to back up his claim of victory. It could provide the legitimacy for the legal battles ahead. The larger the turnout, the greater the legitimacy.

How to find so much evidence?

Relating to the legal battles, Anwar announced on May 7 that Rafizi Ramli would head a team to investigate the electoral fraud.

Rafizi, PKR's director of strategy and one of its new first-timers elected into Parliament as member for Pandan, was widely seen as a good choice. He was smart, sharp and highly lauded for his well-timed exposure of the Cowgate scandal which ranked as a significant factor for BN's worst-ever performance in a general election.

Anwar counted on him to work closely with Bersih and other PR parties to match proof of fraud against empirical analyses of the results of the disputed constituencies. "In the next few weeks, we will present proof to the public that Najib Razak won this election through fraud and irregularities," Anwar declared.

I wondered, though, how this would be accomplished. If there were, as claimed, 30 to 40 constituencies disputed, Rafizi and his team would have to find specific instances of fraud for each specific constituency to support their case. And the number of instances in each constituency would have to be significant enough to justify that the result would have otherwise favoured PR. Finding evidence of enough instances would really take some doing. Presenting it in a few weeks to the public would be almost a miracle.

But of course this was one of the last things the comrades for change and ardent PR supporters cared about. When May 8 came around, they were more excited about the prospect of turning the election result around.

In their minds were these questions: Could the rally turn out to be a game-changer? Could it become a kind of people's revolution against the newly elected government? Could change still come about after all?

As usual, the police warned the public not to attend the rally, calling it illegal. Inspector-General of Police Ismail Omar warned that participants would be arrested. But Rafizi assured everyone that PKR had complied with provisions of the Peaceful Assembly Act by informing the police about the event.

Thus, the stage was set for a highly charged rally. What remained to be seen was how many people would attend. The number would be crucial. It would determine what further action might be taken in the days ahead.

A toll plaza becomes a huge car park!

That memorable evening, I set off with a friend for Kelana Jaya from the suburb of Damansara Jaya at about 6.30pm. I thought we would have ample time as the event would only start two hours later.

We took the New Klang Valley Expressway (NKVE) route to head for the Subang toll exit and then the Kelana Jaya stadium, thinking that this would be a faster way to go. After all, a normal drive from Damansara Jaya to the stadium via that way would normally take only 15 minutes.

As it turned out, we were wrong! Many cars came onto the NKVE that evening, more than I had ever seen before, and they seemed to be headed for the same destination. It was to take us an unprecedented one-and-a-half hours before we got to just the Subang toll plaza!

And when we got to that point, the traffic was at a total standstill. No car could budge. Vehicles were stuck everywhere – after the toll, just right before it, and in long lines behind it! There was a lot of honking but to no avail. So people decided to abandon their cars even right in the middle of the toll lanes and walk instead to the stadium.

As a result, the whole toll plaza became a huge car park!

I had never encountered such a surreal experience before. But after 20 minutes of waiting and moving only a few inches forward, I had to leave my car behind as well. It was already 8.30pm by then, my friend and I were going to be late. But we consoled ourselves that others would speak before Anwar so we could still catch his speech if we started walking now. We had no idea then that the stadium was nearly two kilometres away.

I later found out that cars were also parked on the NKVE itself, causing the three-lane expressway to be reduced to one lane. Unbelievable! But despite the situation, the mood there and at the toll plaza was one of festivity and merry camaraderie.

RALLYING IS THE NEW BLACK

Hundreds of people, mostly dressed in black, were walking towards the stadium. Some were carrying PKR, DAP and PAS flags, some chanting, "*Ubah! Ini kalilah!*" I accosted a Malay couple in their 70s who said they had just come all the way from Johor specially for the rally.

But we also came across a woman in her 30s who complained she could not get home because she was stuck in the standstill. I felt sorry for her because she wasn't going to the rally and she was tired after finishing work, and there was no telling how long it would take before the cars would clear.

Just then a motorcycle flashed by and a loud cry of "*Reformasi!*" rang out, accompanied by applause. We couldn't quite see for sure who were on it, but the pillion rider wearing black looked like Anwar. Someone confirmed it was him. It made sense for him to come to the event on a motorcycle. Otherwise, he would have been terribly late for his own party!

My friend and I trudged the distance to the stadium in semi-darkness, hearing from afar the intermittent roar of the crowd inside it and feeling envious we were not among them. We desperately hoped we would still be in time for a good part of the proceedings and, certainly, the main event.

By the time we finally reached the stadium, however, it was already past 10pm. We managed to push our way through the thick crowd at one of the entrances, but when we got to glimpse the inside of the stadium, we decided not to go in any further. The stadium was jam-packed. And with thousands of vuvuzelas creating a cacophony, it wasn't a comfortable place to be in.

Anwar was speaking, but we couldn't make out the words. People who were inside told us afterwards that they couldn't hear everything he said either because the air was overwhelmed by the noise.

Outside, a few thousand people were milling around. Most of them were also clad in black. I didn't see a single uniformed policeman around, despite the warning issued earlier about this being an illegal rally.

As many as 120,000
The blog *FinanceTwitter* reported afterwards, "Social media research group *Politweet.org* estimated the crowd size in and around the stadium at between

64,000 and 69,000, given that the stadium capacity is about 25,000. Some claimed there were easily 100,000 people ... with thousands more stuck in traffic and couldn't make it to the stadium."

Malaysiakini's estimate was even higher, at a phenomenal 120,000. It also included those who were caught in traffic and therefore unable to make it to the venue.

Whether it was 64,000 or 100,000 or 120,000, the fact remained that for a rally that was called only two days earlier, the response was incredible.

Bersih's co-chairperson Ambiga, who was also present, told *Free Malaysia Today* that the event left her speechless. "I thought Bersih 3 was stunning ... this was unbelievable," she said.

"As I was driving in, I saw lines and lines of people walking towards the stadium ... I felt I had to walk as well ... It was the dignity of the people, moving in harmony, for a single purpose ... People were stuck in massive traffic jams but nobody complained ... they honked in support. The spontaneous camaraderie was unbelievable."

'I never felt more Malaysian'

The next day, Sam, a reader of the blog *anilnetto.com*, wrote, "The crowd at the rally was a good mix. ... Everyone was expressing their disgust at Najib and his cohorts' attempts to stir up racial hatred. ... The gathering will definitely send out a very clear message that Malaysians are united, abhor cheating and thuggery."

Another reader, Ella, reported, "My nephew who was at last night's rally said, 'I never felt more Malaysian after seeing all races unite for one purpose.' And he had this story to tell: 'We were taking photos and several Malay boys came towards us. We asked to borrow one of their PAS flags. They also had a DAP flag. We asked to take a picture together and they said to put the DAP flag in the middle. They said we all must show support for the Chinese. I was touched.'

"Another niece was sitting with a group of Malays and Indians, no

Chinese in the group, and they shouted, 'We are Chinese, we are Chinese.' *Utusan Malaysia*, take a hike!"

Photographs of the scene inside the stadium spoke volumes of the people's commitment to the event. Every inch of space was taken, from the field to the running track to the topmost gallery. The goalposts on the field looked semi-buried in the sea of humanity. People stood shoulder to shoulder. Could they even move?

Looking at these photos, Najib and his colleagues would have been struck with fear and envy. BN had after all lost the popular vote, which raised doubts about its legitimacy as the government. Now it was standing on even more shaky ground. It looked like the people were solidly behind Anwar and PR.

Launch of the Black 505 series

To add to Najib and Co's nightmares, Anwar told the crowd that night, "I want to show and prove to Najib, Umno and BN leaders that this is not a Chinese battle, not a Malay battle … we will go to every nook and corner of the country to show we have the support of all Malaysians." He warned, "This is merely the beginning of the battle between the people and an illegitimate, corrupt and arrogant government. We will continue this struggle and we will never surrender."

He then announced that a series of rallies of a similar nature, dubbed 'Black 505', would be held throughout the country.

The next one was held on May 11 at the Batu Kawan Stadium on the mainland side of Penang. I decided to go for that one, too.

I drove from Kuala Lumpur to Penang island earlier that day and checked into a hotel. Then I decided to leave for the stadium early. So by 5.15pm, I managed to cross the Penang Bridge to get to the mainland. The traffic on the bridge was relatively light then.

It wasn't so when I got near to the turn-off to Batu Kawan on the North-South Expressway. At that point, there were so many cars headed in the same direction, we all had to slow down to a crawl. It was to take me three hours eventually to reach the stadium from the time I set off. Ordinarily, it would have taken 45 minutes.

But that was one traffic jam that those caught in it didn't seem to mind. I was to note in an article I wrote for *MalaysianDigest.com* their buoyant mood: "Everyone was a friend. The four middle-aged Indian men in a car I passed by, the group of young Chinese in another car with PAS and PKR flags sticking out of it, the young Malays on motorcycles bearing PAS and DAP flags – they smiled, they waved, they raised thumbs-up signs. Everyone was in it together. Everyone recognised in one another their common purpose. Even lorry drivers passing by on the North-South Expressway honked in support."

A few kilometres from the stadium, cars were already parked by the side of the road and people were walking to the venue. I passed by thousands, most of them dressed in black, marching resolutely in orderly fashion, some carrying party flags, some blowing vuvuzelas, some spiritedly shouting slogans like "*Hidup! Hidup! Hidup rakyat!*" Most of them were young people.

When I arrived at the stadium, the event was just about to start. I was surprised to get a parking spot quite easily. The stadium wasn't full then, but when it did fill up later that night, the total number of people inside must have been at least 60,000. Outside the stadium were thousands more.

I also heard that many people couldn't make it to the rally because of the massive traffic jam. A friend of mine got stuck right after he drove onto the Penang Bridge. He eventually had to turn back. The same thing happened to his nephew.

'85% were young'

The Star reported the next day that at 10pm, crowds were still pouring into the stadium. "Many had walked for 5km or more, as they had trouble parking their vehicles." Among them were PAS deputy president Mohamad Sabu, popularly known as Mat Sabu, and Penang chief minister Lim Guan Eng.

Susan Loone of *Malaysiakini* reported that "85% of the multi-racial crowd were young men and women". That was very encouraging.

I couldn't say the same, however, of the bluster from the politicians who spoke that night. It was the same old stuff we had heard before. They accused the EC of being complicit in the fraud and demanded that its leaders resign, called on Najib to step down as prime minister, claimed that PR had won the popular vote – and, in fact, the entire general election. But all this talk was just talk.

I wondered how PR would concretely prove the alleged fraud. I wondered how the *ubah* supporters would feel if PR should fail to do it in the end, after having riled them up and made them hunger for a resolution. Would they feel that their support came to nothing? Would they lose their trust in Anwar and turn against PR?

The best thing to emerge from the rallies

As I thought about it while sitting out the jam heading back to Penang island, something else caught my attention.

"It was the sight of the rally participants walking back to their vehicles, in the same orderly manner as before," I wrote in my article. "They showed they were not there to create a disturbance; they were there to assert their right – to be heard. And they were united in spirit.

"It is this that is perhaps the most precious feature of these rallies. And it is this that Malaysia needs to cultivate. If nothing else, Anwar and PR have managed to harness that spirit. And it is perhaps their success in doing so that might exonerate them if nothing comes off in the end.

"As I watched the young rally participants pass by, still energetic despite the long walk, some reluctant to go home, some still waving banners by the side of the expressway to the encouragement of honking motorists, I felt exhilarated by their refreshing vigour.

"I felt I was witness to a revolution of the young. A Budding Sprightly Spring."

Huge crowd at every rally

In the days to come, the rallies went to other towns and cities – Ipoh, Kuantan, Johor Bahru, Seremban, Alor Setar, Kuala Terengganu, Bukit Katil, Petaling Jaya, Kangar, Sungai Petani, Kota Bharu, Batu Pahat.

They never failed to draw huge crowds as Anwar's claim resonated with the people. At each gathering, he and other speakers would invariably whack the EC and demand that its leaders be replaced by a new team chosen in a bipartisan manner. They also called for by-elections to be held for 30 parliamentary seats which PR had marginally lost allegedly because of fraud.

In Alor Setar on May 21, a crowd of about 50,000, mostly Malays, showed up. Sungei Petani MP Johari Abdul was prompted to remark, "This is an extraordinary crowd and it proves people like MCA president Chua Soi Lek wrong. Soi Lek says only the Chinese attend the 'Black 505' rallies but what we saw tonight were the Malays in full force."

On May 25, the tenth rally in the series was held in Petaling Jaya, Selangor, and about 70,000 people came for it. They were as fervent as ever. They cheered when Nurul Izzah declared that the EC must pay for its "crimes".

Then when Anwar came on and asked whether the 'Black 505' rallies should go on or stop, they roared back, "Go on!"

But by the time the rally moved to Kuala Lumpur on June 22, there had already been 14 before it over the previous one-and-a-half months. Although it was to be held in the capital and the organisers expected a moment-defining turnout of 300,000, only 30,000 came.

Stop this 'festival of madness'!

The organisers blamed the low turnout on the haze that had been afflicting the country since a few days before. But lately, BN leaders had been criticising Anwar for challenging the election result by taking it to the streets when that was not the proper way to do it.

Government minister Ahmad Shabery Cheek had said Malaysians must boycott the Opposition's "*pesta kegilaan*" (festival of madness) and accept that BN won GE13. Mahahir Mohamad had remarked sarcastically on his blog, "Perhaps it would be better if governments were chosen through street demonstrations. It would probably be less fraudulent."

Even PKR's own deputy president, Azmin Ali, had tweeted his disapproval of the very first rally. He explained two days later, on May 10, that it was because he felt that PR should instead be collecting information on fraud and working at filing election petitions.

"I am not against the right to assemble, this is enshrined in the Constitution … but are we to rally every day, week and month?" he asked. "We should start working, and not be politicking too much as the next election is just a few years ahead."

Picking up on this, online forums had been questioning what the rallies were meant to achieve since the election result could not be overturned through protests. A couple of academics wanted them to end.

"Stop all this rally nonsense. People are growing tired," said Mustafa Ishak of Universiti Utara Malaysia. "Stop inciting the people. We must respect the rule of law and the people's decision."

Mohamad Zaini Abu Bakar of Universiti Sains Malaysia said, "Let's learn from the West and countries such as Japan and South Korea. They became strong nations because they focused on political stability, which in return facilitated their economic and education development. All these rallies will only contribute to havoc and political uncertainties."

My old friend, academic and political commentator Zaharom Nain, did not agree. He said the rallies were not about Anwar or other PR leaders. "Indeed, Anwar may have inspired them but the rallies are attended by those who are genuinely concerned about the state of our country."

He said the people wanted to keep the issue of electoral irregularities alive, especially when the culprits and their supporters wanted to sweep the matter under the carpet. He also said, "The idiots and sycophants running the show must be replaced by professionals and untainted people. The EC itself must be independent and not beholden to BN."

Anwar salutes the rally participants

In any case, the Kuala Lumpur rally proceeded as planned, right in the heart of the capital at the open area of Padang Merbok. And the call for the leadership of the EC to resign remained as strong as ever, endorsed by the participants emphatically.

"We will push till the end for their resignation," Abdullah Abdul Rahman, a 42-year-old who had come all the way from Alor Setar in the north, told *Malaysiakini*. "If not, it will be like this *sampai kiamat* (until doomsday)."

Wheelchair-bound Fennix Lim, 25, said he had come all the way from Kluang, Johor, just to participate in the rally. "As a Malaysian, I want to show my will to the Government and the EC that we all reject the EC. I came for democracy," he declared.

Anwar paid tribute to the participants for coming despite the haze. "Many made the decision to not join us because of the weather," he said. "To those who are here, who understand the meaning of freedom, I salute you."

He slammed the EC leaders hard and demanded that they step down, particularly its chairman, Abdul Aziz, who had since admitted failure in his handling of the indelible ink controversy. Without pulling any punches, Anwar struck out, "He is more stupid than a primary school student."

Then he gave EC deputy chairman Wan Ahmad a few stinging blows: "Wan Ahmad is a liar, he is arrogant, he insults the *rakyat*. He should be hauled to court."

He announced that the protests would continue. "We have won the elections, we have a clear mandate. If there had been no massive rigging and fraud, everyone knows we would have received 60% of the popular vote," he said.

Claiming 60% of the popular vote seemed far-fetched, and it made Anwar sound like a desperate man. But then that sounded like the kind of bravado that would come from him.

Fortunately, his pledge to continue protesting did not materialise in more 'Black 505' rallies. The signs of fatigue were already starting to show. More significantly, it was also looking more obvious that although the DAP and PAS had been fielding speakers at the rallies, the protests had largely been driven and organised by PKR. It was time to stop before the people got really tired and stopped showing their support.

Besides, there had been a price to pay for organising and taking part in the rallies. The police had been arresting numerous PR leaders as well as activists, mostly for contravening the Peaceful Assembly Act.

The price to pay

The PKR casualty list included its information chief Nik Nazmi Nik Ahmad, deputy youth chief Khairul Anuar Ahmad Zainuddin, Perak state secretary Mohammad Anuar Zakaria, Johor state executive secretary B. Yuvanesh, Negeri Sembilan youth chief Nazree Yunus, Pahang state secretary Kamarzaman Md Yunus, and Rafizi Ramli.

Two DAP MPs, Anthony Loke Siew Fook and Thomas Su Keong Siong, and PAS's Batu Burok assemblyman, Syed Azman Syed Ahmad Nawawi, were also taken in and charged. Along with Muhammad Adib Ishar and Ong Eu Leong, who were staff members of PR.

On June 24, 33 activists were arrested for taking part in an illegal assembly outside Parliament. They were among hundreds of 'Black 505' participants who wanted to hand over a memorandum to MPs who were being sworn in for their first term.

In 2016, five of them were to be found guilty of illegal assembly – Muhamad Aiman Hakim Zainal Arifin, Mah Chee Hoe, Tong Chan Sang, Abdullah Hassan and Annie Ooi Siew Lan, better known as Aunty Bersih for her fervent participation in Bersih rallies.

Ten were to be found guilty of illegal assembly and rioting – Norazimah Mohamad Nor, Ahmad Shauqie Abdul Aziz, Ahmad Syukri Che Ab Razab, Lim Sue Pei, Edy Nor Reduan, Md Sani Md Shah, Muhammad Safwan Anang, Ekhsan Bukharee Badarul Hisham, Adam Adli Abdul Halim and Badrul Hisham Shaharin, popularly known as Chegubard.

Adam Adli, Safwan and Ekhsan Bukharee were also charged with Mohamed Bukhairy Mohamed Sofian and PKR's Khairul Anuar Ahmad Zainuddin for participating in the 'Black 505' rally of June 22. The first four were student activists. All five were to be acquitted in April 2018.

Adam Adli and Safwan also faced the charge of uttering seditious words, which included calling for people to "go to the streets to take back our power", at a public forum in Kuala Lumpur on May 13, 2013.

Also charged for doing the same at the same forum were PKR vice-president Tian Chua, Anything But Umno (ABU) leader Haris Ibrahim, PAS member Tamrin Abdul Ghafar and activist Hishamuddin Rais, who had reportedly told the forum that taking part in street protests was the surest way to bring about a change in government because challenging the election results through legal channels would be futile.

Tian Chua was arrested at an airport. He tweeted afterwards to encourage Malaysians not to be "overtaken by fear but continue to assemble peacefully and have faith". He was sentenced to three months' jail and fined RM1,800. He lodged an appeal. Meanwhile, the Government filed an appeal to enhance the sentence.

Hishamuddin was fined RM5,000. He appealed the conviction and got a heavier sentence of nine months' jail instead. He then took it to the Court of Appeal, which reverted to the RM5,000 fine.

Haris, a lawyer noted for his blog *The People's Parliament* and for his activism, was sentenced to eight months' jail. He appealed and his sentence was replaced by a RM4,000 fine.

Adam Adli, who had first gained public attention for boldly bringing down a flag bearing Najib's portrait at Umno's headquarters in 2011, was sentenced to 12 months' jail. He appealed and had his sentence substituted with a fine of RM5,000. He then brought his case to the Court of Appeal, which summarily acquitted him.

The Court of Appeal also acquitted Safwan after he was first sentenced to 10 months' jail and RM5,000 fine.

People who understood that the action taken against these activists and politicians was motivated by the insecurity of a shaky government and nothing else viewed them not as guilty offenders but as heroes.

The real worth of the rallies

As the days went by, more and more heroes emerged from among concerned citizens to defy the authorities. This greatly heartened the people who still held hope for change and strengthened their resolve.

In the end, it did not really matter so much that the 'Black 505' rallies might not change the GE13 result. What mattered above all was the fact that the people had their say. By showing up in such huge numbers at the rallies, they made it known to the BN government that they were a force to reckon with.

They felt a palpable sense of power, regardless of how small it might actually be. They participated in a democratic act. They established their stake in the country. They rallied to be counted. They were Malaysians.

And, importantly for PR, this collective action would form a collective memory that would be hard to erase soon. When those who took part in the rallies had to decide between BN and PR in future referendums, it would be most unlikely that they would choose BN when they thought back on their 'Black 505' experience.

Also important, most of them were young. Heirs of future Malaysia. They were going to be around for the long run. If they stayed the course, and their numbers increased, they would play a key role in kicking BN out, perhaps at the next general election.

NO DAY IN COURT

As the 'Black 505' protest continued on its nationwide road tour, Rafizi Ramli announced on May 24 that PR intended to file petitions in court to challenge the results of 29 parliamentary constituencies and a number of state seats.

A week later, Najib Razak announced that BN would file more than 50 election petitions. That many? What a surprise! Was it a display of one-upmanship?

However, by the deadline of June 12 set by the EC for filing petitions, the number BN settled on was only 21. Its secretary-general, Tengku Adnan Tengku Mansor, said BN decided to reduce the number by more than half to save the court time and avoid unreasonable costs.

PR, on the other hand, ended up filing against 25 instead of 29 parliamentary seats. It also challenged 10 state seats. The petitions both PR and BN put in added up to make the highest number ever in Malaysian history.

A dicey proposition

For PR, its overall challenge seemed like a touch-and-go prospect. It would have to win 23 of its parliamentary cases in order to take over the government by just the slimmest simple majority. What were the chances? But if it should succeed, the government it would form would be extremely shaky.

In any case, I still had my doubts as to how PR would be able to furnish enough convincing evidence for each specific constituency it challenged. I imagined that if, say, a PR candidate lost in a constituency by, say, 300 votes, it would have to prove that had there been no fraud, 151 of those 300 should have gone its way. It would also have to prove how the fraud prevented it from getting those 151 votes. And it would have to be specific about it.

It could not simply say, for example, that it was robbed of victory because the indelible ink was not indelible and therefore voters could have voted more than once. That would be too general to nullify the election. In fact, even if it produced affidavits from 151 voters in that constituency stating that they managed to wash the ink off their finger immediately after voting, it would still not be enough. It is incumbent on the challenger to prove that these 151 voters voted again, and in doing so affected the outcome of the election.

But I suppose this was only one approach to take. Going by the Election Offences Act, PR could cite other infringements committed by their opponents to make them vacate their seats. These included vote-buying and voter intimidation.

Murder as well!

In addition, even the alleged effects of a murder were considered!

The murder was that of K. Murugan, who was helping PKR's Vasantha Kumar with her campaigning in Tapah despite getting death threats urging him to stop. He was eventually found dead in a river, his hands and feet tied, his body weighed down by scrap metal. "We believe that Murugan was murdered to intimidate the voters," claimed Vasantha.

She submitted a petition to challenge the result of the Tapah parliamentary contest which she had lost to M. Saravanan of BN. But the Election Court dismissed her petition for not adhering to the Election Petition Rules. As it transpired, hers was only one of many more GE13 election petitions that would get thrown out simply because they did not comply strictly with one or two of the rules.

Vasantha then appealed to the Federal Court, which sent the petition back to the Election Court to be heard on its merits. The Election Court judge then found that the facts in the petition were not properly explained. Vasantha claimed that there had been bribery during GE13, but did not make clear who had made the bribe. She also did not explain how her defeat occurred. The judge rejected the petition and ordered Vasantha to pay whopping costs of RM110,000.

Not yet a candidate, not corrupt!

In the case of the Bagan Datoh parliamentary seat, which attracted two petitions, the Election Court initially struck both out, again because of a technicality. Instead of stating the name of the petitioner's lawyer in the petition, which is according to the Election Petition Rules, they had stated the name of the law firm. That was enough to get their case thrown out.

The petitioners then appealed to the Federal Court, which then sent the petitions back to the Election Court and instructed it to hear the merits of the case. The Election Court then found that both the petitioners did not have sufficient facts to support their allegations of corrupt practices, and dismissed the petitions.

In a last-ditch attempt, the petitioners appealed again to the Federal Court. This time, it heard their allegation that the candidate who won, government minister Ahmad Zahid Hamidi, had given out money and bags of rice on April 19, 2013, for the purpose of buying votes. As such, he should be found guilty of bribery and his victory nullified.

However, the five-man panel came up with the reasoning that according to Section 32(c) of the Election Offences Act, only a person who was already a candidate could be held accountable for a corrupt deed, and since nomination day was April 20, it meant that Zahid was not yet a candidate on April 19. He was therefore, by way of definition, not culpable.

Oh, wow! I didn't know whether to laugh or feel outraged.

The petition was dismissed. The petitioners were ordered to pay costs of RM50,000. Zahid must have heaved a sigh of relief. He had escaped on a technicality.

When justice is not served

Indeed, many of PR's petitions suffered dismissal on preliminary objections or on pure technical grounds like not adhering to the Election Petition Rules. As such, the merits of the cases were not even heard.

This was seen to be unfair and antithetical to natural justice, because if the petitioner did have, for example, genuine evidence to prove their case, they would not get their chance to present it. They would not have their day in court.

P. Ramakrishnan, president of the reform movement Aliran, wrote in an article published by *The Malaysian Insider* on October 12:

"Justice is not served when the petitions are dismissed on technical grounds. It is preposterous that a litigant's right to justice should be dismissed because of the failings of his or her counsel. The lawyer concerned ought to know how to file a petition but if for some reason that petition is defective, why deprive the litigant from having the case heard?

"Is it too difficult ... to order the petition to be put right so that the substantive issues in the petition could be addressed by the court? Justice is not hinged on technicalities but on the question of right and wrong. Forfeiting the litigant's right to be heard is a grave injustice. In doing so, isn't the court perpetuating a wrong and upholding an injustice? This is morally repulsive!"

PR petitions that fell victim to technicalities included those challenging the results of contests in Balik Pulau and Teluk Bahang in Penang; Manong, Manjoi, Pasir Panjang and Rungkup in Perak; Air Lanas, Kok Lanas, Ketereh, Bachok and Jelawat in Kelantan; Pulai, Tebrau, Ledang, Pasir Gudang, Nusajaya, Gambir, Labis and Muar in Johor; Setiawangsa and Titiwangsa in Kuala Lumpur; Elopura in Sabah.

To be sure, BN was also not spared. Among the petitions it filed that were thrown out on technical grounds were those concerning the Mengkebang, Manik Urai, Batu, Gaal, Sandakan, Sarikei and Puteri Wangsa seats.

Anwar Ibrahim expressed concern at the Election Court's tendency to "summarily dismiss these petitions purely on so-called technical grounds". He pointed out that some of the technicalities could even be considered "frivolous".

He gave as examples the petitions for Machang and Selising which were struck off because they were not served personally by the petitioners on the respondents. "This is quite ridiculous when everyone understands that parties in court act through lawyers and do not go around trying to serve court documents themselves!" he said in a statement.

Pay high costs for nothing

He also complained about a second trend emerging from the hearings – the awarding of high costs. He cited the case of the petitioner for the Balik Pulau seat being ordered to pay as much as RM120,000 when his petition was dismissed.

Other examples he could have mentioned were those of Titiwangsa (RM70,000), Setiawangsa (RM70,000), Kota Marudu (RM80,000), Air Lanas (RM80,000), Ketereh (RM90,000), Manjoi (RM105,000), Pasir Panjang (RM120,000), and Kuala Berang (a staggering RM150,000).

It seemed unreasonable to have someone pay such huge amounts when they did not even get their day in court.

BN was also punished with high costs. Its petitioner for the Gaal seat was ordered to pay RM80,000. Those challenging the results of the Klias and Batu seats were each slapped with RM50,000.

"I am informed by lawyers that such costs are not in line at all with the trend of costs awarded for similar civil litigation," Anwar said. "For example, similar preliminary objections in the High Court will probably be awarded RM5,000 to RM10,000. Full appeals in the Court of Appeal are awarded RM15,000 to RM20,000.

"Such high costs are oppressive, bearing in mind the public interest nature of the litigation, and invite the inference that there is a decided policy to inflict punitive costs to discourage petitions. ... The pattern of punitive costs suggests that a discussion has taken place amongst the judiciary with a consensus to award such costs. Whether or not that is true, ... costs should be in line with similar civil litigation."

Whatever it was, PR found itself checkmated. It was losing its legal fight at election courts, and was getting financially punished in the process. It needed to launch a new line of attack. The answer lay in indelible ink.

EC commissioners the new target

In July, the three parties in PR along with five individuals – unsuccessful GE13 candidates Dzulkefly Ahmad, M. Manogaran and Saifuddin Nasution Ismail, and voters Arifin Abd Rahman and R. Abbo – filed a civil suit in the High Court. It named the EC's commissioners as respondents for their having committed fraud regarding the use of indelible ink in GE13, and sought to nullify the results of the general election.

In its statement of claim, PR noted that EC chairman Abdul Aziz had announced in 2011 that the indelible ink would have 4 to 7% silver nitrate and would last for seven days when applied on a voter's finger. But in May 2013, Abdul Aziz said the ink contained only 1% silver nitrate.

PR accused the EC of having "dishonestly, maliciously and wilfully decided to reduce the level of silver nitrate in the indelible ink to enable it to be easily washed off so that dishonest voters could vote more than once".

R. Sivarasa, lawyer and PKR Supreme Council member, told reporters afterwards that if PR won the case, it wanted the court to order the EC commissioners to personally pay for the cost of holding a new general election.

He said PR had lost about 30 parliamentary seats each by less than 10% of the votes. "Therefore, even if a small percentage of dishonest voters were able to wrongfully vote more than once because of the deliberate failure of the EC to implement indelible ink, this was sufficient to affect the results in a significant number of seats."

Hmmm ... it sounded speculative to me and, again, too general. I should think PR would have to prove that a large number of people did vote twice, and that of these, a substantial number came from each of the 30 disputed constituencies. Besides, PR would also have to prove that the EC commissioners did wilfully commit the alleged fraud. That would take some doing.

The wrong court

On February 7, 2014, the High Court threw out the case. Judge Rosnaini Saub said the civil suit was "obviously unsustainable" because the court had no jurisdiction to decide on it.

"It seems crystal clear to me that only an election judge can make an order to declare any election null and void. This court is not an election court," she said.

She also commented that it would be "most unfair" to candidates not party to the complaints if the results of an entire general election were nullified.

PR decided to appeal the ruling. Plaintiff Dzulkefly Ahmad of PAS charged that in dismissing the case on technical grounds, the High Court prevented "systemic issues in the election" from being addressed. He also remarked that the Election Court was not the place to bring the claim to because it lacked jurisdiction over matters related to the Federal Constitution.

Plaintiff M. Manogaran of the DAP said the case involved constitutional issues because it was "not just about one particular general election" but about "the entire election process". It was concerned with the issue of indelible ink as a safeguard to the constitutional right of Malaysians to have clean and fair elections, as well as the issue of the appointment of EC commissioners under the Federal Constitution.

On November 7, however, the Court of Appeal concurred with the High Court and upheld its decision. Two of the three judges ruled that under Article 118 of the Federal Constitution, aggrieved parties could only challenge election results through election petitions.

"A civil court has no jurisdiction to hear the matter or the application to remove election commissioners," said judge Alizatul Khair Osman Khairuddin, who was supported by judge Rohana Yusof.

Judge Prasad Sandosham Abraham, however, disagreed. He said the High Court had the jurisidiction to conduct proceedings in order to determine whether the EC breached its constitutional duty. But he was outvoted.

PR's last hope was appealing to the Federal Court. If it failed at that final hurdle, that would spell the end of its legal struggle, the end of its drawn-out bid to prove fraud in GE13 and have another crack at winning Putrajaya.

On June 19, 2015, two long years after the general election and the intense aftermath that was marked by the exuberance and optimism of the 'Black 505' rallies, the Federal Court gave its verdict.

It echoed what the other courts had previously said. The panel of five judges ruled that under the Federal Constitution, questions of conduct related to general elections could only be challenged through an election petition and such petitions had to be heard by the Election Court.

That was it. PR had run out of options. It had been pursuing a wild dream, a wild goose chase. The end-result was disappointing, but not surprising.

Meanwhile, other events had been unravelling that overshadowed the quixotic quest for Putrajaya. Some of them were ominous, some worrying. Some threatened the stability of the Pakatan Rakyat pact and, with that, the hopes of the people.

At this point, the future was not good.

WIN SOME, LOSE SOME, SOME WIN, SOME LOSE

While the legal challenges to nullify GE13 results were going on, BN's elected representative of the state seat of Kuala Besut died. This caused the first by-election to be held, less than 100 days after GE13.

As Kuala Besut was in Terengganu, a state won by BN by the slimmest of margins, with 17 seats to PR's 15 in the state assembly, the stakes were high for both sides. If BN were to lose the by-election, both sides would be tied with 16 seats each and the assembly would be hung. Pressure to win it was therefore great.

As the by-election was to be held on July 24 during the month of Ramadhan, the campaigning got off on a quiet note. The BN candidate, Tengku Zaihan Che Ku Abdul Rahman from Umno, went all out going from door to door while the PR candidate, Azlan Yusof from PAS, targeted crowds at busy places like markets and Ramadhan bazaars.

Azlan, a businessman, made a *faux pas* when he remarked that as he was a busy man, he would need to hire employees to serve his constituents if he should win. His party was shocked by what he said and barred him from speaking to the media after that. But by then, BN had gone to town using his remark to tell voters that he would be unfit as their representative.

Four days into the campaign, BN's by-election deputy director, Idris Jusoh, felt confident. He predicted a higher majority than the 2,434-vote margin obtained by the late A. Rahman Mokhtar in GE13.

"I think voters will not change their minds just two months after the general election. This means we have the 2,000-odd majority in our hands and with the personalised campaign and a young qualified candidate, we should be able to increase the majority," he said.

I remember that campaign. It stuck out because of the laughable rhetoric of Umno Supreme Council member Tajuddin Abdul Rahman. He told the voters, 99% of whom were Malay: Don't vote for PAS, for if PAS should win, it would be manipulated by the DAP, and its chairman, Karpal Singh, could be Malaysia's first president!

"The Sultan is the head of our religion. The King is a Muslim. If we become a republic, Karpal Singh then becomes the president. He would be your chief. Can this be? Can Karpal Singh be the head of Islam? No!" he yelled.

This was idiotic, and Tajuddin was insulting the intelligence of his audience. For how could Malaysia become a republic and Karpal its president? How could the Federal Constitution be so easily changed to boot out the Yang di-Pertuan Agong and the Malay rulers? Would the DAP even dare to dream of it? Would PKR and PAS allow it?

In any case, this was just a by-election, for goodness' sake!

But then, that was the kind of hogwash that would continue to come out of the mouths of Umno's leaders every once in a while. As some of them also held high office in the Federal Government, like Tajuddin who was a deputy minister as well, they came to lose the respect of the *rakyat* as time went on.

In the PAS camp, its by-election director, Husam Musa, was, by comparison to Idris, apprehensive. He feared that once BN started using its "full force", it would include money politics and "the locals, being poor, will not resist".

True enough, an example of it came by way of Terengganu Menteri Besar Ahmad Said. At the launch of a project to build 72 units of affordable housing in Kuala Besut, he promised that 500 more such units would be built if BN won.

And so BN did win. With a slightly higher majority of 2,592 votes, although the turnout was 7% lower than in GE13. BN retained the state government and managed to pass its first test.

Diabetes for Sungai Limau voters?

In the second by-election, PAS was again pitted against Umno-BN, in the state seat of Sungai Limau in Kedah on November 4.

This time it was PAS defending the seat, and the pressure was now on the party and its PR partners to make sure they did not lose it because the pact had lost the Kedah state government to BN in GE13.

Besides, the seat had been with PAS since 1995 and was last held by its previous *menteri besar*, the late Azizan Abdul Razak, so losing it would be bad for PR's morale.

For BN, snatching Sungai Limau from PR would be a triumph for the new Kedah *menteri besar*, Mukhriz, son of former prime minister Mahathir.

The old master showed that he still wielded enough influence over Umno when he managed to get junior the coveted leadership of the state despite word going around that he did not deserve it. A win would silence Mukhriz's doubters and critics, justify his appointment as *menteri besar* by BN chairman Najib Razak, and strengthen his position in the party.

During the campaign, Mukhriz was, according to Zulkifli Sulong of *The Malaysian Insider*, "one of the hardest workers". He was in Sungai Limau from morning till night "to ensure smooth running of the BN machinery". He even brought in his father to win more support for BN.

Zulkifli also observed that "millions of ringgit was spent by both the federal and state governments to 'buy' votes".

Sugar was sold cheaply at RM1 per kilogram to Sungai Limau residents, and yet earlier the Federal Government had removed the sugar subsidy with the explanation that it wanted to cut down the number of diabetic cases in the country. "Does the Government want the voters in Sungai Limau to get diabetes?" Zulkilfi asked.

Despite the low pricing of sugar and the dispensation of other goodies to the locals, BN lost. It did, however, manage to reduce the winning PAS candidate Mohd Azam Samad's majority to 1,084 votes, compared to the GE13 majority of 2,774. So it wasn't such a sweet victory for PR after all.

The infamous Kajang Move

Meanwhile, things were not going well within PKR. Friction had arisen between Khalid Ibrahim, the *menteri besar* of Selangor, and the top PKR leadership, so a plan was afoot to replace him. This would turn out to be the infamous Kajang Move, devised by Rafizi Ramli.

It was aimed at replacing Khalid with none other than Anwar Ibrahim. But first, Anwar would have to be elected to the Selangor state assembly. On January 27, 2014, PKR's Lee Chin Cheh made that possible by resigning as the state assemblyman of Kajang. He didn't give a reason then, but it was already suspected that it was to make way for Anwar.

The next day, the suspicion was confirmed when Khalid announced that Anwar would contest the vacated seat.

Anwar, however, refuted suggestions that his candidacy was to allow him to take over from Khalid. "This decision is for me to help improve the already stellar performance of the state administration under Khalid," he said. "It is to make Selangor a base from which to launch our campaign to take over Putrajaya."

Nobody bought that, of course. And so the Kajang Move came under heavy criticism from political analysts and netizens. Even from within PKR itself.

Bersih's Ambiga demanded to know if PKR had an "overwhelmingly good reason" for a by-election to be forced upon Kajang constituents. She said it appeared as if PKR was using it to resolve an internal leadership crisis. Without due consideration for the waste of public time and funds it would incur.

A 'game-changer'

This compelled Rafizi to publicly defend it on January 29. He said the Kajang Move was meant to be a "game-changer" in PR's quest for Putrajaya.

"While Khalid Ibrahim's administration has set a gold standard in integrity and prudence in managing public funds, we also have to admit there are other areas that we can improve on," he said, stressing that Selangor needed to be made a showcase for PR. "Just as Istanbul was a launchpad for Erdogan and Jakarta is a launchpad for Jokowi, Selangor can be a great launchpad for Pakatan to take over Putrajaya."

He said PR needed to fortify Selangor by expediting reforms and fending off "political attacks and manouevres" from Umno, which was trying to create racial and religious tensions to recapture Selangor. "We need as many of our top leaders around Selangor to defend Selangor because it remains the crown jewel of any political coalition in the country."

The next day, political commentator Nathaniel Tan, who had "for years" defended PKR "until the day came when it became impossible to defend the indefensible", wrote a critical piece about PKR and the Kajang Move in an article published in the blog *Malaysia Flip Flop*.

He said the Kajang Move was the latest in "a culture of cloak and dagger politics within PKR". To try and explain it as "objectively" as he could, he presented two stories.

"The first has been articulated most popularly by Rafizi Ramli ... This story suggests that we are on the edge of a crisis; that forces linked to former prime minister Mahathir Mohamad are looking to dethrone Prime Minister Najib Razak, and instigate an era of unprecedented racial and religious strife. This story has it that in order to take Putrajaya, it is imperative that Anwar be a state assemblyman of Selangor.

"This story also has it that ... somehow the ability to choose between Khalid, Anwar and someone else does not represent potential instability, but is rather some kind of ace up PKR's sleeve against the Umno leviathan. Given the process that needs to be carried out in order to change the *menteri besar*, the Palace dynamics and the uncertain position that PAS will take, it seems to me that this move will actually create great instability all around ...

"Now let's try another story. ... In this story, the most important thing about Khalid is that he does not easily accede to party wishes. ... If you ask his supporters, this applies to how the party wants the state to be a bigger 'resource' for party activities. If you ask a cynic, he or she would say, all the PKR people want is their fingers in the jar that Khalid has kept so tightly closed.

"Is it all just about the money? ... I suppose you will have to look as objectively as you can at the things they are saying. If they make sense to you, then the answer is 'no'. If they do not make sense to you, then the answer is 'yes'."

Well, whether it made sense or not, the Kajang Move was already in the works. The by-election was called, and nomination day was set for March 11, 2014.

But it appeared that Rafizi had failed to consider an all-important factor – the Government's appeal against Anwar's acquittal for sodomy. That could be coming up in the Court of Appeal anytime soon.

The best-laid plans ...

In 2008, Anwar had been charged for sodomising his former aide Mohamad Saiful Bukhari on June 26 that year. This was the second time he had been charged with sodomy. The first time had ended with his being sentenced to six years in jail (also for corruption) in 1999.

His supporters screamed conspiracy. Anwar applied to the court to strike out the charge on grounds that it was "a travesty, a complete farce with absolutely no basis". Some people suggested that Najib and his wife, Rosmah, had set it up because Saiful had met with Najib to tell him about the alleged sodomy before he reported it to the police. Intriguing.

The trial proceeded in 2010, but it was interrupted numerous times by the defence team's attempts to have the charge struck out, or to have the judge recuse himself from the case on grounds of bias, or to have the case dropped on the allegation that Saiful was having an affair with a member of the prosecution team!

Finally, in January 2012, High Court judge Mohamad Zabidin Mohd Diah gave his verdict. He said that after going through the evidence, the court decided it could not be 100% certain of making a conviction. He thus acquitted and discharged Anwar.

THE PEOPLE'S VICTORY

Many people were surprised by the verdict, including, reportedly, Anwar himself. Eight months earlier, during the trial, the judge had ruled that Saiful was a truthful and credible witness. But now he felt that Saiful's testimony was not enough to convict Anwar because it was uncorroborated.

For the 7,000 supporters waiting outside the courthouse, it was a moment of jubilation. They mobbed Anwar when he came out to greet them. As far as they were concerned, he had been the victim of a political conspiracy, and his protests of innocence over the last three-and-a-half years had now been vindicated.

Six months later, the prosecution filed an appeal against the verdict.

The Court of Appeal set the first hearing for February, seven months after the filing of the appeal. It appeared to be in no hurry. The case dragged on further when Anwar tried to get senior lawyer Muhammad Shafee Abdullah disqualified from appearing as *ad hoc* deputy public prosecutor leading the prosecution. He tried it twice, and failed both times, in September and December.

The next hearing was then set for April 2014. But on February 28, the Court of Appeal suddenly decided to change it to March 6 and 7, one month earlier than scheduled. Why the hurry this time? Was it dictated by the upcoming Kajang by-election?

Whether or not it was, on March 7, 2014, just four days before Anwar was to be nominated as PKR's candidate, the Court of Appeal swiftly delivered its verdict. It overturned the High Court's acquittal and found Anwar guilty of sodomy. It sentenced him to five years' jail. That was a massive double blow for him.

The delivery of the verdict and sentencing hearing were conducted on the same day. Before the sentencing hearing, the defence requested time to prepare for mitigation, but the court would not allow it. After a one-hour recess, the sentencing hearing was conducted. And then it was all over. The court was suspiciously in a real hurry to get it over and done with.

Anwar was done for. He could no longer stand for the by-election, even though he submitted an appeal to the Federal Court against the verdict. The Kajang Move had been derailed.

Ooi Kee Beng of Singapore's Institute of Southeast Asian Studies inferred from the court's ruling that BN's leaders might have been greatly worried about Anwar becoming *menteri besar* of Selangor as he "would be able to play a real Malay leader and not just a politician who just promises things". But, he also said, BN could face a backlash at the by-election because the ruling would be viewed as political manoeuvring by the Government.

Did the judges act hastily?

On the question of hastiness to get the case settled, the Court of Appeal uncharacteristically addressed it when its written judgement was released on April 18.

The panel of three judges comprising Balia Yusof Wahi, Aziah Ali and Mohd Zawawi Salleh defended its move to quickly hear and decide on the case by saying that delays raised doubts about the administration of justice.

They tried to pin it on the defence for having caused the case to be dragged out from July 2013 to February 2014: "As is often pointed out, 'delay is a known defence tactic'. It is not proper for a counsel to routinely fail to expedite hearing an appeal solely for the convenience of his client. Nor will a failure to expedite be reasonable, if done for the purpose of frustrating an opposing party to obtain rightful redress. Counsel should not intentionally use procedural devices to delay proceedings without any legal basis."

They therefore found it justified to conclude, "Based on the above facts, it would be stretching it too far to say that this appeal has been disposed of in haste."

Lawyer and PKR MP N. Surendran was not convinced. "It is highly inappropriate for the judges to respond to criticism of their conduct in such a manner," he said. It only reinforced doubts about their impartiality.

PKR names a substitute

With Anwar out of the picture, PKR now had to find a substitute. Two days later, Anwar himself announced the new candidate. "The judiciary was manipulated by Umno to prevent me from contesting. So I am announcing Wan Azizah as our candidate for the by-election," he said.

This was to be the second time his wife would be stepping in for him. In 1999, when he was sent to jail for sodomy and corruption, she stood in the subsequent by-election for the Permatang Pauh parliamentary seat and won.

On March 23 in Kajang, she won again, but with a majority less than that obtained by Lee Chin Cheh in GE13.

BN's candidate from the MCA, Chew Mei Fun, claimed that the Chinese vote for MCA-BN had gone up from 18% in GE13 to 24.8%. "This is considered quite a good result," she said.

So, what would happen now in the bid to oust Khalid as Selangor *menteri besar*?

MB crisis gets messy

In July, the PKR Supreme Council publicly endorsed Azizah as a candidate for MB (*menteri besar*) of Selangor. Then on August 10, Khalid was sacked from the party for refusing to vacate his MB position. He said his sacking was "flawed and illegal", but he acknowledged the decision.

He also said, "Until such a time as this issue is resolved in accordance with proper procedures, laws and conventions, particularly in the Selangor Constitution, I will continue to perform my duty to the people as the *menteri besar* of Selangor to the best of my ability."

In response, PAS's spiritual adviser, Nik Abdul Aziz Nik Mat, said his party would stick to its stand that Khalid should remain as *menteri besar*. Things got messier when the Sultan of Selangor said the next day that he, too, wanted Khalid to stay on.

On August 14, Wan Azizah declared that 30 state assemblymen no longer had the confidence in Khalid to continue as MB. "They have also expressed their support for me to take over the post," she said.

Among the 30 who signed their declaration of support for her were two PAS assemblymen, Saari Sungib and Hasnul Baharuddin.

Three days later, PAS's central committee finally agreed to have Khalid replaced and decided to nominate both Wan Azizah and PKR deputy president Azmin Ali as replacement. The announcement was made by PAS deputy president Mat Sabu.

But the next day, at the PR Leadership Council meeting, Azmin declined the nomination, so PR decided to go ahead with just Wan Azizah.

On August 26, Khalid tendered his resignation, but the Sultan asked him to defer stepping down until a new MB had been found. The Sultan then asked each of the three PR parties to name at least three candidates as Khalid's replacement.

PKR and the DAP named only Wan Azizah. This upset the Sultan. He accused the two parties of showing arrogance and *derhaka* (disloyalty) to the royal institution.

DAP secretary-general Lim Guan Eng apologised to the Sultan. After that, Anwar also apologised. He, however, pointed out that providing one name had been the practice since the days of the Alliance and then BN, even for the post of prime minister. PKR and the DAP were therefore merely following convention.

Well, if that were so, and they were right in doing what had been done since Independence, why should he and Lim even have to apologise?

In fact, in 2008, after PR captured Selangor from BN, it had also submitted only one name, Khalid's, to the same sultan and the latter had accepted it without any fuss. Surely, PKR and the DAP could not be fairly accused of showing arrogance or disloyalty for doing the same thing this time?

Hadi does not want to go to hell

The problem was with the PAS president and the party's *ulama* (religious clergy) faction. They were not in accord with the other PR parties on the issue, nor with their own central committee, to nominate Wan Azizah and Azmin.

On September 4, the deadline given by the Sultan, PAS president

Abdul Hadi Awang acted independently of the PR Leadership Council and submitted three names to the palace. They were reportedly the names of three of PAS's executive councillors in the state government. Hadi's deputy, Mat Sabu, was not even informed of this.

On September 6, Hadi let on that he had snubbed Wan Azizah as she was not qualified. He said the main criteria for an MB were ability and the confidence to lead, qualities which he claimed she did not possess. He was also opposed to the possibility of her functioning as Anwar's proxy in the state's administration.

Two weeks later, at the PAS *muktamar* (annual congress), he defended his disagreement with the decision of the party's central committee.

"Whoever appoints an individual based merely on inclinations and not on qualifications, Allah would not forgive such an act and would condemn that party to hell," he said. "I do not want to drag PAS and our members to hell."

He went on to scathingly attack the party's PR allies. Referring to the two PAS assemblymen who had signed declarations supporting Wan Azizah, he said they were "stolen" and "bought" by "brokers" and "pimps". At this, his audience responded with thunderous applause and shouts of "*Allah-u-Akbar*" (Allah is great).

As if that was not enough, he went on to warn PKR and the DAP not to exploit PAS for their own political gains. "Do not use us as a hotel to have your meals and stay comfortably in and then leave, or use us as a bridge to cross the river before disappearing into the forest," he said.

This sounded ominous. Would it lead to dire consequences in the near future?

Why won't the palace appoint Wan Azizah?

In the end, the final selection of the MB was accomplished in the least desirable way. The Sultan intervened and reportedly interviewed three potential candidates.

They were PAS state executive councillors Iskandar Samad and Ahmad

Yunus Hairi, and PKR's Azmin, who had not even been nominated by his own party. His inclusion was therefore a surprise.

On September 21, PKR secretary-general Saifuddin Nasution maintained that the party would not support any candidate for the post other than Wan Azizah. As such, Azmin did not have the party's blessing to be MB.

But did the Sultan heed that? No.

PKR asked for an audience to present the declaration of support for Wan Azizah by the 30 state assemblymen, which was clear proof that she commanded the majority support of the elected representatives. He did not grant it.

PKR legal adviser R. Sivarasa then asked for an explanation from the palace because it appeared that the Sultan was not proceeding like a constitutional monarch should.

He pointed out that Selangor's constitution allowed the Sultan to appoint a person as *menteri besar* if he or she commanded the confidence of most of the elected representatives, but although Wan Azizah had that support, she had not been called for an interview.

"If Wan Azizah is to be refused her appointment as the next *menteri besar*, there ought to be at the very least an explanation as to which provision of the State Constitution is being invoked to prevent her from being considered for the appointment and why," Sivarasa said.

This was indirectly telling the Sultan that he was not following the State Constitution, but it did not cut any ice with him. Ultimately, his decision to make Azmin *menteri besar* came as a *fait accompli* to everyone, and on September 23, Azmin was sworn in by the ruler.

Those who disagreed with the way the decision was arrived at did not dare to say too much for fear that it might be misconstrued as insulting the Selangor royalty and cause them to be arrested under the dreaded Sedition Act.

Similarly, Wan Azizah had to accept Azmin's appointment. She could have challenged this transgression of constitutional law, but that would have risked incurring the loss of Malay support for PKR because going against royalty was an emotional issue in the feudal scheme of things.

It must, however, have been painful for her to have to say that she accepted the decision "with an open heart" and that she took this decision "for the good of the people and with the realisation that this crisis must be resolved as quickly as possible".

And yet for all her graciousness, the palace still blamed PKR and the DAP for having complicated the appointment process and thereby delaying the swearing-in of the new MB. The Sultan's private secretary, Mohamad Munir Bani, said that because the two parties refused to obey his boss's decree to nominate more candidates, the Sultan was forced to look for likely candidates other than the one name they gave.

In the first place, why was there a need to name more candidates when naming only one supported by the majority of the elected representatives was enough and in accordance with the State Constitution?

No one forced the Sultan to look for more candidates afterwards. As a constitutional monarch, that was outside his brief, anyway. But Munir of course denied allegations that the Sultan had interfered in the selection process. And that was the end of the matter.

Rakyat the biggest loser

So, finally, Azmin was the surprise winner, Wan Azizah was the one left in the lurch, and Anwar was the one who also felt the blow.

The State Government, duly elected by the people, had lost its once unassailable right to name its own leader – to a ruler who should be above politics. And Anwar, as the leader of the pact that formed the state government, had shown his inability to stand his ground and uphold the principles of a parliamentary democracy.

But, according to P. Gunasegaram, founding editor of online business news portal *KiniBiz*, "The biggest loser from this prolonged crisis and its eventual unsatisfactory outcome is the *rakyat*, because the people's right to choose their leaders has been eroded. An incident like this one is only likely to encourage the palace's greater interference in choosing the country's leaders. And in future, together with the politics of brinkmanship which Malaysia is increasingly heading towards, one wonders what this means towards a smooth transition of power according to the wishes of the people."

Indeed, a few years from then, the thought in his last two sentences would prove to be prescient for an even more significant act of power transition, and it would take a stout-hearted face-off with royalty to ensure that the right and proper measures were eventually taken.

The Kajang Move failed

Meanwhile, analysts declared the Kajang Move a faliure.

It had failed to get Anwar to become Selangor MB and later Wan Azizah. It resulted in a costly by-election which incurred RM1.6 million of public funds to resolve an internal party conflict that was, in the end, not satisfactorily resolved. It received brickbats from the public as a result and lost PR some support, as was partly evidenced in the outcome of the by-election.

Perhaps more serious than anything else, it triggered infighting between the parties and also within them. Due to PAS's role in the move, tension between PAS and the other PR parties was heightened as well.

Lastly, for all we knew, it might even have expedited Anwar's conviction for sodomy.

"The Kajang Move has obviously not worked," said Wan Saiful Wan Jan, chief executive of the Institute for Democracy and Economic Affairs (IDEAS).

He believed that Azmin was possibly a better candidate than Wan Azizah for the MB post, but he felt Azmin should not have accepted it. "I do feel it's wrong as a matter of principle in democratic practices because Wan Azizah had the required majority support."

Speaking of Anwar, Wan Saiful said, "This is a clear case where he was defeated."

Adding further humiliation to Anwar, the Sultan of Selangor stripped him of the Datuk Seri title that had been conferred by his late father in 1992.

A statement from the palace said, "The decision is based on Anwar's repeated questioning of the integrity of the Selangor Sultan and royal institution in resolving the Selangor *menteri besar* crisis, as well as his questioning of issues related to Islam."

It was not made clear what Islamic issues Anwar had been questioning. And the media did not seem to ask for clarification. The message the public got from this episode was, do not cross the Selangor Sultan or you will face the consequences.

Could the "defeated" Anwar now quell the factional strife within PKR and bring all the three parties in PR back to an amicable relationship again? Could they all recover from the ravages of the Selangor MB crisis, patch up and move forward? Would they be able to reorganise and become the united and forceful Opposition they needed to be to topple BN at the next general election?

The coming months would show the way to brightness or to gloom.

THE WORST THAT COULD HAPPEN

Gloom loomed ahead for PR after the end of the Selangor MB crisis. Instead of mending ties with one another, PAS and its partners intensified their conflict. At the same time, the Islamist party was torn by internal strife.

A conservative faction within it was getting more intent on cooperating with Umno, continuing a process that had actually started way back in 2008, after GE12, when PAS held secret talks with Umno to discuss political power-sharing with the blessing of PAS president Abdul Hadi Awang and his then deputy, Nasharuddin Mat Isa.

Nothing came of it then, but right after GE13, Nasharuddin brought it up again, in the interest of protecting Islam and Malay rights, which, he said, the struggles of both parties were founded on.

Umno's deputy president, Muhyiddin Yassin, responded positively to the suggestion, saying that PAS and Umno needed to cooperate to overcome problems faced by Muslims.

PAS vice-president Husam Musa, however, argued against the notion of PAS uniting with Umno, because he said the latter was "not a species to be trusted". And PAS spiritual adviser Nik Aziz Nik Mat declared, "The call to have a unity government with Umno is ridiculous."

Nik Aziz, who had then just relinquished his Kelantan *menteri besar* post, had been fighting against Umno's attempts to co-opt PAS into its camp since 2008. In fact, he was committed to seeing Umno defeated. He not only considered it an apostate and infidel party, he had also seen how Umno betrayed PAS in the 1970s when the latter was part of the BN coalition.

In 2009, he strongly chided Nasharuddin for pursuing the PAS-Umno unity government agenda: "If it's true that he is agreeable to it, then he had better join Umno, resign from his posts as deputy president and MP for Bachok."

The spiritual adviser fondly known as Tok Guru understood, despite his conservative leanings, that working with multi-racial parties was a necessity for forming the federal government. As such, he was strongly in favour of having his party join PR – and remaining in it.

As long as he was still around, his wish would be respected by his party as he was highly revered as a leader. But he was already in his 80s and ailing. If he should pass on, there would be no one as staunch as he to hold up the wall against Umno and maintain the partnership in PR.

Umno suddenly supports PAS on *hudud*

Meanwhile, something else started to brew towards the end of 2013. Members of the *ulama* felt that the party was losing support among the Malays. In GE13, Malay support for PAS dropped by 2%, and the party retained power in Kelantan with seven fewer state seats than in GE12. The conservatives attributed it to PAS having shifted its mission of pursuing an Islamic State to that of a Benevolent or Welfare State.

They thus clamoured for a return to the party's original struggle and the implementation of *hudud*, which they felt was integral to the concept of an Islamic State.

When Umno got wind of the changing sentiment in November 2013, its MP Annuar Musa unexpectedly came out to declare that if PAS intended to introduce *hudud* in Kelantan, Umno would support it.

In Kelantan, *hudud* offences were contained in the set of legislation known as the Syariah Criminal Code (II) Enactment, which was passed by the state in 1993. This dictates that offences such as theft, robbery, illicit sex, alcohol consumption and apostasy could be punished by amputation of limbs, whipping, stoning to death.

Its detractors, including the Malaysian Bar Council, had time and again argued, however, that the Syariah Criminal Code (II) Enactment goes against the secular nature of the Federal Constitution.

The NGO Lawyers for Liberty asserted, "Malaysia is a country founded on parliamentary democracy where the Federal Constitution, which is secular in nature, reigns supreme. Any attempt to introduce *hudud* would be unconstitutional as *hudud* derives its ultimate authority from the Quran and therefore only possible under a theocracy.

"In order for *hudud* to be implemented, the Constitution and its legislature, executive and judiciary, all other structures and institutions that make up Malaysia would need to be reconstituted as being based on Islam and the Quran, and that would not be possible, short of an Islamic revolution as in Iran or Afghanistan."

But PAS was now nonetheless adamant in pushing for *hudud*. And Umno was suddenly giving its support. It looked like Najib's talk of "national reconciliation" on May 6 after the GE13 results came out was plain hogwash. Allowing *hudud* to be implemented even just in Kelantan would rock the basic foundation of the country.

Najib had said 'no' in 2011

In fact, Najib himself had said in 2011 that the Government would not enforce *hudud* in Malaysia "as we have to take into consideration the environment and the reality".

So why the move to support PAS now? Was he planning ahead for the next general election?

On March 27, 2014, Jamil Khir Baharom, the minister in charge of Islamic affairs, confirmed BN's turnaround when he said in Parliament that the Government was willing to work with PAS to implement *hudud*.

But for that to happen, he said a PAS MP would first have to table a private member's bill to invoke Article 76(A) of the Federal Constitution. This would pave the way for Parliament to extend Kelantan's state legislative powers to enable it to legislate on *hudud*.

The procedure was essential because a number of *hudud* offences are deemed criminal offences legislated in the Penal Code, which could otherwise only be legislated by Parliament and tried in the civil court.

Within a week, Kelantan Menteri Besar Ahmad Yakob announced that two private member's bills would be tabled in Parliament to enable *hudud* to be implemented in Kelantan by 2015.

The first was to invoke Article 76(A), and the second, to amend the Syariah Courts (Criminal Jurisdiction) Act 1965, also known as Act 355, to authorise a wider scope of punishments to be issued by the *syariah* court.

After that, Najib appeared to imply agreement by saying that the Government had never rejected *hudud* as divine law. He was clever enough not to express his outright backing of PAS's move, but this was enough to prompt his deputy, Muhyiddin, to suggest that Kelantan PAS form a national-level technical committee to study how *hudud* could be implemented in the state. PAS agreed, and decided to postpone its announced tabling of the private member's bills.

The pro-*ulama* versus the progressives

Other than *hudud*, an issue that would soon prove thorny for PAS-PR relations was the anxiety felt among the pro-*ulama* conservatives in PAS about some of the party's members becoming what was termed "Anwarinas", meaning those who supported Anwar. They saw this threat reflected particularly in the party's progressives, also known as "the Erdogan group", who comprised mostly professionals and technocrats.

In 2011, the progressives did well at the party elections, with Mat Sabu getting elected as deputy president over Nasharuddin and Husam Musa being endorsed as one of the three vice-presidents.

Then at the next party polls in 2013, Mat Sabu retained his position easily and the progressives captured 11 of the 18 leadership positions, winning 45% of the votes in comparison to the pro-*ulama* group's 30% score.

This intensified the internal strife between the two groups. When the

'Black 505' rallies protesting against the alleged electoral fraud committed in GE13 were being held, the *ulama* wing cautioned the party against getting involved, but the central committee, which was dominated by the progressives, declared support for it. *Ulama* chief Harun Taib was quick to point out that the party was apparently influenced by "Anwarinas".

It might not have been support for Anwar *per se* that mattered so much to the progressives; more important to them was their belief that PAS should remain in PR to realise its political aims. This caused them to further clash with the conservatives.

PKR and DAP accused of 'bullying' PAS

On September 28, something happened that made things worse between PAS and its partners. Conservative hardliner Nik Abduh, the son of spiritual adviser Nik Aziz, accused PKR and the DAP of behaving like "bullies". In a Facebook post, he hit out at DAP leaders who had said that PAS would be punished for going against its allies in the MB crisis.

"They said PAS would be dead and buried in Selangor and eventually in Malaysia. But the DAP needs to know that PAS will not die," he wrote. "They're turning into Umno, getting arrogant when they're in power."

He claimed that PKR also wanted to bully PAS. In calumnious fashion, he charged, "They're stealing while bullying." Now, that was severe.

What he wrote next bordered on insult: "It's a good thing that PKR has its own internal problems so they're not as strong as the DAP. Some of them don't even see eye to eye. So their bullying isn't really working."

Sarawak DAP threatens to pull out

In October, the DAP did not help matters when its Sarawak chapter announced that it would not associate itself with PAS and PKR until the two parties had clarified their respective stands on *hudud*.

Local chairman Chong Chieng Jen also threatened to pull Sarawak DAP out of PR if the PAS *ulama* group, which had been pushing for *hudud*, were to take control of the party at its elections in eight months' time.

He said that if, however, the progressives won control instead, then there would be "no reason for us to go out".

This was an open declaration of aligning with the progressives that could not have gone down well with the PAS conservatives. Might it not lead to consequences later that the DAP would not appreciate?

Or was the DAP already making plans, just as PAS was also making their own? Because come November, it became publicly known that Hadi had not been attending PR Leadership Council meetings. Why was he avoiding them?

DAP secretary-general Lim Guan Eng requested his attendance: "This is a reasonable request as Hadi is the only person in PAS with the sole authority to make decisions. This makes his presence at the meetings necessarily compulsory if PR is to function in concert as a coalition as well as to ensure policy coherence and cohesion."

But to no avail. Hadi kept away, and an impasse set in.

Two pivotal moments

Then in February 2015, two things happened that were to prove pivotal in determining PR's future course.

One concerned Anwar Ibrahim and the other, Nik Aziz.

In Anwar's case, it started much earlier, on October 28 the previous year, when his appeal against his conviction for sodomy came up for hearing in the Federal Court.

At the time, he told *TIME* magazine he was not optimistic of winning the appeal, "Most of Malaysia does not believe that I will get a fair trial or a decision based on the facts of the law. But I want to show young people that my conviction is a small price to pay in the struggle for freedom and justice."

Over eight days, the prosecution and the defence went over the evidence and the previous trial proceedings as each made a case for and against conviction.

Was there penetration? Was Saiful's testimony reliable? Did the DNA profile found in Saiful's rectum belong to Anwar? Was the integrity of the

DNA samples compromised before they reached the chemistry department for analysis? Why did Anwar not call his alibi witnesses to prove he was not at the place where the alleged sodomy took place at the alleged time? Why did Anwar opt not to be cross-examined and instead gave a statement in his defence from the dock? Was it all a political conspiracy?

The five Federal Court judges, comprising Chief Justice Arifin Zakaria, Md Raus Shariff, Abdull Hamid Embong, Suriyadi Halim Omar and Ramly Ali, heard all this and reserved their judgement.

They were to deliver their verdict three months later, on February 10, 2015.

'Bebas Anwar!' versus *'Tangkap Anwar!'*

That day, the police presence was strong, with about 300 officers stationed in the vicinity of the Palace of Justice. The road leading to the venue had been blocked since the night before. Barriers were set up in front of the court complex to keep Anwar's supporters at bay.

About a thousand of them showed up, marching from the nearby mosque where they had gathered since 6am and shouting *"Bebas Anwar!"* (Free Anwar!) and *"Reformasi"*.

Saiful's supporters also came along. About 200 of them. Chanting *"Tangkap Anwar!"* (Arrest Anwar!) and *"Hukum Peliwat!"* (Punish the sodomite). One of them told *Malaysiakini*, "We came to prove that Saiful is not alone."

The court was called to order a little after 10am. Then Arifin started reading from the 116-page judgement. Nearly an hour later, he came to the part where it said, "Saiful is not an accomplice and there is enough corroborative evidence to support his testimony."

This sounded like bad news for Anwar. Rafizi Ramli tweeted, "Doesn't look good now. … Judges are saying Saiful is credible."

Journalist Beh Lih Yi tweeted, "Looks like it will be a guilty verdict based on what's reported so far. Malaysia to be in spotlight for all the wrong reasons again."

The judge went on to read, "We hold there is no merit in the complaint of political conspiracy. ... The allegation remains unsubstantiated."

'Beyond reasonable doubt'

Finally, after two hours of reading, Arifin arrived at the verdict. He said there was overwhelming scientific and corroborative evidence to show that Saiful was sodomised by Anwar. "We agree with the Court of Appeal that the case was proven beyond reasonable doubt. The appeal against the conviction is dismissed."

The decision was unanimous among the five judges.

Tears flowed. Anwar's immediate family, his father-in-law, his friends, his supporters, leaders of PR component parties, leaders of NGOs were deeply affected by the verdict.

Anwar hugged his wife and daughter Nurul Izzah as the two struggled to fight back tears. He waved to the public gallery and said, "See you in some years."

Did the Government know the verdict earlier?

Within minutes, the Prime Minister's Department issued a three-paragraph press statement which asserted that "Malaysia has an independent judiciary". It also saw it fit to remind everyone that the case against Anwar was brought by a private individual, "not by the Government".

It concluded, "In this case, exhaustive and comprehensive due process has been followed over many years. That process is now complete, and we call on all parties involved to respect the legal process and the judgment."

Why the defensive tone, the eagerness to highlight the impartiality of the judges? And how did the statement manage to be released so soon after the verdict was announced? Surely, it must have been written sometime before. Would that imply that the Prime Minister's Department knew beforehand what the verdict would be?

'You chose to remain on the dark side'

Next, during mitigation proceedings, the lead defence counsel, Gopal Sri Ram, asked the judges to consider Anwar's contribution to the country and argued against enhancing the sentence to be passed on him based on the facts of the case.

However, lead prosecutor Muhammad Shafee Abdullah reminded the court that the maximum sentence was 20 years' imprisonment and argued that since Anwar was not repentant, five years was "manifestly inadequate". He asked for a sentence of above six years.

Anwar then made a request to address the court, and Arifin allowed it.

Anwar said he would accept the decision and be patient, but he maintained his innocence and his belief that this was all a conspiracy "to stop my political career".

Then he launched a broadside at the judges, "You could have carved your names. But in bowing to the dictates of your political masters, you have become partners in the murder of the judiciary. You chose to remain on the dark side."

Arifin told him to stop. But Anwar refused. The judges stood up and walked out. One of them said: "I don't need to hear all this."

Anwar carried on speaking loudly, "Allah be my witness. I pledge that I will not be silenced. I will fight on for freedom and justice. I will never surrender."

When the judges returned, Arifin announced that the five-year jail sentence imposed by the Court of Appeal would not be enhanced.

And so Anwar was sent to Sungai Buloh prison.

With him out of the way, PR was effectively crippled. If Najib had planned it, it was a masterstroke. It nicely complemented Umno's simultaneous courting of PAS with *hudud* as the bait.

As for Anwar, it looked like his political career could be over. Facing five years in prison at the age of 68 and another five years after that of a mandatory prohibition on running for political office, he might only be eligible to take part in the 2023 general election at the earliest. By then, he would be 76.

Meanwhile, he had to vacate his Permatang Pauh parliamentary seat, and his wife, Wan Azizah, had to yet again step in to contest and win it, and become the new Opposition Leader in Parliament.

Death of a guiding light

Two days after Anwar was sent to prison, the other pivotal moment occurred. Nik Aziz died.

Highly respected by all the factions in PAS as well as by all PKR and DAP leaders, he was a great guiding light for both his party and the pact. Even non-Muslims who were just a little politically savvy admired him. They saw him as a humble and incorruptible leader, a rare breed.

His death would deprive his party of the crucial moderating influence between the conservatives and the progressives. And it would provide the leeway for Hadi and Najib to cooperate politically even if their parties were not joined by a formal union.

These twin developments would soon spell trouble for PR. And make it look even more unlikely that the wounded and weakened alliance would ever succeed in winning Putrajaya.

'An act of provocation'

Things came to a head on March 18, 2015, when Kelantan PAS tabled amendments to the Syariah Criminal Code (II), the version of *hudud* which the PAS state government of the time had passed in 1993.

Six days earlier, PKR and the DAP had urged PAS not to table it when the PR Leadership Council was briefed on the amendments. They viewed it as going against the agreement the three parties had made in 2008 on not making *hudud* a part of PR's common policy framework. PAS's representatives at the council meeting understood the argument and a consensus was then reached to put the bill on hold.

But that consensus was betrayed on March 18 when PAS tabled the bill regardless. The DAP was livid and protested for having been stabbed in the back.

"It is an act of provocation to break up Pakatan Rakyat," the party's national organising secretary, Anthony Loke, said.

He accused "enemies" from within PAS of putting aside the consensus reached with its partners in order to comply with Umno's schemes.

PAS, however, did not heed the DAP's protest. The next day, the bill was unanimously passed by the 44 assemblymen in the Kelantan State Assembly. History was created with all the 12 BN assemblymen from Umno supporting the bill. The other votes comprised 31 from PAS and one from the lone PKR representative.

At around the same time, Hadi submitted a private member's bill in Parliament to amend the Syariah Courts (Criminal Jurisdiction) Act 1965 (Revised 1988). If these amendments were to be passed in Parliament, it would allow for four offences in the *hudud* bill to be implemented in Kelantan.

DAP cuts ties with Hadi

On March 24, the DAP central committee held an emergency meeting and passed a resolution to cut ties with Hadi.

Guan Eng said his party deplored Hadi's "dishonest and dishonourable acts" of violating the spirit of consensus within the PR pact.

Sarawak DAP also said it could no longer work with PAS and made the "painful decision" to pull out of PR in the state.

On May 22, Hadi responded by saying that his party was willing to sever ties with the DAP, which he accused of being arrogant.

In contrast to Hadi, Mat Sabu, his deputy, was supportive of PR. He cautioned his party not to be "arrogant". He said the *rakyat* were committed to changing the government and they would succeed with or without PAS.

Progressives swept out of PAS

Mat Sabu's days in the PAS leadership were, however, numbered. Also those of other progressives.

On June 4, 2015, at the party elections, Mat Sabu was trounced in his bid to defend his deputy presidency. He managed to get only 279 votes whereas his rival, Tuan Ibrahim Tuan Man, obtained three times that number, with 881.

The other progressives were also roundly rejected. The support they got from the voting was only about 20%.

Hadi won re-election by a landslide. Candidates endorsed by the powerful *ulama* wing captured all key leadership positions and almost all the seats in the central committee. It was a decisive victory for the conservatives.

The day before, the *ulama* accepted a motion to sever ties with the DAP but to remain in PR. Its over-600 members sanctioned it. The motion would eventually go to the Syura Council, the highest decision-making body in the party, for deliberation and approval.

On June 6, DAP adviser Lim Kit Siang portended the death of PR. The veteran had seen enough of such things happening throughout his years in politics to sense what was coming.

On June 18, his son, Guan Eng, who was also Penang chief minister, reiterated that PR was dead "for real".

He said the DAP would continue to work with PKR and other parties "to reshape and realign Malaysian politics with the aim of winning Putrajaya for the people".

The Opposition was on the verge of breaking up.

On July 11, PAS's Syura Council practically sealed it when it passed the motion to cut ties with the DAP. It, however, ruled that PAS would maintain ties with PKR in the spirit of *tahaluf siyasi* (political cooperation).

That was it. After this bitter blow-up, how would the DAP and PAS be able to return to normal relations? How would they continue to be partners in the pact? More importantly, how could they convince the *rakyat* to vote for a shattered PR at the next general election?

The answer was blowing in the wind.

ACTS OF BLAME, ACTS OF SHAME

Najib Razak was not having an easy time either.

With BN having secured 60% of parliamentary seats with only 47.38% of the popular vote, he was coming under heavy pressure from numerous quarters questioning the legitimacy of his government and his own eligibility as prime minister and Umno president.

His face and that of his deputy, Muhyiddin Yassin, on a huge poster outside a busy shopping mall in Kuala Lumpur were rudely defaced. Scrawled over the poster was the derisive comment: "47% PM".

He faced pressure from his mentor, Mahathir Mohamad, who watched him like a hawk. Three weeks after the elections, Mahathir told the media that Najib was "not in a very strong position", and that he faced the risk of BN elected representatives defecting to PR.

"When you are concerned about that, the focus on development, economy and all will be affected," he said. "That is Najib's problem." There would be other Mahathir criticisms to come.

Out in the streets all over the country, there was another big problem. Anwar Ibrahim and his supporters were running down Najib and accusing him of electoral fraud. This was embarrassing. But worse than that, the huge turnouts at the rallies boded ill for BN.

Why apply heat on *The Heat*?

Najib must have felt he was losing his grip as leader of the country. Even the weekly publication *The Heat* had the audacity to question his extravagant spending and that of his wife, Rosmah Mansor.

It did it in its November 2013 issue, with its front page screaming, 'All eyes on big spending PM Najib'. This was intolerable!

Action had to be taken, so the weekly's publishing licence was of course suspended, thanks to the handy availability of the Printing Presses and Publications Act (PPPA).

I had been following *The Heat*'s progress since it was launched three months earlier and applauding it for its boldness in encouraging discussion on current issues. So I was incensed by the Government's move to silence the newsweekly.

In a commentary I wrote for *Yahoo! Malaysia*, I questioned why *The Heat* deserved such punishment.

"There is nothing in the article that breaks the law," I wrote. "In fact, in publishing it, *The Heat* was providing a public service in informing its readers about what the prime minister has been doing with our money. If Najib and Rosmah are displeased with *The Heat* for exposing their extravagance, they should sue the weekly. No government agency should intervene in the matter instead."

I called on the media and all journalists to stop the "tyranny" against media freedom. "Stand up and take back your right to freedom of speech and expression. Push for the repeal of the PPPA," I wrote.

"So often, mainstream media journalists complain to me about having to take bullshit from their bosses, about having to do things that grate against their journalistic beliefs. So often, they say they are fed up. Now is the time for them to say, 'Enough is enough!'"

RM140,000 for a night in a hotel

I suspect the tough action on *The Heat* was taken because it held Rosmah up to public view in a way that was unflattering.

It talked about RM17 million of the people's money having been spent on her overseas travel with Najib between 2008 and 2011, followed by RM134,317 for her trip in 2012 to Saudi Arabia, Oman and Bangladesh, plus RM140,000 for just an overnight stay in Dubai's luxury hotel Atlantis.

"Doesn't this go beyond the bounds of decency and the limits of the *rakyat's* tolerance? Why should we have to pay for these expenses when Rosmah holds no public office and is therefore not a representative of the Malaysian government?" I asked.

I also warned against returning to the culture of fear that Mahathir imposed on the country when he was prime minister. "Whether it is Rosmah being criticised or otherwise, we cannot tolerate such authoritarian interference with the media. It's now 2013, coming to 2014, not 1984 and the era of Mahathir Mohamad anymore."

Seven weeks later, on February 15, 2014, the suspension was lifted. To *The Heat's* credit, it was uncowed by the experience. It vowed to continue to "speak up against corruption, injustice and the forces that seek to divide our nation". And its comeback issue carried articles focusing on the theme of freedom – for the media and for public university students.

I welcomed its return in a piece for *MSN Malaysia*. I said the suspension was "an exercise in stupidity" and that the Home Ministry lied when it said that *The Heat* did not adhere to the conditions of its publishing licence.

Placed 147th out of 180

I also pointed out that the newsweekly's timely return coincided with the release of the 2014 World Press Freedom Index which showed that Malaysia's press freedom index had plunged to the low position of 147th out of 180 countries. "This is the lowest the country has fallen to. And – would you believe it? – we are now even lower than Cambodia (132rd) and Myanmar (145th)."

This brought me to the action taken a few days earlier by the Malaysian Communications and Multimedia Commission to bar the radio station BFM from broadcasting its interview with Anwar Ibrahim. I said it had made the Government look bad.

"And yet the next day, the Prime Minister's Office had the gumption to say that the media in Malaysia is 'freer than it has ever been'. This is either self-denial or a downright lie or a ploy to deceive Malaysians who are poorly informed," I charged.

Clearly, Najib's administration was running scared when it would not even allow an interview with Anwar to be aired. And yet ironically, in his New Year message just one-and-a-half months earlier, Najib had said that "encouraging public debate" was a great part of rebuilding national unity. What bullshit!

The dreaded tax cometh

On October 25, 2013, however, he meant business when he tabled the Budget for 2014 in Parliament and announced that the Goods and Services Tax (GST) would come into force on April 1, 2015, fixed at 6%.

GST would, however, prove to be a most unpopular tax because it was feared that the low-income group would suffer from it the most. But public debt had been rising to an alarming degree because of continuous budget deficits for many years, so the Government felt it had to broaden its tax base and collect additional revenue to reduce the budget deficit.

Furthermore, the country had become too dependent on revenue from state-owned oil company Petronas. It was hoped that the implementation of GST would reduce this dependency.

In any case, GST was not really a new form of tax on the consumer. There were already the existing sales tax of between 5 and 10% and the service tax of 6%. GST would be replacing these.

Besides, collecting GST would be more efficient than collecting SST as the system was more transparent and regulated. It made for easier accounting. Consumers would know exactly how much tax they were paying for the product or service they were purchasing. SST was more susceptible to fraud and dishonest practices.

As for the poor, the Government assured they would be protected from too much tax by its move to exempt from GST essential goods like sugar, flour, rice, vegetables, salt, cooking oils, eggs, fish and unprocessed meat.

Government services such as for the issuance of passports and licences, health services, school education and public transportation services would also be exempted.

Najib debunked the false impression being given by certain quarters that the imposition of GST would cause the prices of goods to rise.

"If we buy a carbonated drink in a restaurant today, we are paying double taxes – sales tax and service tax," he explained. "With the GST system, consumers will only need to pay tax once, and the prices of goods should be cheaper."

He said the proposed rate of 6% was the lowest among Asean countries, compared with 10% in Indonesia, Vietnam, Cambodia, the Philippines and Laos, and 7% in Singapore and Thailand.

He also pledged that low-income households would be assisted during the "transition period" with, among other things, a one-off cash payment of RM300.

The people rally against GST

His assurances were not well received, however. GST had been dreaded by many Malaysians ever since it was first touted. While some had welcomed it as a fair system that taxed everyone alike, the Opposition had been playing up the negative impact of the tax, especially on the poor.

PR harped on the point that if the Government could instead put a stop to all the wastage and leakages exposed by the Auditor-General's Report of 2012 amounting to millions of ringgit, it would not need to impose GST and make the people pay for the irresponsible spending of government departments.

PAS president Hadi Awang said the Government was going to use GST as a "painkiller" while it continued to misuse public funds. He warned that it would weaken the economy by lowering the spending power of the people.

Despite all the criticisms, the Goods and Services Tax (GST) Bill was passed in Parliament on April 7, 2014, by 119 votes to 81. To show their disagreement, Opposition MPs held up placards and banners in the House displaying the words "*Tolak GST*" (Reject GST).

On May 1, 2014, protestors poured onto the streets around Dataran Merdeka in Kuala Lumpur to express their feelings against the new tax: "Down with GST! Down with BN!" The rally was reportedly organised by a coalition of 89 NGOs.

Malaysiakini claimed that as many as 50,000 people showed up. However, the state-owned news agency Bernama quoted Dang Wangi police chief ACP Zainuddin Ahmad as saying that the turnout was 15,000. The truth was probably somewhere in the middle.

The people rally against rising costs

Meanwhile, Najib's ratings were dropping. From 62% in August 2013 to 52% three months later. They would drop further to 48% in October 2014 and then 44% in January 2015.

The people lost faith in the Government's credibility and its concern for them. The prices of goods and services were rising and nothing seemed to be done to lower them.

They blamed the price upsurge on the cut in the subsidy prices of diesel and RON 95 petrol by 20 sen per litre for both in September 2013, followed by the termination of the sugar subsidy the following month.

Although these cuts were made in tandem with the Government's GST initiative to address the pressing issues of rising debt and the need to reduce the budget deficit – and therefore financially necessary – the immediate effects of the cuts were being severely felt.

On top of that, the Government announced that effective January 1, electricity rates would go up by 15%. This made the situation worse.

Najib had to greet 2014 confronted by a protest rally called '*Turun*' (Go down) held at Dataran Merdeka, organised by a loose group comprising student movements and a few NGOs. Attended by nearly 10,000 people, it directed "the people's anger" at the unjustified increases in living costs.

Najib the *kangkung* PM

On January 13, unluckily for him, Najib became a laughing stock when he made his famous statement responding to the public anger over price increases.

He said, "When the price of vegetables goes up, the price of *sawi* (Chinese flowering cabbage) goes up, that of *kangkung* (water spinach) goes up. There are times when it goes up, times when it goes down. Today, I read in the newspapers that the prices of some vegetables have dropped. The price of *kangkung* went up previously, now it has gone down. When this happens, why not praise the Government? But when it rises, blame the Government! This is not fair because it's due to weather conditions."

He was caught on video saying that and it went viral. Even the BBC picked up the story, and more than just Malaysians had a good laugh at the "*kangkung*" leader of the country.

Many criticised him for being out of touch with the feelings of the common people regarding rising food prices, and therefore not sympathetic towards their hardship.

Several facetious '*Kangkung*' fan pages popped up on Facebook, getting tens of thousands of 'likes'. Netizens declared January 13 as 'World *Kangkung* Day'. Some enterprising entrepreneur even sold T-shirts emblazoned with '*Kangkung* for #breakfast #lunch #dinner'.

Farawahida Mohd Fauzi wrote on Facebook that she felt sad having a prime minister like Najib: "*Sedih rasa ada PM macam ini.*"

Another Facebook user, Muhammad Nadzmi, called Najib "*Johan Raja Lawak Sedunia*" (World Champion Comedian).

Malaysians also made fun of the prime minister in various lampoons. One was a hilarious *kangkung* remix video featuring him saying words extracted from his speech but autotuned and set to an electronica track. Another was a remix video of Najib and Rosmah dancing a folksy jig but with the original number replaced by the favourite children's song 'Lenggang Lenggang Kangkung'.

A flashmob was staged in a busy area in Penang with the participants stuffing *kangkung* into the mouth of a mock effigy of Najib's face while singing that same children's song.

With Mahathir around, who needs enemies?

With so much going against him, Najib could have done without further aggravation. But this was not to be.

According to the online news platform *Asia Sentinel*, around May or June 2014, Mahathir sent Najib a letter "bristling with a list of demands to change his ways".

This was the last thing Najib needed – pressure from within his party – so he sent an emissary to ask Mahathir to withdraw the letter, but the elder man refused.

It is interesting to note that one of the demands involved 1MDB (1Malaysia Development Berhad), the strategic development company wholly owned by the Minister of Finance (Incorporated) set up to boost the country's economic development. In the days to come, it was to become the focus of the biggest scandal in Malaysian history.

For now, Mahathir wanted Najib to address the heavy debts 1MDB had incurred after having funded a string of controversial projects.

He next wanted more contracts from Petronas to go to *Bumiputeras* instead of to more neutral parties. He also wanted his 2003 idea of building a "crooked bridge" to link Singapore and Malaysia over the Johor Strait revived. He was angry at Najib for "bending to Singapore's wishes" and cancelling it.

On domestic issues, he objected to the BRIM cash handouts being used by the Government as an election sweetener because, at a cost of RM4 billion, it was "breaking the budget".

Finally, Mahathir criticised Najib over "the breakdown in racial and religious relations" that had grown progressively "more poisonous".

On this, *Asia Sentinel* commented, "That seems to be a striking obtuseness on Mahathir's part, since he has backed the Malay-supremacy

NGO Perkasa, headed by firebrand Ibrahim Ali, and has made incendiary statements about racial superiority on his own."

It went on to disclose that before GE13, Mahathir had even sought to lead a major rally on May 13, the anniversary of the 1969 racial riots, but Najib intervened and cancelled it.

The letter spoke volumes about Mahathir's trademark penchant for wanting things done his way. But after receiving it, Najib apparently did nothing to entertain his demands. This must have riled Mahathir even more.

So on August 18, he wrote in his blog that he was withdrawing his support for Najib's administration.

He started by saying that Najib was his choice to take over from Abdullah. In fact, it was open knowledge that Mahathir was influential in compelling Abdullah to step down after BN fared badly at the 2008 general election.

But now he lamented that Najib's performance as prime minister had so far turned out to be no more effective than Abdullah's. He said he had also not expected the performance at GE13 to be worse.

He had hoped that Najib would learn from the poor performance but that had not been the case, even though he had tried to give Najib his views directly. "I have no other choice but to withdraw my support," he declared.

Mahathir then proceeded to pound Najib with what he considered the prime minister did wrong. He accused Najib of listening to his enemies by repealing the Internal Security Act (ISA) and the Restrictive Residents Act in 2011, both of which allowed for detention without trial.

He mentioned some of the other grouses contained in his earlier letter and new ones as well. His overall point was clear. Many of Najib's policies, approaches and actions were destroying the country. And, implicitly, the party, I suppose.

Year of the sedition dragnet

With so much pressure bulding up against him, Najib must have felt exasperated. No other prime minister had had to face such a slew of protests springing up one after another in such a short space of time. And with Mahathir as well as the public insinuating that he was weak, he must have felt the need to show them he was boss.

So he got down to action and 2014 was to become the year of the sedition dragnet.

Numerous Opposition politicians, activists and dissenters were probed for sedition, some eventually charged. One of them was my friend Azmi Sharom, a prominent law lecturer who was charged in September for his comments in an online news report. Looking at what Azmi had reportedly said, I could only say that the charge was "crazy".

I wondered if Azmi was being singled out for persecution because he had been critical of the Government through his column 'Brave New World' published in *The Star* and his participation as a speaker in numerous political forums.

The Sedition Act was introduced in 1948 by the British colonial administration to criminalise any act, speech, words, etc, that would "bring into hatred or contempt or to excite disaffection against" the Government or engender "feelings of ill-will and hostility between different races or classes".

In 1970, after the May 13 racial riots, the Act was amended to add citizenship, language, the special position of *Bumiputeras* and the sovereignty of the Malay rulers to the list of seditious matters.

Section 3(1) of the Act spells out the definition of "seditious tendency", but 3(2) provides exceptions. It is important to note that it is not seditious for anyone to point out that a ruler "has been misled or mistaken in any of his measures". It is also not seditious "to point out errors or defects in the Government or Constitution as by law established".

In Azmi's case, he was merely calling for transparency in the handling of the Selangor MB crisis and cautioning against doing it the way it was done during the Perak MB crisis in 2009. He did not think that BN's takeover of the Perak state government from PR at the time was legally done.

So, what was seditious about that? Was it considered so because Azmi's comment implicated the then Perak sultan who was involved in the takeover discussion? Because Azmi said the discussion was done at "a secret meeting" and that was considered rude to royalty?

I slammed the stupidity of the charge in an article I wrote for *Yahoo! Malaysia* and posited that "in the absence of the Internal Security Act (ISA), the Government seems to be resorting to the Sedition Act to silence dissent".

I pointed out that just the month before, Opposition politicians N. Surendran, Khalid Samad and R.S.N. Rayer had also been arrested and charged with sedition.

"In Rayer's case, he was charged for uttering the words 'Umno *celaka*'. What, pray tell, is seditious about calling a political party '*celaka*' (damned)? It may be considered rude, but surely not seditious."

I asked if Najib was flexing his muscles to rebut Mahathir's recent criticism of him as a weak leader. I said Najib would be a stronger leader if he ignored Mahathir's rantings and became his own man. A true reflection of his strength would be repealing, finally, the Sedition Act he had promised to do two years before.

Najib promised to repeal Act

Malaysians were filled with hope when Najib announced on July 11, 2012, that he would repeal the Sedition Act, which he said, correctly, represented a bygone era.

However, he also said he would replace it with a new National Harmony Act, which would "balance the right of freedom of expression as enshrined in the Constitution, while at the same time ensuring that all races and religions are protected".

But then after that, nothing happened. Nonetheless, in July 2013, Najib still peddled hope when he told the BBC that the repeal was "coming".

Around the same time, however, government minister Ahmad Zahid Hamidi contradicted his boss by publicly declaring, "I think the Sedition Act need not be abolished. Otherwise, what is there left?" He said sedition would then be "legitimised" and that was "not what democracy requires".

Saying that showed that he sorely needed a tutorial on Democracy 101. But then Zahid was noted for saying stupid things. Yet even so, what he said actually carried dark implications. Because when 2014 came around, not only was there still no repeal, the Act came to be used wantonly.

Calling IGP Himmler lands man in court!

The sedition investigations that emerged from February to December that year were not just related to politics. Some were for insulting religion, insulting royalty and, unbelievably, insulting the Inspector-General of Police (IGP)!

Another unbelievable case was the investigation of a 17-year-old boy allegedly clicking 'like' on the 'I Love Israel' page on Facebook. *Alamak!* Was that seditious because Malaysia does not recognise Israel? Did the police have nothing better to do than to frighten a teenager with a serious action like that?

Out of the numerous investigations, several politicians were charged. They included Rayer, Ng Wei Aik and Teresa Kok from the DAP, Surendran and Rafizi (with the latter being charged eventually under the Penal Code instead) from PKR, Khalid Samad and Nizar Jamaluddin (also under the Penal Code) from PAS, and David Orok from the State Reform Party in Sabah.

Others charged for sedition included Azmi, Safwan Anang, political activist Ali Abd Jalil, Wan Ji Wan Hussin, Gopinath Jayaratnam, Hidayat Mohamed and Abdullah Zaik Abd Rahman.

In the case of the insult to the IGP, Wong Hoi Cheng, director of the think tank Inter-Research and Studies, was eventually charged under the Penal Code for his tweet calling IGP Khalid Abu Bakar "the Henrich Himmler of Malaysia" and holding him responsible for the "bastardisation" of the police force. That was the funniest of the charges.

Minister makes unbelievable statement

Three people were convicted for sedition in 2014 – the late Karpal Singh from the DAP, and student activists Safwan Anang and Adam Adli.

In view of all that had transpired, MP Tony Pua was prompted to declare: "It is clear from the actions of the Najib administration that he has no intention to repeal the Act. Instead the Act will be used more viciously against BN's political opponents to curtail the freedom of speech and the country's democratic space."

As if to affirm that, minister Shahidan Kassim made an unbelievable statement on September 5. He said the Government never promised to abolish the Act, only to review it. Was he zonked out when Najib made the announcement in 2012?

Amazingly, that very September day, Najib reiterated his pledge and again said it would be replaced with the National Harmony Act. So whom were Malaysians to believe? Were Najib and his ministers playing games?

Najib finally breaks his promise

Two-and-a-half months later, on November 27, the promise was finally broken. At the Umno general assembly of 2014, the platform at which Najib knew he would score high for making the announcement, he said the Sedition Act would remain.

What's more, he added two special provisions to the Act – one, to safeguard the sanctity of Islam, as well as other religions, and the other, to take action against anyone who tried to incite Sabah and Sarawak to secede.

In an article I wrote for *Yahoo! Malaysia* published three days later, I called Najib "a most untrustworthy prime minister" and "a false democrat".

I disagreed with the new provisions: "The phrase 'sanctity of Islam', in particular, could carry quite a load … with religion included in the Act, imagine if you will the endless ominous possibilities of religious politicisation. Already, there are too many sacred cows to uphold; why do we want to further constrict our democratic space?"

Umno's partners not consulted

I also noted his disrespect for Umno's partners by not having consulted them first. "It is telling them that they have no say although they are supposedly part of the Government, that Umno calls all the shots, take it or leave it."

MIC president and government minister S. Subramaniam told the media that Najib did not even discuss the matter with the Cabinet.

Gerakan president Mah Siew Keong was forced to now backtrack on what he had said in September, when he urged the Government to drop all the existing sedition charges. Not only that, he had to welcome the new provisions.

I wondered how they felt about Najib's admission that he came to the decision "after listening to the Umno leadership, wing leaders, grassroots and NGOs". These people obviously had more clout.

But which NGOs were these when two months earlier, 112 multi-racial NGOs had issued a strong statement against the Act, saying it was "clearly being misused to protect the Government and its interests, make certain issues off limits, and create a climate of fear"?

Najib assured that the Act would be "implemented fairly and not harm the innocent". I asked in my article, "Can we still trust whatever he says?"

"This is the start of authoritarian rule by Najib," said Anwar Ibrahim, who was also under investigation for alleged seditious remarks made in 2011 alluding to the murder of the Mongolian model Altantuya Shaariibuu which was linked to Najib. "They will use the sedition law to intimidate the legitimate voice of the Opposition."

It turned out to be true for the next few years. Among those who would come to be charged for sedition were outspoken cartoonist Zunar (Zulkifi Anwar Ulhaque) who faced nine charges; politicians Mohd Fakhrulrazi Mohd Mokhtar, Mat Sabu, Hassan Karim and S. Arutchelvan; activists Khalid Ismath, Lawrence Jayaraj, Jemmy Liku Markus Ratu, Erick Jack William, Joseph Kolis and Azrie Situ; and lawyer Eric Paulsen.

A number of these charges were simply for criticising the Federal Court's 2015 ruling that sent Anwar to jail for five years. When was criticising the judiciary considered seditious? Why should it be?

The plan to destroy PR

Writing for Aliran's online newsletter in March 2015, Francis Loh explained why the BN government was using the Sedition Act to arrest people at this time. He said that with Anwar in jail, it was the right time to destroy him and his party.

This was part of the overall plan since BN's poor performance at GE13 to also split the PR pact, "to isolate the DAP by painting it as a chauvinistic party, to drive a wedge into PAS to break it up, to arrest and destroy the young enthusiastic leaders of PKR while their leader is in jail again, and to break up the Pakatan Rakyat ultimately".

DAP MP and strategist Liew Chin Tong expanded on this. He saw Najib as having succeeded in removing a leader with prime ministerial appeal from PR, and one seen as a central Malay figure as well. At the same time, he was splitting the Opposition along ethnic and religious lines by luring PAS with *hudud* and thereby causing friction between it and the DAP. Eventually, with PAS out of PR, the pact would be left with no Malay giants to lead it. This would make it even easier to thenceforth target the Opposition as being "Chinese" and DAP-dominated in order to frighten the Malays into voting for BN.

"In short, Najib planned to win GE14 by default, by systematically dismantling the Opposition," he said.

Sure enough, PAS did break up.

Those of the progressive faction found it counter-productive to stay on in an environment that was becoming increasingly difficult for them to operate in. So most of them opted to leave to create first a group called G18, in reference to the 18 leaders who were ousted at the PAS 2015 party polls, and later a movement called Gerakan Harapan Baru (GHB), or New Hope Movement.

One of them, Dzulkefly Ahmad, told *The Malaysian Insider*, "Over the years, we have been effecting reforms and changes in PAS. Very recently, all these seemed to be in danger of being rolled back. Now we are free to embark on a new endeavour that is more inclusive or all-encompassing. We believe this platform will be better accepted by the people because it is the friendly face of Islam, inclusive and adapting to a multi-religious and multi-ethnic nation."

In July, to gain public support, GHB launched a series of roadshows nationwide, beginning with Kangar in Perlis. It was attended by representatives from PKR and the DAP, indicating that both parties were seriously considering it as a new potential partner.

After a month of canvassing in other states as well, GHB announced that it had submitted an application to the Registrar of Societies (RoS) to form a new political party.

A new party is born

On August 31, Mat Sabu announced the birth of Parti Amanah Negara (Amanah), or National Trust Party, which had taken over the registration of the old Malaysian Workers' Party (MWP) and applied to RoS to rename it.

It had had to take this measure of appropriating MWP, a near-defunct party founded in 1978, because the Home Ministry had rejected its application to set up a new party called Parti Progresif Islam.

The ever jocund Mat Sabu said MWP gave GHB only one condition in agreeing to the takeover, "They told us not to ever cooperate with BN and Umno, and that was it."

The event was welcomed especially by the DAP. With the party's secretary-general, Lim Guan Eng, having declared on June 18 that PR was "dead" after its fallout with PAS, Amanah seemed like the ideal party to take PAS's place. Its members were, after all, familiar and friendly, and Mat Sabu and Guan Eng had been bosom buddies since they were both detained under the ISA at the Kamunting Detention Centre in 1987 as a result of Operation Lalang.

Anwar, however, said from prison that PAS was still a part of PR, even as he welcomed Amanah to be part of the pact. "Amanah will further strengthen the national Opposition, together with PKR, PAS, DAP," he said while also adding that PR would be open to "other committed non-governmental organisations (NGOs) which share our common objectives".

On September 16, 2015, Amanah was officially launched to coincide with Malaysia Day, with Mat Sabu as president and Salahuddin Ayub as his deputy.

A new pact is forged

Six days later, on September 22, PKR, the DAP and Amanah met for a roundtable discussion. Right after that, Wan Azizah announced that they had agreed to form a new pact to replace the now-defunct Pakatan Rakyat.

It was called Pakatan Harapan (PH), or Pact of Hope.

"We understand the need to have this coalition. We are not going to sugarcoat it and deny we had differences in the past, but this time around we will make it better," she said. "The people have high hopes of seeing the Opposition working together. This is for the people."

All three parties unanimously agreed that if the pact should win GE14, Anwar would be prime minister. One would assume that with him in jail and disqualified from standing for office for five years upon release, the only way that could be realised was if they managed to get him a full pardon from the King. It seemed like a long shot.

Wan Azizah said PAS was also welcome to join the new pact. In fact, the party was invited to the roundtable meeting but it declined to attend. "Yes, as long as they are in the Opposition, we welcome them," she affirmed.

PAS deputy president Tuan Ibrahim Tuan Man responded, saying that his party was still "united with the Opposition" in fighting for the *rakyat* in opposing corruption, abuse of power and the misuse of public funds. It still considered PKR a political friend, but it would not cooperate with the DAP or Amanah.

And so there it was. A new pact. A pact of hope. But would this bring real hope for the people?

Not so a year later when PH was tested at the Sarawak state elections and two by-elections in Peninsular Malaysia. The voting outcome from these was to prove disappointing for it and presage uncertain prospects for the pact at the next general election.

After that, the people again braced themselves for dark days ahead. Some felt there was no real improvement in the new set-up because Amanah was, to begin with, only a small part of PAS and by no means as strong as the parent it broke away from. Some gave up hope after feeling demoralised by the many disappointments they had experienced over time. Some succumbed to political fatigue.

It had been a long, hard struggle since May 6, the day after GE13, with no promise of success. And the future was not bright. If there was one word to describe the mood of the people at this point, it would have to be: Despair.

ACT 2
HOPE

THE BIG STEAL

Despair turned to hope for the people on July 2, 2015.

The hope came in the form of a simple abbreviation – 1MDB.

It would stand for the world's biggest financial scandal.

That fateful day, *The Wall Street Journal* (WSJ) exposed the shocking news that Najib Razak had received RM2.6 billion (US$681 million) in his private bank accounts in March 2013.

Quoting from what Malaysian investigations into 1MDB had so far discovered, the paper reported, "The cash came from a company registered in the British Virgin Islands via a Swiss bank owned by an Abu Dhabi state fund."

That was not all. Another amount totalling RM42 million (US$11.1 million) had also gone into Najib's private bank accounts between December 2014 and February 2015.

That money allegedly came from SRC International Sdn Bhd, a company that was originally controlled by 1MDB but later transferred to the Finance Ministry.

The same day, *Sarawak Report*, an online investigative journalism website operated from London by Clare Rewcastle Brown, revealed that the source of the RM2.6 billion was linked to 1MDB.

It said the transfer of the money took place just days after the signing of a "strategic partnership" in 2013 between Malaysia and Abu Dhabi. A US$3 billion bond was then issued, guaranteed by the Malaysian Government as part of a "50-50 joint venture" between 1MDB and Aabar Investments PJS to develop the Tun Razak Exchange project.

Aabar was a subsidiary of Abu Dhabi's sovereign wealth fund, International Petroleum Investment Co (IPIC).

"However, there have been many queries since about what happened to the money; about the failure to develop the Tun Razak Exchange project and about why Aabar itself never contributed, as promised, to the so-called joint venture," *Sarawak Report* pointed out.

It said the connections between 1MDB projects and the prime minister's personal finances "transforms the 1MDB investigation into a political crisis of the gravest magnitude in Malaysia".

"Whatever the excuses (and of course there will be attempts at plenty), such vast transfers of money into a sitting prime minister's private account cannot be ignored."

Absolutely not. Najib was, after all, chairman of 1MDB's board of advisors, and the company belonged to the Minister of Finance (Incorporated) (MOF (Inc)). He was finance minister as well.

The first to dig up the dirt

Actually, long before *WSJ* and *Sarawak Report* exposed the scandal, DAP MP Tony Pua had been nosing around and doggedly asking questions about 1MDB. He found out things that did not look right.

I remember hearing him say at a DAP fund-raising dinner even before GE13 that Malaysians should keep an eye on 1MDB because it would soon be at the centre of "the mother of all scandals".

He deserves credit for being the first to raise awareness about the dealings of the company and afterwards relentlessly digging up the dirt surrounding it.

As early as 2010, he asked Najib in Parliament twice, once in March and then again in June, for an update on 1MDB's investments and performance as well as its financial standing. And in October, he called for the full accounts and annual report of 1MDB to be made public.

In 2014, he also trained his guns on SRC International. When it belonged to 1MDB, it secured a RM4 billion loan guaranteed by the

Federal Government from Kumpulan Wang Amanah Persaraan (KWAP), or Retirement Trust Fund. But after it had received the first tranche of the loan, amounting to RM2 billion, in March 2012, the Finance Ministry hastily took over the company from 1MDB.

Pua suspected that the RM4 billion loaned to SRC might have been misappropriated, which was why the ministry hastily acquired the company, so that the deed would not be reflected in 1MDB's consolidated accounts.

It led him to ask the important question, "What has happened to the RM4 billion since March 2012?"

Another person who should be credited for diligently raising awareness and asking critical questions about 1MDB and its dubious dealings from early on is Rafizi Ramli.

Apart from speaking up in Parliament, he wrote extensively on 1MDB in his blog. His first entry on the company was on April 23, 2013, in which he noted with concern why, despite its burgeoning debt, 1MDB invested RM7 billion in shares in a Cayman Islands fund instead of bringing the money home.

In November 2016, Rafizi was found guilty of possessing a classified audit report on 1MDB and leaking it to the media. He was sentenced to 18 months' jail. But in June 2018, the Court of Appeal was to spare him the jail sentence. He was then bound over for two years on a good behaviour bond of RM10,000 in one surety.

From TIA to 1MDB

1MDB had actually been rebranded from the Terengganu Investment Authority (TIA), which was set up in February 2009 as a sovereign wealth fund aimed at facilitating the economic development of the northeastern state.

TIA hired Shahrol Azral Ibrahim Halmi as CEO. It also had as one of its two special advisers a young economist named Low Taek Jho, better known as Jho Low. He came from a wealthy Penang family and attended elite schools in the U.K. and the U.S. While studying at the prestigious

Wharton business school, he made friends with royalty from Saudi Arabia, Kuwait and Abu Dhabi.

In July, MOF (Inc) took over TIA and turned it into 1MDB (1Malaysia Development Berhad), a government-owned strategic development company given the mission "to drive the sustainable long-term economic development and growth of Malaysia".

A statement from the Prime Minister's Office (PMO) said the company would invest billions of ringgit in energy, real estate and hospitality sectors in the country.

1MDB would report directly to the prime minister, while having an eight-member board of advisors and a five-member board of directors.

Enter a prince of Arabia

Less than a month after 1MDB was established, Najib received a letter from a Prince Turki bin Abdullah, co-founder of the private company PetroSaudi International, proposing a business venture.

This same Prince Turki was to be arrested on an unrelated matter in 2018 by the Saudi Arabian government for alleged corruption and taking advantage of his influence to award contracts to his own companies.

In August 2009, he and his company's CEO, Tarek Obaid, met with Najib and Jho Low on board a mega-yacht off the coast of Monaco.

Tarek was no stranger to the Malaysian set-up; Low had earlier introduced him to TIA. What he now proposed to Najib was a joint venture between 1MDB and PetroSaudi to "make strategic investments in high-impact projects".

1MDB would contribute US$1 billion cash for a 40% stake in a joint-venture company while PetroSaudi Holdings, registered in the Cayman Islands, would put in its oil fields in Turkmenistan and Argentina valued at US$3.6 billion.

Both parties concurred and soon signed an agreement in September. The new joint-venture company, called 1MDB PetroSaudi Ltd, was registered in the British Virgin Islands and made a subsidiary of PetroSaudi Holdings.

As it turned out, PetroSaudi Holdings did not own the Turkmenistan assets. It was a scam. But this was not made known to 1MDB's board of directors.

The next scam was a loan of US$700 million that the joint-venture company supposedly took from its parent company, PetroSaudi Holdings. But it turned out to be a fake loan. The money went to Good Star Limited instead of 1MDB PetroSaudi Ltd. It came out of the US$1 billion 1MDB had paid up for the joint venture. And Good Star was controlled by Jho Low!

The 1MDB board was upset when it found out that US$700 million went to Good Star. They would have been more upset if they had known that Tarek's benefit from this was a cool broker's fee of US$85 million.

In 2010, 1MDB decided to invest an additional US$830 million, taking its total investment to US$1.83 billion. Out of that total amount, between 2009 and 2011, Good Star was to receive about US$1.03 billion. Of this, US$529 million went to Low. The rest went to others like Tarek, Prince Turki and PetroSaudi executive Patrick Mahony.

In September 2012, 1MDB and PetroSaudi ended their joint venture. 1MDB declared later that it received US$2.318 billion (RM7 billion), which included a US$488 million profit on its original investment. It invested the amount in a fund in the Cayman Islands.

This was the money Rafizi asked about in his blog, wondering why it was not brought home to pay off 1MDB's debts instead.

In debt by RM42 billion

Moving onward from 2009, 1MDB made various business dealings, including buying overpriced power plants, and acquiring property assets, like the Tun Razak Exchange (TRX) and Bandar Malaysia, as well as land in various places. It took out loans to pay for its property assets.

In just a few years, from 2010 to 2014, it came to accumulate a whopping debt of RM42.88 billion (about US$11 billion).

It had to use some of the funds meant for project development to pay interest on its loans. Faced with cash flow problems, it could hardly get started on developing Bandar Malaysia and TRX, which was planned to be a new financial district on prime land in the heart of Kuala Lumpur.

Sarawak Report drops bombshell

Then the inevitable happened. On February 28, 2015, *Sarawak Report* sent tremors across the world when it dropped a bombshell about Jho Low.

In an article entitled 'Heist of the century', Clare Rewcastle Brown said she had worked together with London's *The Sunday Times* to establish that Low was the one who conceived, managed and drove through the 1MDB-PetroSaudi joint-venture scam, with PetroSaudi agreeing to act as "a front" for the deals.

The e-mail exchanges between Low and Patrick Mahony disclosed by *Sarawak Report* were revealing. They showed how Low deviously connived to use the name of Saudi's King Abdullah to impress the Malaysian side and make it seem as if this would be a Saudi-Malaysia bilateral venture.

The report also described in detail how the US$700 million so-called loan ended up in the bank account of Low's Good Star Limited.

It was able to piece together the whole scam from "thousands of documents and e-mails" related to the transactions.

All these, amounting to 90GB of data, had been passed on to her in January 2015 by Xavier Justo, who was hired to be a director with PetroSaudi by Tarek in 2010. But when Justo resigned in 2011, he felt cheated by Tarek, who cut his severance pay by almost half the amount that was promised.

Angered by this, Justo took a copy of the data on the PetroSaudi servers before he left the company. Rewcastle Brown found out about what he possessed two years later and realised it was going to make a big story. She managed to set up a meeting with Justo in Bangkok in October 2014, during which he said he would give her the data for US$2 million.

Rewcastle Brown had to find someone to sponsor it. She found Tong Kooi Ong, a tycoon who also owned Malaysian business weekly *The Edge*.

They all met in January 2015 in Singapore, and Tong agreed to pay

Justo the US$2 million. Rewcastle Brown got the documents she needed and posted her first story in February.

In June 2015, Justo was arrested in Thailand, where he had been living for the past four years, and charged with an attempt to blackmail his former employer. He was sentenced to three years' imprisonment.

In July, Tong admitted in an article in *The Edge* that he never paid Justo the US$2 million. "Yes, we misled him. But that was the only way to get hold of the evidence to expose how a small group of Malaysians and foreigners cheated the people of Malaysia of US$1.83 billion (RM6.97 billion)."

Attorney-general sets up task force

Meanwhile, in March 2015, Najib made a move to show that he was responding to the allegations against 1MDB by instructing the auditor-general to "independently verify" the financial accounts of the company, and the bipartisan Public Accounts Committee (PAC) of Parliament to examine the auditor-general's report afterwards.

He promised that "if any wrongdoing is proven, the law will be enforced without exception".

On March 10, the attorney-general, Abdul Gani Patail, set up a special task force comprising officials from the police, the Malaysian Anti-Corruption Commission (MACC) and the Attorney-General's Chambers to investigate 1MDB.

In April, Mahathir called on Najib to resign. He also riled Najib by raising questions about the gruesome murder of Mongolian model Altantuya Shaariibuu in 2006.

She was connected to allegations of high-level corruption involving Malaysia's purchase of two submarines when Najib was defence minister. Razak Baginda, an adviser and close confidant to Najib who was in on the deal, was charged for her murder but later acquitted.

Najib refused to bow to pressure and hit back at Mahathir. He said when Mahathir was prime minister, "we supported him to stay on" when he faced troubled times. Otherwise, he "would not have lasted 22 years" in that position. So now, if Mahathir "cannot support, then don't make so much noise", he said.

Najib also said that "no individual has the right to ask for the removal of a democratically elected leader". But in that, he was patently wrong. In a democracy, everybody has the right to do that.

Deputy prime minister speaks up

In May, Rafizi questioned what had happened to some RM3.5 billion in funds raised by 1MDB over the past four years to develop Bandar Malaysia into an optimal business and residential district of Kuala Lumpur, when there had been no progress on it at all.

But more disturbing for Najib was criticism coming from his own camp, especially from his own deputy, Muhyiddin Yassin, who openly warned that the scandal and the way it was being handled had become so toxic, it might have a negative impact on the people as well as Umno.

Muhyiddin wanted transparency from his boss on what was happening with 1MDB because he himself was clueless about it. He recounted that when campaigning at the recent Permatang Pauh by-election, he was not even able to explain what was going on with 1MDB because "I didn't know what to say".

On another occasion, he told Umno members at a closed-door event that he had told Najib to sack 1MDB's board of directors and its CEO.

"If the company were mine, with the CEO causing a stir by borrowing up to RM10 billion, and every month having to pay interest of RM100 million to RM200 million, what would I do? Throw it away! This CEO – throw away! And not just throw away, ask the police to investigate! Take action so the *rakyat* can see that the Government is responsible. If not, this burden will drag us down. We cannot have the 'never mind, give it some time' attitude – we cannot!"

Something2Hide

But Najib remained impervious to the criticisms. Then something happened on June 5 that turned out to be a pivotal moment.

Najib was invited to a dialogue session called 'Nothing2Hide', organised by an NGO to provide him a platform to answer questions about 1MDB. According to the organisers, he said he would come.

It drew a standing-room-only crowd of more than 2,000 people eager to hear Najib out. Including Mahathir. But an hour before it was to start, IGP Khalid Abu Bakar sent out a tweet calling for the event to be cancelled – for security reasons.

Everyone was appalled. It turned out that Khalid had advised Najib not to show up, and perhaps to save him face called off the dialogue session.

Mahathir took the opportunity to go on stage to address the audience. But the police stopped him after several minutes. This infuriated the crowd, some of whom had come from as far as Johor and Perlis. They jeered the police and cheered Mahathir.

A press conference was then held with Mahathir. One of the questions asked of him was whether Najib feared him. He cannily replied, "I am just an ordinary man, why be afraid of me?"

He had everyone eating out of his hands. When he left after the press conference, the crowd followed him out of the building, shouting "*Hidup Tun!*" (Long live Tun! Tun being his awarded title.)

The episode gave Mahathir the opportunity to steal the show and be lionised. Najib and the IGP had miscalculated. The cancellation of the event also reinforced the notion that Najib must have something to hide, and that he was too afraid to face the people.

It was ironic and shameful that just the day before, he had told a gathering of 10,000 in Kuching, Sarawak, that he would fight to stay on as prime minister because "the blood in me is not any blood, I have warrior spirit".

Lawyer and political commentator Art Harun tweeted, "Can you imagine a warrior declaring war and not turn up for the 1st battle? LOL!"

The crown prince of Johor, Tunku Ismail Sultan Ibrahim, who was supposed to be above politics, posted on Facebook, "How can you have a dialogue called 'Nothing2Hide' featuring a person who has everything to hide? Obviously he won't show up."

In an article I wrote for *Malaysiakini* on what had transpired, I said:

"It is really tragic for Malaysians that because we have such a weak prime minister in Najib that Mahathir is able to capitalise on the situation in order to worm his way back into the public's good books.

"It is really tragic that there should arise a 1MDB scandal of such mega proportions to give Mahathir the chance to use it to gain the public's forgiveness for his past misdeeds.

"It is really sad to see Malaysians cheer Mahathir when he calls on the police to investigate 1MDB when instead they should be telling the old man that during his tenure as prime minister, investigations were not conducted on the misuse of billions of the public's ringgit in the Perwaja Scandal, the Port Klang Free Trade Zone (PKFZ) scandal, the Tajuddin Ramli bailout, the alleged losses in currency speculation, just to name a few cases."

'1MDB funds used by BN for GE13'

More trouble came for Najib on June 18. *WSJ* published a damning report by Tom Wright that revealed that 1MDB funds were used to finance BN's GE13 campaign.

This was done indirectly, through 1MDB paying an inflated price for a power plant purchased from the powerful Genting Group. After that, Genting made a handsome donation to a foundation of which Najib was chairman. Najib then announced that the foundation would be making donations to two Chinese-medium schools. This was part of his plan to woo Chinese voters for the general election.

More than that, the foundation and other charity bodies linked to Najib, together with Jho Low, also spent millions of ringgit on BN's campaign to win back the state of Penang.

They staged concerts featuring international artists like the Korean pop sensation Psy, organised charity buffets with lucky draws, and distributed grants ranging from RM5,000 to RM200,000 to various NGOs and welfare bodies – all aimed at pleasing Penangites while spreading the BN propaganda.

A-G confirms receiving documents

Then July 2 came. That fateful day when *WSJ* and *Sarawak Report* alleged that RM2.6 billion went into Najib's personal bank accounts. Now how was Najib going to hide?

Attorney-general Abdul Gani Patail released a statement saying that the task force investigating 1MDB had given him documents "connected to allegations that money was transferred into the accounts of the prime minister". It all seemed to add up.

The same day, however, the PMO issued a statement claiming that the allegations were part of "concerted efforts by certain individuals to undermine confidence in our economy, tarnish the Government, and remove a democratically elected prime minister".

But that was the PMO. Why wasn't Najib making a personal statement?

People were dissatisfied with that and challenged him to sue *WSJ* if the report was false.

Najib does not deny receiving RM2.6 billion

Then late that night, Najib posted a personal message on his Facebook page. He obviously did not have the courage to do it at a press conference so he resorted to social media.

He accused Mahathir of having mounted "unsubstantiated" and "outrageous" attacks against him and his family over the past several months, and of "working hand in glove with foreign nationals" to create "this latest lie".

This was an insinuation that Mahathir was involved in the leaking of information obtained from the ongoing investigation into the scandal to *Sarawak Report*.

He also wrote: "Let me be very clear: I have never taken funds for personal gain …" And he repeated the PMO's earlier claim of "political sabotage".

But he did not do the one thing expected of an innocent party, he did not deny receiving the RM2.6 billion.

On July 6, Muhyiddin added pressure when he called on the task force to investigate *WSJ*'s allegations. "We want the truth. This is a very serious allegation that can jeopardise Najib's credibility and integrity as prime minister and leader of the government," he said.

Najib was then in Besut, Kelantan, where he declared, "I did not betray the people. I will find ways to uphold the truth." Again, no categorical denial. In fact, in the weeks to come, he would maintain this refusal to say "yes" or "no". Which of course merely intensified public suspicion of his culpability.

'Najib said 100% not true'

On July 7, *WSJ* uploaded documents sourced from a "Malaysian government investigation" which showed the RM2.6 billion money trail that led to Najib's personal bank accounts.

But three days later, deputy minister Ahmad Maslan, one of Najib's most laughed-at lieutenants for numerous comments he had made previously on other matters, assured the public that the *WSJ* report could not be true.

"What kind of stupid prime minister would take RM2.6 billion in funds from a government agency into his personal account?" he asked. "This is an improbability of the greatest kind. If it is true, it is stupidity of the greatest kind."

What he said next was most curious. "The prime minister has told us that the information is 100% not true. Don't worry, he is not that kind of person."

So, it sounded like Najib had denied to Ahmad Maslan and presumably others in Umno that he received the money. Then why could he not tell the public the same? Or was Ahmad Maslan's information unreliable?

Najib's lawyer sends *WSJ* a stupid letter

Meanwhile, as people waited for Najib to decide whether he would sue *WSJ*, Najib's lawyer, Mohd Hafarizam Harun, sent *WSJ* a letter on July 8. But instead of issuing a legal challenge, it stupidly asked the paper "to state unequivocally and with clarity as to whether it is your contention that our Client misappropriated about USD700 million belonging to 1Malaysia Development Berhad", so that this "confirmation" would "enable us to advise our Client on the appropriate legal recourse he can take to seek redress".

I laughed out loud. And when *WSJ* replied in no uncertain terms that the request was "unnecessary" as what it had published spoke for itself, I laughed even louder. How else did Hafarizam expect *WSJ* to reply?

So, naturally, Najib did not sue the paper. I suspect what Najib wanted to achieve in sending that letter was to get an answer from *WSJ* saying that it did not accuse him of misappropriating the US$700 million. Then he could tell Malaysians, "See! *WSJ* has admitted I did not steal any money!"

In any case, suing *WSJ* would have opened a can of worms. I doubt he would have wanted that.

Access to *Sarawak Report* barred

Neither would he have wanted to sue *Sarawak Report*. Instead, he instructed the Malaysian Communications and Multimedia Commission (MCMC) to bar Malaysians' access to the whistleblowing website.

This was done on July 20 on the grounds that *Sarawak Report*'s "unverified content" could "create unrest and threaten national stability, public order and economic stability".

Subsequently, a warrant would be issued for Rewcastle Brown's arrest under Section 124B of the Penal Code for carrying out activities detrimental to parliamentary democracy.

In response, Rewcastle Brown called it an "irrational" action, "an Orwellian charge", and said, "I'm not scared. I don't think they have got a chance in hell of extraditing me from the UK … this isn't about intimidating me, this is about intimidating Najib's own domestic population." She was right.

Malaysians owe Clare and her source a great debt

Actually, although *WSJ* appears to be in the limelight over the issue, Clare Rewcastle Brown was the first person to get the story about the RM2.6 billion.

She describes it in her book *The Sarawak Report* that was launched in September 2018.

It was not *WSJ* that got it first. She was given the revealing documents by her Malaysian source through an intermediary she refers to as "Din" and told it was hers to run the story. But she decided to get *WSJ* on board because, as she describes it in her book, she felt that "a bigger player" making it an "international story" would be more impactful than if it were published in just her own "small platform". So that's how *WSJ* got into it.

As for her source, the people who gave her the story, who risked their own safety and that of their family members – they are heroes. Malaysians owe Rewcastle Brown a great debt for exposing the story, but they owe her source an even greater debt.

The Edge gets suspended

On July 24, the Home Ministry announced that it was suspending the publishing permit of *The Edge Weekly* and *The Edge Financial Daily* for three months from July 27.

This was because of their reporting on 1MDB, which was deemed to be "prejudicial or likely to be prejudicial to public order, security or likely to alarm public opinion or is likely to be prejudicial to public and national interest".

The people wondered if it was national interest that was the issue or Najib's interest.

Deputy prime minister speaks up again

On July 26, Muhyiddin spoke up again, this time telling Umno members that the Government should not underestimate the people's negative sentiments towards the party because of the 1MDB controversy.

"Don't underestimate the people, we cannot lie … so who is going to tell us the real facts? It should be the Prime Minister, true or not?" he asked.

He assured his audience that he was not out to overthrow Najib, and warned that because Umno was being wrongly perceived in light of the 1MDB controversy and also the implementation of GST, BN could lose if elections were called now.

Najib sacks his deputy and A-G

Two days later, on July 28, Najib sent shock waves throughout the nation by sacking Muhyiddin from the Cabinet and replacing him with Ahmad Zahid Hamidi, who was told of it only a few hours before Najib made the announcement.

On national television, Najib said, "The decision to replace Muhyiddin was a difficult one, but I was forced to do so to ensure the Cabinet is a united team."

Mohd Shafie Apdal, who had also been vocal about 1MDB, was also sacked from his position of rural and regional development minister.

Najib took the action at a rapid pace because he had earlier been tipped off that attorney-general Gani Patail was about to charge him with criminal misappropriation. Gani had apparently also shown Muhyiddin evidence of this previously.

So, that same day, Najib terminated Gani's contract prematurely, giving "health reasons" as the excuse, and had him replaced by former Federal Court judge Mohamed Apandi Ali.

Four PAC members promoted to the Cabinet

In another major move, Najib promoted to the Cabinet four of the members of the PAC currently investigating 1MDB, including its chairman, Nur

Jazlan Mohamed, who had so far been acknowledged even by the Opposition as doing a good job helming the investigation.

The promotion manoeuvre would stall the PAC proceedings until replacements were appointed. Sceptics feared that Najib was playing for time and that he would select his loyalists to join the committee.

Najib wants loyalty from now on

On August 1, Najib laid it down to Umno members that he would brook no dissent. But the way he put it sounded ludicrous. He said he valued people who were loyal more than those who were smart and of high calibre. Nonetheless, this statement would clearly establish what he expected of his lieutenants from now on.

In a racist tone, he also demanded that "white people" stay out of Malaysia's affairs. "Everything is being exposed in *Sarawak Report* as if foreigners are deciding how we should run the country. What is their right? I cannot allow this to continue. I cannot allow white people to determine our future," he declaimed.

After that, Najib had a legion of yes-men bending over backwards to prove their loyalty by spewing rubbish about the RM2.6 billion and 1MDB controversy.

New education minister Mahdzir Khalid accused Jews, Christians and *Sarawak Report* of having a clear agenda to destabilise Malaysia as a Muslim country.

Deputy minister Abdul Aziz Kaprawi said Jews were trying to bring about the downfall of Muslims and Malays with the help of the Western media and – believe it or not – the DAP.

MACC says it was a 'donation'

On August 3, the MACC announced a bewildering revelation. The RM2.6 billion did not come from 1MDB, it was a "donation".

This made people wonder what sort of donation it was.

If it was a personal one, then, according to the MACC Act 2009,

Najib would be prosecutable for corruption. The Act states that public officials who receive gratification, including donations, are "presumed to have done so corruptly", thus committing "an offence punishable by 20 years' imprisonment".

However, if it was a political donation for Umno, how come other party leaders, especially Muhyiddin, did not know about it?

Most pertinent of all, when *WSJ* broke the story, why did Najib not come clean and say straight away that the money was a political contribution to Umno? Why was it left to the MACC to announce that the money was a contribution from donors one whole month later?

Was it truly a donation?

But then again, was it truly a donation? Did the MACC mean it? Was there interference in the announcement of its findings?

Journalist Hafiz Yatim wrote in *Malaysiakini*:

"According to those who claim to be in the know, there was a high-powered meeting held on Monday, July 27, comprising the police led by Khalid, the Armed Forces chief Zulkefli Mohd Zin, the MACC and Gani over what may happen the week after that date.

"MACC officers investigating SRC International Sdn Bhd, a former subsidiary of 1MDB, who were present at the meeting told Gani that they had strong evidence against the sitting prime minister, enough to charge him with corruption. Since the MACC cannot charge an individual unless it gets the consent to prosecute from the attorney-general, Gani offered to charge the PM himself."

Hafiz's report then speculated that someone snitched to Najib about this, and we know what happened after that.

It was later widely rumoured that the snitch was IGP Khalid, but there was no evidence to back that up.

'Hidden hands' hamper probe on SRC

Things took a dramatic turn on July 30. *Sarawak Report* posted a charge sheet said to have been prepared by the MACC and the A-G's Chambers to be served on Najib and another SRC director, Shamsul Anuar bin Sulaiman.

This was another shocker for the unknowing public. It enhanced suspicion that Najib was culpable, and that his swift action in removing Gani was to save himself from prosecution.

Apandi did what was expected of a loyal lieutenant, he dismissed the charge sheet as being false. And the police were called to investigate the leak. But then, if it was false, why consider it a "leak"?

Several MACC officers were summarily hauled up for questioning and evidence they had gathered on SRC was seized. Their investigation into the SRC case was consequently hampered. The authorities' real intent was therefore not to investigate the so-called leak but something more sinister.

This became clearer when a former MACC adviser, an MACC deputy public prosecutor and an officer from the A-G's Chambers were also arrested.

They and the MACC officers were declared by police to be investigated under Section 124B of the Penal Code for alleged activities detrimental to parliamentary democracy.

MACC special operations division director Bahri Mohamad Zain, who was among those questioned, was furious at the harassment. He suggested that there were hidden hands behind the police action. He vowed, "I will find the perpetrators who are ordering the arrests. By God, I will hound them till Kingdom Come."

A few days later, he and his colleague Rohaizad Yaakob were abruptly transferred to the Prime Minister's Department.

MACC deputy commissioner Shukri Abdull, who was in the U.S. then, negotiated for the immediate return of the two officers.

On August 10, they were reinstated to their original positions at the MACC. The chief secretary, Ali Hamsa, and the director-general of the Public Services Department, Mohamad Zabidi Zainal, must have realised that in issuing the transfer orders, they had committed the offence of obstructing the two public servants in the discharge of their public functions. The enraged Shukri would probably not have let them off the hook.

Now it seemed clear that the MACC was trying to do its job properly, but other agencies in the Government were trying to subvert it.

Donation is from the Middle East

Prior to all these shenanigans, on August 5, the MACC made another eyebrow-raising declaration – that the RM2.6 billion was a donation from the Middle East.

It said in a statement, "The MACC has obtained explanation from the donors who originated from the Middle East, and they have verified the donation. The RM2.6 billion donation has no connection at all to 1MDB."

Was the MACC pressured to put out such a claim? Again, was there interference?

Mahathir responded to the claim by calling it "bullshit".

He wrote in his blog: "Arabs are generous, but not that generous. I could not raise even a single dollar from them for the Malaysian International Islamic University or for the Oxford Islamic Centre. This claim that Arabs donated billions is what people describe as hogwash or bullshit. Certainly I don't believe it and neither can the majority of Malaysians if we go by the comments on social media. The world had a good laugh."

Najib finally admits he received money

On August 8, after five weeks of not saying "yes" or "no", Najib finally admitted that he had received money, but the MACC had cleared him of corruption for it and said it was not money from 1MDB.

He said he had received the money not for himself but on behalf of the party. He did not mention it was RM2.6 billion.

"Don't say I sell the country, I won't sell the country. I'm a prime minister who will take responsibility for whatever I do," he told Umno members in Pasir Gudang, Johor.

'Stop thinking that Malaysians are stupid'

Najib's sycophants came out with a new spin. Kuantan Umno division chief Wan Adnan Wan Mamat disclosed that Najib had told him and 145 other Umno divisional leaders at a meeting on August 13 that the RM2.6 billion came from Saudi Arabia as "an appreciation to Malaysia for championing Islam and for practising Sunni Islam". And also for Malaysia's efforts in combating Islamic State (IS) threats.

But then IS was only formed a month after Najib received the money, so the spin sounded more like a lie.

The Arab angle was further exploited when the new deputy prime minister announced he had actually met with the Arab donors. He said they were from a wealthy Arab family, and that they had donated the money because they were impressed with Malaysia and its commitment to fighting terrorism.

He said the first US$100 million was given via a cheque under Najib's name and the rest through other channels. "I saw the documents myself – the original documents, not photostat ones – and I also saw the money trail."

He also said, perhaps unadvisedly, "They want Umno and BN to continue ruling the country."

This immediately raised a serious issue. It clearly meant that Najib had allowed a foreign party to interfere in Malaysia's internal affairs. If a party other than Umno had done that, the Government would have charged that party for treason.

Zahid's and the other Umno leaders' complicity in this spin showed that they were either uncritically accepting of the proposal that the money actually did come from an Arab donor or that they were nonetheless uncertain or even suspicious but chose instead to protect Najib.

Because at the base of it all, if it was all so innocent and legal and so Islamic, why did Najib keep the source of the RM2.6 billion secret from everyone for so long and come up with the Arab story only now?

Mahathir had an apt response to all that spin, "Stop thinking that Malaysians are stupid."

Bersih 4 rally calls for Najib to step down

And because Malaysians refused to believe the bullshit, many of them joined the Bersih 4 rally held on August 29 and 30 in Sabah, Sarawak and the heart of Kuala Lumpur to demand Najib's resignation.

I was at the Kuala Lumpur rally on both days and saw tens of thousands on the streets, some bedding down in the open overnight on August 29, including future Parti Amanah Negara president Mat Sabu and 56-year-old Koh Joo Hoo who said he was at the rally for the sake of his "grandchildren's future".

As the rally was a 34-hour marathon event, it was difficult to ascertain how many actually attended, but *Politweet.Org* measured the total attendance, using a scientific method, as "between 79,919 and 108,125".

Thousands more rallied in about 70 cities around the world in solidarity with the Malaysian ones. The biggest turnout was in Melbourne, where 5,000 people took part.

Surprise! Surprise!

A surprise visitor at the Kuala Lumpur rally was Mahathir. His arrival was met with frenzied roars of approval by rally participants. When asked why he was there, he said, "I just came to see."

He left after 20 minutes but returned the next day. He walked among the crowd and spoke to the media. "The only way for the people to get back to the old system is for them to remove this prime minister. And to remove him, the people must show people power. The people as a whole do not want this kind of corrupt leader," he said.

PKR vice-president Tian Chua, who helped escort Mahathir on the first day of his visit, said he was thankful for the latter's support "but it does not mean the *rakyat* have forgotten that part of the problem today is due to the system he built that closed our democratic space and contributed to the people's uprising today".

Umno vice-president Hishammuddin Hussein reacted by saying

Mahathir had "crossed the line" by attending the rally. He said, "His action has gone against the values he promulgated when he was prime minister. During his administration, he clearly stated that street demonstrations were not the approach to voice dissatisfaction."

Umno man's fight for the truth

In September, Hong Kong police said it had begun investigations into bank deposits of more than US$250 million allegedly made at a Credit Suisse branch there.

This was in response to a police report lodged in Hong Kong on August 30 by Khairuddin Abu Hassan, an Umno man and former deputy chief of the party's Batu Kawan division.

In fact, between July and September, Khairuddin was busy lodging reports against 1MDB to authorities in other countries as well, including Switzerland, Singapore, France and the U.K.

He was prompted to do so because no action had been taken in Malaysia after he had made seven police reports since December 2014. This was remarkably way before anyone else in Umno had drawn attention to 1MDB. Before Muhyiddin started asking pointed questions.

When Khairuddin made that initial report alleging improprieties in the management of the company, Umno secretary-general Tengku Adnan Tengku Mansor asked him to withdraw it, but he refused. Two months later, he was sacked from his Umno post.

Khairuddin told *The Malaysian Insider* that he felt compelled to go outside Malaysia to lodge reports after Gani was removed and the special task force investigating the RM2.6 billion and 1MDB scandal got derailed, followed by the postponement of the PAC probe.

He was "perplexed" that some PAC members, including Nur Jazlan, were appointed to the Cabinet. "They accepted the posts and the PAC investigation stopped, what was the motive? So when there was no action, I was confident that money was being laundered overseas," he said.

Asked why he was insistent on lodging reports about 1MDB, he said,

"This is about saving our country, not bringing down the Government or Umno. This is a struggle, and I want to fight for the truth."

I suspect he must have had backing from powerful people with means and influence to pursue his quest. Mahathir's and Daim's names come to mind.

On September 18, he and his lawyer, Matthias Chang, were about to leave for New York to meet with agents of the Federal Bureau of Investigation (FBI) there, but they were stopped. The Immigration Department told them they had been barred from travelling abroad by the police.

That night, Khairuddin was arrested. At first, the charge against him was for carrying out activities detrimental to parliamentary democracy, but on September 23, he was charged under SOSMA (Security Offences (Special Measures) Act 2012) for sabotaging banking and financial services.

This was alarming. SOSMA was a controversial law supposed to be specifically targeted at terrorism. It allowed up to 28 days of detention without trial. When it was tabled in Parliament, government leaders guaranteed that it would be used specific to terrorism and not for political reasons. But now Najib was going back on that promise.

On October 8, Chang was also arrested under SOSMA for the same offence as Khairuddin's. Chang was just his lawyer, why was he being punished with something so severe? It is interesting to note that Chang was political secretary to Mahathir when the latter was prime minister.

On November 18, however, the High Court ruled that the charge of sabotaging banking and financial services did not fall under SOSMA. It ordered the release of both men on bail and the case to be tried at the Sessions Court.

In May 2017, Khairuddin and Chang were to be acquitted and discharged.

'Get rid of the cancer and pus'

In December 2015, Najib showed his undemocratic and authoritarian side yet again when he got Umno to bar its deputy president, who was still

Muhyiddin, from speaking at the party's annual general assembly. This was an unwarranted break from a decades-old tradition.

However, Muhyiddin found an alternative platform at a function hall in Kuala Lumpur to address his supporters within the party just days before the assembly started.

He told them, "I would like to suggest that the prime minister take a rest for now. Allow the investigations to proceed freely, transparently and fairly ... go on leave until the case is over. I would rather appeal to Umno to undergo painful surgery than face the uncertain future in a state of coma and slow death later. Let me be straight ... whoever is the cancer and pus in Umno must be discarded. In order to save the party, race and country, we must get rid of the cancer and pus."

But Muhyiddin's speech achieved little immediate effect. As expected, it was brought to the scrutiny of the party's disciplinary committee. It was to result in Muhyiddin being suspended as deputy president in February 2016.

At last, Najib says 2.6 billion

On December 8, the day after Muhyiddin made his speech, Najib went on television to be interviewed by Mohd Ashraf Abdullah, Abdul Jalil Hamid and Abdul Aziz Ishak, three top editors of BN-owned media organisations. It looked obviously set up for him to say openly at last that he did receive RM2.6 billion in his personal bank accounts, six months after it had been exposed by *Sarawak Report* and *Wall Street Journal*.

Asked why he had received the funds in his own bank accounts, he replied: "That is what the donors wanted. The donation to me was on a personal basis."

I recalled what Ahmad Maslan had said in July – "What kind of stupid prime minister would take RM2.6 billion ... into his personal account?" – and had a good laugh.

Najib said the donors did not want anything in return. But I inferred that was to pre-empt accusations of his having been bribed or having sold out the country to foreigners.

He also said, "I have not committed any offence or malpractice, and this has been explained in Parliament by the deputy prime minister."

No guts to face Parliament

Indeed, on December 3, Zahid did face the House on Najib's behalf and spoke for five minutes. He touched on what was safe, such as the money not being from 1MDB, the donor having been identified by the MACC, the legal acceptability of political donations, and ended with the excuse that he could not elaborate more because of ongoing investigations. It was hardly an explanation. Everything Zahid said was what everybody already knew.

Opposition MPs objected and asked why Najib was not present to address the matter himself. He did not have the courage?

Journalists or lackeys?

He obviously felt safer talking to the three journalists who, on their part, looked obeisant and scared to ask him questions that cried out to be asked.

For example, they did not ask him if the Inland Revenue Board was informed of the donation, because donations were not tax-exempt. Or why he did not inform Umno about the donation. Or why he did not admit to it immediately after *WSJ* broke the story.

When he said, "A donation is not illegal under any legal provision", they did not remind him that as in this case the money was given to him "on a personal basis", he could be charged with corruption. Just check the Penal Code and the Malaysian Anti-Corruption Commission Act 2009.

They were derelict in their duty as journalists. Or they were just dancing to their master's tune. One of them even asked him if his conscience was clear. How else would he have replied but "Yes, absolutely clear. I have done what I did with full responsibility and I am confident that after the investigation is completed, the truth will prevail."? It just gave him opportunity to come off looking good.

Najib firmly in control

So, the interview was a boon for him ahead of the Umno general assembly, which started the next day. He said, "I want the party to remain united. I do not want to see the party in chaos or divided … I want party members to close ranks."

As a result, what was expected to be an event full of fireworks turned out to be a tame affair. The movement set up by some branch chiefs in late November to pressure Najib to resign as party president seemed to have fizzled out. Umno leaders and members responded to his call to close ranks.

In his speech to the party faithfuls, Najib focused on the threat posed by the DAP, and strongly proposed cooperating with PAS to win Malay votes at the next general election.

"We in Umno feel relieved, and even happy, that PAS is now no longer with the Opposition," he said. "With open hearts, we extend to them the ties of *ukhuwah* (brotherhood) towards the ideal of building Malaysia based on Islamic principles."

The delegates joined in to support the idea of working towards Muslim unity. By and large, party members seemed to have put the RM2.6 billion and 1MDB scandal behind them, and were heeding the president's call to move on. All was well for Najib. He looked firmly in control of the party.

Najib cleared by A-G

That was, however, not enough. To make doubly sure that Najib was out of the woods, new A-G Apandi brought good news for him in 2016.

On January 26, in a hurriedly gathered press conference, he declared that Najib did not commit any offence in receiving the RM2.6 billion "donation" and the RM42 million from SRC in his personal bank accounts.

This was a shocking moment, but not an unexpected one.

Apandi said he was convinced that the RM2.6 billion was donated to Najib by the Saudi royal family, and that it was not given as an inducement or reward for doing anything in return.

Apandi also said – to many people's surprise – that Najib had on August 2013 returned a sum of US$620 million (RM2.03 billion) to the Saudi royal family as the money was not utilised.

That straight away begged a few questions. If he had returned the money, why did he never mention it earlier so that the public would know and he would have looked better? What about the remaining US$61 million? What was the money used for? Did Apandi ask for a proper accounting of it to make sure it was not corruptly used?

As for the RM42 million from SRC, Apandi said Najib was not aware that the money went into his bank account. I had a good laugh. That much amount of money and Najib was unaware?

Is Apandi covering up for Najib?

I did not believe a word of all the things Apandi said. Besides, he was in too much of a hurry to get things over and done with.

In December, the MACC had presented him with evidence of Najib having received the RM42 million from SRC and recommended further investigations, but Apandi had rejected it.

He also rejected numerous requests from the MACC to seek legal assistance from foreign governments to trace missing 1MDB funds that were outside the country.

Out of defiance or frustration, MACC's Shukri made a public statement on December 31 declaring that the RM2.6 billion probe was still incomplete because it needed documents and statements involving several overseas financial institutions.

"These documents and statements can only be taken through mutual legal assistance (MLA) as this is tied to the banking laws of the countries involved," he said, and added that the MACC had filed a request with Apandi to get the MLA.

Why did Apandi reject the MACC's request to get the MLA? Furthermore, if three-and-a-half weeks before he cleared Najib, the MACC had said its investigations were incomplete, how could he be sure of his current conclusions in the short interim?

Apandi had apparently covered things up. And now he wanted the MACC to close the case. He said there was no need for Malaysia to request mutual legal assistance from any foreign state for the purpose of completing the criminal investigation.

Why was he so hasty to close the case when there were still unanswered questions and the money trail outside the country was not investigated?

Tony Pua was most unsatisfied with Apandi's conclusions. He said the basis to absolve Najib of any wrongdoing was "utterly without merit" because Apandi had provided "no new or convincing information or arguments on whether the massive funds were *bona fide*" or free of corrupt motives.

Najib, on the other hand, said Apandi's conclusions "confirmed what I have maintained all along: that no crime was committed".

"This issue has been an unnecessary distraction for the country. Now that the matter has been comprehensively put to rest, it is time for us to unite and move on," he said.

The MACC asked for a review of Apandi's decision to close the case. In February, the independent eight-member review panel that studied the investigations recommended that the MACC continue the probe as it was "still incomplete", and advised the commission to seek Apandi's help to obtain MLA to get access to evidence from banks overseas to follow the money trail.

However, the panel lacked the power to enforce its recommendations.

One of the panel members, lawyer Lim Chee Wee, would reveal in 2018 that the MACC was "very professional, they did a very good job" on the case but their hands were tied. "To us, the biggest disappointment was Apandi," he said.

Apandi was the one who would call the shots ultimately, and if he refused to take further action, nothing could be done to compel him to do so.

'Is 1MDB a kind of BR1M?'

So, Najib had pulled it off. He had been absolved by the attorney-general, the only person who could have had him prosecuted.

The people could now see he had much power he could manipulate as prime minister to absolve himself from wrongdoing, and also to punish anyone who tried to go against him. The police were with him, so were the A-G and some members of the judiciary. And the mainstream media controlled by BN parties were ever cooperative in killing reports that might hurt him. He was almost invincible.

The RM2.6 billion exposé that had appeared unexpectedly had not succeeded in bringing him down. Now it seemed nothing could. The people feared that in time the scandal would fade out and he would be back to winning ways.

In any case, Rafizi shared with attendees at a DAP fund-raising dinner that 1MDB might not have produced a devastating effect after all. The complexities of its financial transactions and problems were not comprehensible to many rural people, so the scandal might not be as far-reaching as the Opposition had hoped.

He gave an anecdotal example of what he meant. When he asked a rural respondent to one of his surveys what she thought about 1MDB, she gave him a blank stare. Then she asked him back if it was another BR1M cash handout.

This was of course an extreme example but it nonetheless evoked a sense of pessismism, and in the days ahead, the pessismism would increase as extensive BN propaganda spun the scandal as something cooked up by the Opposition to topple a democratically elected government. And some people would, sadly, fall for that. Some would actually believe that the money came from an Arab donor.

It all boiled down to who controlled the narrative. In this case, Najib and his myrmidons did. But would this narrative last for long, till the next general election, and would more people believe it?

That was the billion-ringgit question.

RULE BY THIEVES

Fortunately, the 1MDB fire was kept alive in other countries.

Singapore had started investigating 1MDB-related fund flows since March 2015, and Switzerland since July. Hong Kong, the U.K. and the U.S. joined in later in the year.

In January 2016, the Swiss attorney-general's office revealed that as much as US$4 billion appeared to have been misappropriated from 1MDB, and a small portion of the money had been transferred to accounts held in Switzerland.

Swiss attorney-general Michael Lauber requested Malaysia's cooperation for its own investigations into the involvement of Swiss banks in alleged criminal activities linked to 1MDB. He asked twice, first in January and then again in November 2016, but attorney-general Apandi Ali turned him down.

Singapore did not waste time getting down to brass tacks. In over just a year, from May 2016 to 2017, the Monetary Authority of Singapore (MAS) ordered the closure of Switzerland's BSI Bank and Falcon Bank over, among other things, "serious breaches of anti-money laundering requirements".

Six other banking and financial services companies were fined for breaches of MAS's anti-money laundering requirements in allowing fund flows related to 1MDB.

Singapore also banned at least eight people from the financial industry, including ex-Goldman Sachs banker Tim Leissner, and took some to court. Among those convicted was Yeo Jiawei, who was identified as a central figure linked to Jho Low.

Yeo admitted to money laundering and cheating, and was sentenced to four-and-a-half years' jail, on top of a 30-month jail sentence for perverting the course of justice by urging witnesses to lie to police and destroy evidence during the investigation into 1MDB.

The Wolf, according to *WSJ*

In April 2016, *WSJ* reported that global investigators believed that some of the money used to make the Hollywood movie *The Wolf of Wall Street*, starring Leonardo DiCaprio and directed by Martin Scorsese, might have come from 1MDB.

It said US$155 million allegedly flowed in 2012 through several offshore shell companies to the film's production company, Red Granite Pictures, which was co-founded by Riza Aziz, son of Rosmah Mansor and stepson of Najib. Among the people the movie thanks in its closing credits is Jho Low.

Riza had, however, told *The New York Times* in 2014 that the investment for the movie came mainly from Mohamed Ahmed Badawy Al-Husseiny, former head of an Abu Dhabi sovereign wealth fund.

Responding to the *WSJ* report, Najib denied any involvement in the affairs of Red Granite, and 1MDB said it had never funded the movie nor transferred money to the production company.

Auditor-general's report ready, but classified

Earlier in March, the auditor-general's report on 1MDB, which had been commissioned by Najib a year before, was finally presented to the PAC. But it was classified under the Official Secrets Act (OSA) by auditor-general Ambrin Buang himself to prevent leakage.

He, however, specified that the report should be declassified when the PAC eventually tabled its own findings in Parliament. The new PAC chairman, Hasan Arifin, of course a BN man, gave the undertaking that it would be done when the time came.

Najib not implicated

On April 7, the PAC tabled its report. It found that as of January 2016, 1MDB's debt had risen to RM50 billion while its assets amounted to RM53 billion. The company's debt and interest payments of RM3.3 billion were too high compared to its cash flow.

This undesirable situation had come to pass because of poor management and governance. Several large investments and loans were made without detailed assessments. On some occasions, the management did not comply with the decisions and instructions of the board of directors. It even made its own decisions without obtaining the board's approval. The board, on its part, was not proactive or stringent in monitoring the activities of the management and the company's cash flow.

The PAC did not implicate Najib in 1MDB's dealings. Instead, it urged the authorities to investigate the company's former CEO, Shahrol Azral Ibrahim Halmi.

Hearings were flawed

But the PAC hearings were flawed. The committee got no access to important documents that would give a fuller picture of 1MDB's dealings because the company and the Finance Ministry could not produce them. Some key witnesses were also not called. Despite the urgings of some committee members to call them, the chairman refused.

Committee member Tony Pua told the media after the tabling that he was only "80% happy" with the report. He maintained that the PAC "failed" to clear Najib's name because the documents were not made available. Statements from 1MBD's overseas bank accounts were also not provided, nor documents requested from Bank Negara.

He said although the report did not explicitly implicate Najib in any wrongdoing, he should, as finance minister, be held, "at the very least" ministerially accountable.

PAC chairman accused of lying

There was also strong disagreement between the chairman and the committee members from the Opposition.

They accused him of misrepresenting the committee's views and lying when he had told the media that the committee unanimously found no evidence to indicate wrongdoing or abuse of power by Najib, and that it also found no evidence of criminal misconduct related to 1MDB's transactions.

They also expressed shock and disappointment at Hasan's failure to honour his pledge to declassify the auditor-general's report and table it together with the PAC report.

They revealed that the auditor-general and the PAC found "many questionable and suspicious transactions, amounting to billions of ringgit, to foreign firms of which the ownerships are unverified, including Good Star Limited and Aabar Investment PJS Ltd".

A total of US$7 billion of 1MDB cash and liquid assets could not be verified, raising concerns that it had "disappeared without a trace", but the PAC report made no mention of it. The report merely said an unspecified amount of money was unaccounted for.

The assets were US$1.03 billion paid to Good Star, US$3.51 billion paid to Aabar Investment PJS Ltd, US$940 million worth of "units" in BSI Bank, Singapore, and US$1.56 billion worth of investments by 1MDB Global Investment Ltd.

Hasan also did not inform the committee of a letter he had received from a senior Bank Negara official on April 6 telling him that US$1.03 billion in 1MDB funds meant for the joint venture with PetroSaudi had been transferred to an offshore company named Good Star owned by Jho Low, a close associate of Najib's.

Low's name was never mentioned in the PAC report. The Opposition MPs in the PAC accused Hasan of removing without their knowledge sentences from the report that were crucial.

As for Najib, committee members repeatedly asked Hasan to call him to give testimony, but he did not accede to their request.

'Cari makan' PAC chairman

On that point, the media did ask Hasan the previous November why Najib was not called. He replied: *"Janganlah, saya pun cari makan."* (Please don't, I too need to make a living.)

He tried to wriggle out of it later by saying he was making a joke, that he actually meant "looking for food". But that was not what it sounded like in the video that was posted on the Internet.

Hasan also turned down calls to summon other key witnesses like Low, the Bank Negara governor, one of 1MDB's former auditors, and Mohd Hazem Abdul Rahman, who took over as CEO from Shahrol Azral.

What Hasan did as chairman on the whole was severely condemned by Tony Pua: "He lied to the committee, suppressed evidence, covered up wrongdoing and obstructed investigations into 1MDB."

Najib has done it again

For all that anyone said, however, Hasan had served his purpose and Najib had done it yet again. He had stalled the PAC's work the previous July by appointing four of its members to the Cabinet, including its chairman. Then he had installed a new chairman who apparently knew which side his bread was buttered.

After the tabling of the report, Najib could now gloat. He made a statement denouncing Mahathir's allegations against 1MDB and accused him of having been "motivated by personal interest, not the national interest, and a desire to unseat the Government".

Najib also reiterated what he had said before about the Government taking action if wrongdoing was found. But as time went on, no action was ever taken against Shahrol Azral despite the PAC's recommendation to investigate him.

To be sure, Najib wanted the whole 1MDB issue to be buried for good, so that it would soon recede from the public consciousness. He wanted people to know that he had been "cleared of wrongdoing", that was the magic phrase. He was innocent. Let's move on.

Another horrible July

But it was not going to happen. July came, and it turned out to be a horrible month for Najib for the second year running. This time, it was more serious than a newspaper exposé.

On July 20, U.S. attorney-general Loretta E. Lynch announced the largest single action ever taken by the country's Department of Justice (DoJ) under its Kleptocracy Asset Recovery Initiative (KARI). And it involved 1MDB.

Lynch said the DoJ was filing civil forfeiture suits seeking the recovery of more than US$1 billion in assets related to an international conspiracy to launder funds misappropriated from the company.

It said the amount pilfered from 1MDB between 2009 and 2013 was more than US$3.5 billion, allegedly by high-level company officials, their relatives and other associates.

The money was then allegedly laundered through complex transactions and fraudulent shell companies with bank accounts located in Singapore, Switzerland, Luxembourg and the U.S. These transactions were allegedly used to acquire assets located in the U.S. and elsewhere.

These assets allegedly included high-end real estate and hotel properties, such as Parklane Hotel and a luxury condominium in New York, and a mansion in Beverly Hills; a US$35 million jet aircraft; works of art by Vincent van Gogh and Claude Monet; a US$176 million interest in the music publishing rights of EMI Music; and the production of the 2013 film *The Wolf of Wall Street*.

The embezzled money was also used to pay gambling debts in Las Vegas casinos and interior decorators in London, and to buy a townhouse in the U.K. and a luxury yacht.

Assistant attorney-general Leslie R. Caldwell put it beautifully when she said, "The associates of these corrupt 1MDB officials are alleged to have used some of the illicit proceeds of their fraud scheme to fund the production of *The Wolf of Wall Street*, a movie about a corrupt stockbroker who tried to hide his own illicit profits in a perceived foreign safe haven. But whether corrupt officials try to hide stolen assets across international borders –

or behind the silver screen – the Department of Justice is committed to ensuring that there is no safe haven."

Najib's stepson and Jho Low named

The details from the KARI lawsuits got spicier. They named Riza Aziz as a "relevant individual" in the investigations and referred to him as a "close relative of a senior 1MDB official".

They also named Jho Low, and Khadem Abdulla Al-Qubaisi and Mohammed Ahmed Badawy Al-Husseiny, former officials at a sovereign fund in Abu Dhabi that participated in deals with 1MDB.

And there's also 'Malaysian Official 1'

But the spiciest allegation was this – US$731 million was siphoned out of 1MDB and transferred to the bank accounts of "Malaysian Official 1" (MO1), described as "a high-ranking official in the Malaysian Government who also held a position of authority with 1MDB".

Of this amount, US$20 million came from Good Star Limited via a Saudi prince in 2011; US$30 million from Aabar Investments PJS Ltd (British Virgin Islands) in 2012; and US$681 million from Tanore Finance Corporation in 2013.

That revelation set off a buzz throughout the country. The US$681 million, equivalent to RM2.6 billion, corroborated the amount received by Najib in 2013, as reported by *WSJ* and *Sarawak Report*. The dates of the transaction given by both reports also matched those of the DoJ's.

It seemed true after all, even though the recipient was only referred to as "MO1". Anyone with any sense would have concluded straight away that MO1 was none other than the Malaysian prime minister.

Who else could MO1 be?

But the next day, no one would say so publicly. So I was prompted to write an article and say it. The article, entitled 'Who else could "Malaysian Official 1" be?', was published in *Malaysiakini*.

In it, I said the DoJ might not have named him but it did say that the Malaysian A-G declared that MO1 returned US$620 million of the money and ultimately characterised the payment of US$681 million as a personal donation from the Saudi royal family. "For crying out loud," I wrote, "it has to be Najib!"

I went on to ask, "How is the Malaysian Government going to hide from the DoJ's findings now? Is the Malaysian Government going to accuse the U.S. of attempting to topple a legitimately elected government? More importantly, is it still going to hide the truth from the Malaysian people?"

I censured the government ministers who had been misleading the people into thinking that the scandal was a deception conjured by traitors, Hasan for his conduct as PAC chairman, and current 1MDB CEO Arul Kanda Kandasamy for having steadfastly maintained that 1MDB had committed no wrongdoing.

I said Apandi should be sacked.

Blame it on Mahathir's allies

Meanwhile, Najib's lackeys and bootlickers came out to defuse the DoJ's findings.

First up was minister Abdul Rahman Dahlan, who sighed with relief that Najib was not implicated. "The important thing is that in the released documents, the prime minister is not involved in the investigation. In fact, the prime minister's name is not mentioned at all," he said.

Shahrizat Abdul Jalil, leader of the Umno women's wing, was also eager to point out that Najib's name was not mentioned. Then she hit out at "certain quarters who are trying to use foreign powers to overthrow the government that the people have elected".

Najib champion Salleh Said Keruak, writing in his blog, was more specific in referring to them as Mahathir's allies. He said he was made to understand that they had lodged complaints with the U.S. Government, and the action being taken was based on those complaints.

What about Apandi? What did he have to say? He still maintained that "to date, there has been no evidence from any investigation conducted by any law enforcement agencies in various jurisdictions which shows that money has been misappropriated from 1MDB".

'MO1 is the Agong'

In August, BN MP Nawawi Ahmad, apparently a Najib bootlicker, stupidly wrote on his Facebook page that MO1 was the King!

"According to the Federal Constitution, Malaysia's government was formed with three separate and independent entities, the judiciary headed by the chief justice, the legislative led by the Parliament speaker, and the executive directed by the prime minister. All three entities are responsible to the Agong. Hence, according to the constitution, MO1 is the Agong," he reasoned.

A few hours later, he must have realised the potential trouble he could get into for what he had written, so he took out the reference to the King and changed the last line to: "Hence, according to the constitution, Najib is not MO1, as he is either MO2, MO3, or MO4."

It was hilarious, but the consequences were not funny for Nawawi. It is interesting to note that as an Umno man, he tried the Umno trick of worming out of a sticky situation by dissembling that he was not talking about MO1 in the context of the DoJ lawsuits but rather in terms of the Federal Constitution. But it did not work, and he ended up having to apologise profusely to the King.

The government man spills it

On the other side of the fence, Tony Pua called on Najib to instruct the police and the MACC to follow the leads provided by the DoJ to find out the identity of MO1. Najib must have guffawed at the idea.

But on September 1 – wonder of wonders! – ardent Najib defender Rahman Dahlan surprisingly and strangely spilled the beans!

He was being interviewed by the British Broadcasting Corporation (BBC) and was asked if he knew MO1's identity. He tried to deflect it at first, but when the interviewer asked again, he replied, "Well, I've said it openly and publicly. If you read the documents, people say obviously that is the prime minister ..."

There it was! Straight from the mouth of a government man.

He immediately tried to sideline this issue by pushing the point that the identity of MO1 was not as important as why the official was not explicitly named by DoJ. "That tells you that the Department of Justice feels that whoever is supposed to be MO1 is not involved in the 1MDB saga ... he is not a focus of this investigation," he said.

But it was obvious he was being disingenuous. He was not so stupid as not to know that although Najib a.k.a. MO1 was not being investigated, it did not mean that he was not involved in the 1MDB saga. The money trail allegedly led to him.

Najib was not named, I gathered, because he did not hold the alleged illegal assets or directly launder the alleged stolen money in the U.S. But that did not exclude him as an alleged recipient of the money.

Reacting to Rahman Dahlan's revelation, PAS deputy president Tuan Ibrahim Tuan Man pointedly asked, "Confirmed, Malaysian Official 1 is the PM. So is the money in his account, Arab donation or 1MDB funds?"

He insisted that the MACC re-open its investigations into 1MDB and the "donation" story as well as the DoJ's claims "so that we can prevent foreign interference in our internal affairs". He said the MACC should also call upon Apandi to re-evaluate the case.

But of course, nothing would come of that.

'Kleptocracy at its worst'

And so, to the world, Malaysia became a kleptocracy, defined as "rule by thieves". Or, according to the *Cambridge English Dictionary*, "a society whose leaders make themselves rich and powerful by stealing from the rest of the people".

This demeaning tag brought shame to the country and its people. To the extent that several fellow citizens I know dared not identify themselves as being from Malaysia when they went on trips abroad and foreigners asked them where they came from. They would instead fib that they were from either Singapore or Brunei.

Malaysians felt more shame when U.S. attorney-general Jeff Sessions was to describe 1MDB's dealings at a global forum in this sentence: "This is kleptocracy at its worst."

But at least, the U.S. Department of Justice was working to "return the stolen assets to their legitimate owners, the Malaysian people". The Malaysian Government, on the other hand, was ironically working to prevent justice from being done, in its own home for its own people.

Indeed, many people wondered what would eventually happen to the assets when they were recovered by the DoJ – if the Malaysian Government and 1MDB continued to protest that nothing went missing from the company. And, furthermore, if they were eventually returned, would it be safe – or right – to hand them to Najib's BN government?

This was a government that could not be trusted. It needed to be replaced. But the general election was due in less than a couple of years. Would the Opposition be ready by then to vanquish Najib and his juggernaut? Did it have a leader who was strong enough to spur the team on to victory?

Unfortunately, the one person who had the greatest likelihood of doing that was now in prison. And there was no one else in the team who could take his place. He had been the Opposition's most credible choice. Its only choice. Whence comes such another?

EARTHQUAKES AND REALIGNMENTS

"In the wake of an earthquake, tectonic plates will shift and realign." It will also leave "a huge vacuum" waiting to be filled.

That was how brilliant strategist Liew Chin Tong metaphorised the Malaysian political landscape in October 2015.

At the time, a few earthquakes had taken place, in his estimation. One was the sacking of Muhyiddin Yassin and Shafie Apdal from the Cabinet.

Chin Tong said it was so significant that Umno members were still "shell-shocked" by it and unable to express themselves openly. This was because it was something "not seen since September 1998", when Mahathir sacked Anwar.

Another earthquake was the defeat of the progressive faction by the conservatives within PAS. This led to the formation of Amanah, which then joined PKR and the DAP in a new alignment called Pakatan Harapan.

Chin Tong predicted that PAS without the progressive faction would not win the middle-ground Malay votes, and certainly not the non-Malay ones. So it was now looking set to realign with Umno, which had also suffered the earthquake caused by the megascale 1MDB and RM2.6 billion scandal.

Both were seeking to save each other by consolidating their commonly shared ethnocentric views. But, observed Chin Tong, "These views are not even representative of the many voices among the Malay community, not to mention the wider society."

He said the "racial version of Malaysia" promoted by both of them was "a recipe for disaster electorally" as any coalition "should know they need support from across ethnic groups in the Peninsula, and win votes from Sabah and Sarawak".

Given that the battle for Malaysia was increasingly "between the conservatives and the progressives, between those who push for Malay/ Muslim dominance without a moral compass and those who push for a better Malaysia for all", there was a huge vacuum waiting to be filled. And, according to Chin Tong, "no one is sure how to fill it".

He, however, felt that "the final countdown" for change was imminent, and if Najib were to lead Umno into the next general election, Chin Tong predicted it would lose. "An Umno led by Najib is a Titanic on the way to doom."

He pointed out that with the ringgit and oil prices falling, and endless scandals involving Najib surfacing, there was "a huge space outside Umno" waiting to be filled as "millions of Malaysians, especially Malay voters", were upset with the prime minister and his party. Considering that Muhyiddin and Shafie would not have much of a future left in Umno, other realignments could soon shape up.

All the points made by Chin Tong were incisive, and the most challenging one was the question of filling the huge "vacuum" outside Umno. How would his thesis pan out in the days to come?

Remove Najib but keep the government

For starters, in August 2015, Mahathir reached out to the Opposition to propose a vote of no-confidence in Parliament to remove Najib. He said there were BN MPs who would support it, namely, those who did not believe "the nonsensical explanations" about the disappearance of 1MDB money or the RM2.6 billion in Najib's private bank accounts.

However, because the BN MPs "would not like to become instrumental in bringing down a BN government", the no-confidence motion would be targeted at removing only Najib, which meant that the Opposition would have to accept that the current government would remain in power.

Of course, the Opposition did not welcome the idea. PAS's deputy president, Tuan Ibrahim, described the proposal as "half-baked" because "the main issue affecting the country is not only due to Najib but stems from a culture and a corrupt governance system inherited from Mahathir".

He said PAS viewed the proposal as an attempt by Mahathir "to use the Opposition" to remove Najib and "rescue his beloved Umno, which is no longer capable of correcting itself due to money politics".

The DAP's Tony Pua agreed. "It will be old wine in a new bottle," he said. "Umno is rotten, there is no hope for another leader from BN to fix it."

PAS's Shah Alam MP Khalid Samad described the proposal as "odd". He said, quite correctly, "It would be meaningless for us to do a vote of no-confidence to get just Najib out and after that, BN carries on like business as usual."

In any case, the idea was not a feasible one. The country's Parliament system did not allow for a no-confidence vote against an individual. It would have to be against the entire government. So the plot did not materialise.

Then on January 20, Mahathir's son Mukhriz was asked to step down as *menteri besar* of Kedah by state Umno leaders giving flimsy reasons. Mukhriz refused.

But two weeks later, he was informed he had lost the support of the state assembly. He had no choice but to resign.

That was hard for Mahathir to take. He had worked hard, with the help of former finance minister Daim Zainuddin, to deliver Kedah to BN at GE13 and Mukhriz's appointment as *menteri besar* had been the reward. His removal now was the unkindest cut. Even more so because he was being unjustly victimised for the ongoing feud between his father and Najib.

Mahathir quits Umno

So on February 29, 2016, Mahathir resigned from Umno.

When he announced his resignation, he said, "The organisation that is led by Najib today is no longer the Umno which was founded on May 11, 1946. I have always supported Umno, but Umno is no more. I feel embarrassed to be associated with a party that is seen as supporting corruption. It has caused me to feel ashamed."

He said he would not join another party or start a new one, but two days earlier, he had met with DAP adviser Lim Kit Siang to discuss current issues and problems to find a way out of "the national *cul-de-sac*". The same Kit Siang whom he had put under ISA detention for 17 months in 1987 and vilified in the past, the same Kit Siang he had warned voters in Gelang Patah not to vote for in GE13 because if he won, there would be racial violence.

But now the situation in the country was getting dire, and both men knew that something had to be done to set things right. Kit Siang was willing to forgive the man who had put him under detention and denigrated him in untold numbers of ways over the decades. He was even willing to work with the man he called "the number one racist in Malaysia" in 2010.

Actually, Kit Siang had expressed his readiness to bury the hatchet about a year before, in March 2015, when he proposed the formation of a grand coalition of MPs from both sides of the political divide called 'Save Malaysia' whose ultimate aim would be to defend the rule of law and constitutionalism.

Kit Siang said even then that he was willing to work with Mahathir on this idea. So now both men were talking.

An unprecedented move

A few days later, on March 4, Mahathir came up with an overt political move – the Citizens' Declaration, calling for the removal of Najib.

And to many people's surprise, 45 civil society leaders and politicians from both sides of the political divide showed up to give their support and sign the Declaration.

It was launched in conjunction with Gerakan Selamatkan Malaysia (GSM), or Save Malaysia Movement, which sounded like the idea that Kit Siang first broached a year before.

The representatives from the Opposition included Kit Siang,

Teresa Kok and Anthony Loke from the DAP, Azmin Ali, Tian Chua and Rafizi Ramli from PKR, and Mat Sabu and Salahuddin Ayub from Amanah.

From the BN side were Muhyiddin, former MCA president Ling Liong Sik, former deputy minister Wan Abu Bakar Wan Mohamed and Mahathir's son, Mukhriz.

PAS's MP Mahfuz Omar and its elections director, Mustafa Ali, were also present in their individual capacities as concerned citizens because their party had chosen not to show support.

This coming together of BN and Opposition politicians for a common cause was unprecedented. But what was even more amazing was the presence as well of civil society leaders and activists who had been Mahathir's staunchest critics for years.

These critics included former Bersih chairperson Ambiga Sreenevasan, current Bersih chairperson Maria Chin Abdullah, activist Hishamuddin Rais and former law minister Zaid Ibrahim, who was now one of Mahathr's biggest supporters.

Surprised by Ambiga's involvement, I asked her why she got in. She gave the analogy of World War Two in which the Allied forces were even willing to team up with Stalin to fight Hitler. "Now is the time to fight Najib before he finishes the country," she said. "I assure you it was a difficult decision, but we said we would only join if the reform agenda was there."

Mahathir told the media, "As you can all see, this is a very strange group of people. There is only one thing we have in common, we are citizens of this country. We are not here as representatives of any party or NGO. We are here as citizens of Malaysia."

The Declaration set forth four demands. One, remove Najib. Two, remove those who had acted in concert with him and those who "covered up his misdeeds".

The next two called for reform, and were not in Mahathir's original plan. They were inserted at the request of reform-minded civil society leaders almost at the eleventh hour.

They called for the repeal of laws which violated the Federal Constitution, and the restoration of the integrity of institutions that had been undermined under Najib's administration, such as the police, the MACC, Bank Negara and the Public Accounts Committee (PAC).

Ambiga was emphatic about adding the release of Anwar from prison to the list as well, but Mahathir was noncommittal about it. So it was not included.

Beware of Mahathir

The signing of the Declaration was not quite welcomed by Opposition and civil society figures who were wary of Mahathir's involvement.

Lawyer and leader of Anything But Umno (ABU) Haris Ibrahim said he opposed the movement because he felt it carried a "hidden agenda" to save Umno and BN.

"I don't believe in any effort led by Mahathir and I see that it will not achieve the reforms demanded by the people ... Umno and BN must be taken down, not just Najib," he said.

Charles Santiago of the DAP agreed that Najib had to be removed for the good of the country and the people, but he cautioned that Mahathir was "the root cause of the rot" affecting every Malaysian.

"Mahathir introduced money politics in Umno, robbed the judiciary of its independence, clamped down on street protests, used draconian laws to jail dissidents and critics," he said.

PKR's *reformasi* activists, including Badrul Hisham Shaharin, fondly known as Chegubard, rejected Mahathir. Some of them booed the former prime minister when he spoke at an anti-GST rally in April. They shouted "*Undur, Mahathir!*" (Back off, Mahathir!) and called him "*Mahafiraun*" (Great Pharaoh), a derogatory insult levelled at him in the past for his autocratic premiership.

Nonetheless, GSM went ahead with its mission to get the *rakyat* to sign the Declaration. Its goal was to get one million signatures. Then it would hand the Declaration over to the Conference of Rulers.

This actually did not seem like a sound idea. The rulers were constitutional monarchs, they had no power under the Federal Constitution to remove the prime minister. What good would Mahathir's petition do in their hands, even if it carried a million signatures?

"I believe if a million sign it, and it is presented to the rulers, they can see how much the *rakyat* want Najib to be removed and come up with efforts to make that happen," he said.

It sounded like wishful thinking, like his suggestion of moving that no-confidence vote in Parliament solely against Najib. He was grabbing at straws.

In any case, some people were hesitant to sign the Declaration because they found it odd for Mahathir to be in league with Opposition leaders. There were also those, according to him, who were afraid to do so for fear of getting into trouble with the Government. Ironically, that culture of fear was what he had created when he was prime minister.

GSM held its first gathering on March 27 at Shah Alam in Selangor, and invited the public to attend and listen to its cause. After that, it embarked on a nationwide roadshow to garner more support for the Declaration.

In May, Anwar wrote a long letter from prison warning his party colleagues to "set a distance" from the Declaration.

"Essentially, it remains Mahathir's document, defective and incoherent viewed in the context of reform. Its only focus is the removal of Najib as PM due to the 1MDB fiasco. This is obviously a departure from the *raison d'etre* of our struggle: for freedom and justice, rule of law, combating abuse of power and corruption and distributive justice!" he wrote.

He urged his party to steer clear of "the danger of falling into the games of the power elites and their skilful trickery to maintain an outdated system". He named Mahathir and Daim Zainuddin as the architects and aggressive exponents of crony capitalism. He felt it was disturbing that neither man had expressed remorse for what they did or come out to give unequivocal support for systemic reform.

"The Citizens' Declaration group, including Mahathir, can be part of our struggle, but our agenda must be for change, not to advance the Citizens' Declaration," he wrote.

After that, Wan Azizah told Opposition party leaders to be wary of Mahathir's agenda. She said without elaborating, "Be wary, that's all."

In September, Mahathir had an audience with the King to hand over the Citizens' Declaration, bearing 1.4 million signatures. He was accompanied by Khairuddin Abu Hassan, the former Umno man who was arrested and charged for lodging reports about 1MDB outside Malaysia.

Three weeks later, Mahathir announced that he had failed to convince the King about removing Najib. "Unfortunately, we could not get a positive answer," he said.

All that effort had been in vain. But he should have seen that coming from the very start.

BN wins big in Sarawak

Earlier in May 2016, Sarawak held its state elections.

BN won yet again, as expected. But it did better than in the last contest in 2011. It captured 72 of the 82 seats in the state assembly. Its leader, Adenan Satem, was very popular among the people so they gave him a strong mandate.

The Opposition suffered a crushing defeat. It lost in all the *Bumiputera* seats it contested, and the DAP lost five out of the 12 urban seats it had previously held. The party ended up with only seven seats in total, out of the 31 it contested.

PKR managed to defend all three of its seats, but did not manage to win any new ones.

The Opposition was hugely disappointed by the election outcome. It looked like the 1MDB and RM2.6 billion scandal and the imposition of GST had had no effect on the electorate. But perhaps Sarawakians were more swayed by the Adenan Satem factor and the positive measures he was taking to develop the state.

BN wins two by-elections

The next electoral test was in June. Two by-elections came up in Peninsular Malaysia and they were held simultaneously on June 18, one in Sungai Besar in Selangor and the other in Kuala Kangsar in Perak.

BN, which fielded candidates from Umno, won both convincingly. The Opposition vote was split this time because PAS, now out of Pakatan Rakyat, and Amanah, the new member in the reconstituted Pakatan Harapan (PH), threw their hats in the ring to generate three-cornered fights.

Even so, BN's vote scores in both constituencies easily outnumbered the combined totals of PAS and Amanah's, which gave BN a big confidence boost for now and the next general election.

Mahathir's campaigning for the Amanah candidates did not seem to affect the outcome. And the bad news for Amanah was that the party was not getting substantial support among Malay voters. It came out the worst of the three parties in Kuala Kangsar, but did slightly better than PAS in Sungai Besar.

MIC president S. Subramaniam claimed that about 70 to 75% of Indians voted for BN in both seats. He called for the momentum to be maintained till the next general election.

The MCA also claimed that Chinese votes had swung back to BN, increasing from 12% in GE13 to 37% in the by-elections. This posed another worry for PH.

Mahathir had declared during campaigning that the by-elections would be a referendum on Najib, but as it turned out, BN had won well, despite the scandal, GST and other negative issues arising from Najib's administration of the country.

BN was naturally pleased with the results. If the pattern of three-cornered fights among the three parties vying for Malay support was going to carry on to the general election, BN's place in Putrajaya would appear secure.

Mahathir forms new party

A week after the by-elections, Mukhriz and Muhyiddin were sacked from Umno for having appeared on the same stage with Opposition leaders to criticise the party and its leadership.

Mahathir's last link with Umno was gone. If he had harboured any ambition for Mukhriz to become prime minister one day, it would not be realised now with his old party.

So he negotiated with Muhyiddin to set up a new Malay party called Parti Pribumi Bersatu Malaysia (PPBM), or Malaysian United Indigenous Party, of which the younger man would be president and Mukhriz his deputy. Mahathir would be the chairman.

It would be a race-based party strategically targeting Umno's main vote bank, the Malay rural heartland. So its mission was to defend Islam, the special position of the Malays and the *Bumiputera* community.

On September 9, 2016, the RoS offically approved PPBM's application for registration, but it stipulated that the party would not be allowed to be promoted as "Bersatu" because there were other parties using the same word.

With that done, PPBM would need to join up with other Opposition parties to form a strong offensive force against BN at the next general election, due in about one-and-a-half years. The natural choice was of course PH.

To seal that, Mahathir would need to do something that demanded great humility on his part. He needed to meet up with Anwar, the man he had sent to jail nearly 20 years earlier, the man he still ran down from time to time.

As recent as April 2016, he had told *The Australian* that at the age of 74, Anwar was "too old" to be prime minister. He was apparently mistaken because Anwar was only 68.

"When I was in my 70s, I announced I can't be PM at the age of 80 so I indicated that I was going to step down and I did before I was 80," he said.

He also said he sacked Anwar in 1998 because "people complained about his moral behaviour" and for him, that behaviour was "not acceptable" for a person who would lead the country.

That was bad enough. Mahathir rubbed Anwar the wrong way even more when he also told the paper that with regard to GSM and the Citizens' Declaration, "I am not in partnership with him. He agreed to support the removal of Najib. I cannot afford to reject any support so I can't just tell him 'please don't support me because I don't like you'. I can't do that."

Was that the slur that prompted Anwar to write that letter from prison in May urging his party to distance itself from the Declaration? If it was, how would it pan out for Mahathir if he went to see Anwar just a few months after all that and asked him to go into partnership with him to fight Najib at the next general election?

Mahathir was game to try. What other avenue was left open to him, anyway? He chose for the occasion the hearing at the High Court of Anwar's application to stop the implementation of the National Security Council (NSC) Act 2016 on the grounds that it was unconstitutional.

The Act empowered the prime minister to declare an area a security area and deploy security forces there up to six months at a time. This was aimed at strengthening the Government's ability to address threats to the nation's security, including threats of terrorism and extremism.

The Opposition had strongly objected to it because it claimed the Act conferred wide-ranging powers to the prime minister and allowed him to declare a state of emergency without needing to seek the consent of the King. The Opposition feared that Najib might abuse the Act to his advantage if BN were to lose GE14. But its objections proved to be useless when the law was hastily pushed through Parliament and passed in December 2015.

First face-to-face in 18 years

On September 5, 2016, Mahathir walked into the courtroom accompanied by Azmin Ali and Khairuddin Abu Hassan, the man who had lodged reports about 1MDB overseas and who now seemed to accompany Mahathir almost everywhere. Their entrance caught everyone present by surprise.

They proceeded to the front row and waited. At 3.09pm, Anwar came in with a police escort. He shook hands with his supporters and then walked towards Mahathir.

They both smiled warmly and shook hands. Mahathir wished Anwar luck with his case and asked about it. They both talked, as if like old friends.

It was the first time they had met face-to-face in 18 years, since September 3, 1998. Wan Azizah later described it to the media as "a pleasant surprise".

PKR MP N. Surendran, who was acting as Anwar's lawyer on the NSC case and was present in the courtroom, said it was a moving moment. "No one expected in their life to see these two men burying the hatchet and shaking hands," he said.

People around them took the opportunity to take photos of the two men, ignoring the ruling that the taking of photographs was not allowed inside a courtroom. It made a valuable photo op. Newspapers all over the world carried the image of the moment afterwards.

That image brought cheer to Malaysians praying for a game-changer to overturn the Opposition's fortunes and brighten its prospects of forming the next government. While many still doubted Mahathir and distrusted him, they nonetheless saw him as the only person left to revive the Opposition's fading hopes. They rationalised it would be all right to "use" him as a means to their desired end.

Mahathir, however, did not confirm to the media that he was making peace with Anwar. He merely said he came to the High Court because he was interested in the case initiated by Anwar.

"This is about the NSC Act. As you know, I have written about the Act in my blog and he is doing the same thing – trying to stop the Act. So I met him and had a long chat with him about what he's doing," he said.

Asked if he and Anwar were now friends or partners in the Opposition, he replied, "I don't know about friends. I talked to him, that's it. I endorse his actions against the NSC Act."

Anwar told the media outside the courtroom he was touched by Mahathir's visit, "He showed his preparedness to come, and he pledged his support for the court application and wished me success. I presume, therefore, that he supports the reform agenda. Anyone who supports the reform agenda must be given a chance."

Lawyer Eric Paulsen tweeted a photo of the handshake and said, "Now I think I have seen everything."

Netizen Faizal Hamssin tweeted, jokingly, "To those still hung over their exes, look at Anwar and Mahathir, reuniting after 18 years. There's still hope for you all."

Ibrahim Suffian of Merdeka Centre said it was a sign of the compromises Mahathir had been forced to make by working with the Opposition. He had limited options left, this was "the only option" he had now.

As for the Opposition, its fundamental problem was that Mahathir and Anwar could not get along. "Their shaking hands means their interests have converged," said Ibrahim.

He also said the challenge for Mahathir would be whether he could reunite the Opposition forces which had splintered since Anwar's imprisonment. If they could be galvanised, Mahathir, who still commanded substantial support from within Umno, might be able "to shave enough support off Umno to give the Opposition a real chance of taking power".

As time went on, PPBM and PH drew nearer to each other. PH could see that PPBM had the ability to penetrate the rural Malay heartland and appeal to voters there. The problem was PAS. It, too, had a respectable share of the Malay rural market, so if PPBM were to contest against it and BN in three-cornered fights, the outcome could benefit BN. This lesson had already been learnt from the June by-elections.

The only way to avoid that was to draw PAS back to the Pakatan fold. PKR's Azmin set about to try that. So did Muhyiddin of PPBM. But PAS was at the same time being lured by BN. Earlier in May, the Government had prioritised Hadi Awang's private member's bill to amend the Syariah Courts (Criminal Jurisdiction) Act 1965 (also known as RUU 355) over its own bills and allowed it to be tabled in Parliament. This was a signal of some kind of cooperation brewing between PAS and BN.

New kid on the block

Come November, Mahathir decided that PPBM was ready to join PH. He said the only way to win the coming general election was for the Opposition parties to "unite under one coalition, one logo and one common manifesto".

But he was still willing to give PAS time to consider coming on board as well. "If PAS does not join the Opposition, there will be three-cornered fights in at least 40 constituencies," he warned.

Hisomuddin Bakar of the think tank Ilham Centre was, however, confident that the PAS factor could be neutralised. But this could happen only as long as PH and PPBM were unified and committed to presenting a common policy platform to the public.

"In a national election, voters will look at which coalition or force can win and form the Government. Voters will view a third party that can't form the Government as a spoiler – they will be ignored," he reassured.

With or without PAS, PPBM and the three parties in PH decided to seal a deal to take on BN in GE14 anyway. On December 13, 2016, they signed a cooperation agreement based on seven points.

One of them was ensuring straight fights against BN in all the electoral contests. Another was resolving disputes through collective negotiation.

And since Mahathir had been pushing the idea for all four parties to contest as a coalition, like BN, it was agreed that this would be established before GE14. Not only was this strategically sound, it would also facilitate the formation of a new government should PH win.

They also agreed to set up a joint technical committee to discuss seat allocations and a common manifesto. A common logo would also be designed.

The mood was buoyant and hopeful. Asked why PPBM was not yet part of PH, Wan Azizah said, "We are already working together, the coalition is just a formality. ... Today, we have a new kid on the block. We have PPBM," she said.

Three months later, on March 20, 2017, PH officially welcomed PPBM as it fourth component party.

Going by Liew Chin Tong's thesis, this event must surely be an earthquake, not just a tectonic shift or realignment. But whatever anyone might call it, one thing was for certain.

The fight for Putrajaya was definitely on.

BRAVEHEARTS, STOOGES AND A COMEBACK KID

Overnight, Mahathir became the focus of heated debate. He was adulated by those who saw him as the only person who could save Malaysia, and rejected by those who remembered him as the man who damaged the country's institutions and committed other sins during his 22-year reign as prime minister.

Political blogger Din Merican put out this sober reminder, "We Malaysians must be a bunch of sentimental fools and free riders. It speaks volumes of who we are that we have to depend on a 91-year-old politician to bring about change. In the first place, he created this situation by removing all his rivals like Tengku Razaleigh Hamzah, Musa Hitam and Anwar Ibrahim in Umno, and second by dismantling our system of checks and balances to create a powerful Executive Branch."

Din did not think Mahathir would change the Malaysian political landscape: "He is not a Renaissance man. He is an old-school politician through and through."

Journalist P. Gunasegaram was scathing: "If anyone takes the trouble to remember what this man did and stood for, he would be mad to think that Mahathir is the solution – he was, and is, the problem. Without him and his 22 years of misrule, Malaysia would not have descended to what it is today."

He said Mahathir was not accountable to anyone when he was prime minister. He could do almost anything he pleased and get away with it using the controls he had put in place. He made opaque government decisions and marked secret under the law anything that could embarrass his government and expose its corrupt ways.

THE PEOPLE'S VICTORY

"That was the legacy he left behind – and a leader who followed him used it to do nasty things, some worse than those by Mahathir. Now we expect Mahathir – the source of all this – to save us from Najib!"

But these views were countered by those of "sentimental fools" and pragmatists. Many people felt that the only person who could take on Najib now was Mahathir. And if so, why not let him? They did not care about the consequences that could come later. They only thought of kicking Najib out.

Another political blogger, Mariam Mokhtar, quoted a senior civil servant who alleged, "Mahathir was corrupt, but he did it for the nation. On the other hand, Najib's corruption serves only himself."

In other words, it did not matter that corruption in itself is wrong. Mahathir's corruption could be overlooked in light of present circumstances.

Mariam did not condone that; corruption, to her, "is theft, immoral and a sin". But she also acknowledged that "we need all the help we can get to regain our democracy", so if Mahathir "wants to be part of the greater struggle to reclaim our democracy, then use him to the hilt, like he once used us".

That encapsulated the current general feeling about Mahathir. Never mind what he did in the past, what mattered now was his new mission. Never mind if he was tainted, use him, ride on him to achieve the larger cause. No matter what it cost.

Bersih 5 proceeds without Maria

On November 19, 2016, Bersih held its fifth rally to call for Najib's resignation yet again, and a few days before the event, Mahathir appeared in a video wearing a Bersih 5 T-shirt to urge Malaysians to join the rally and show their dissatisfaction with the Government.

He said he would not be able to attend the event itself as he would be speaking at a conference overseas, but in the afternoon of November 19, he made a surprise appearance at the rally after his return from Sudan. Wearing the same T-shirt as in the video, he was accompanied by Mukhriz and Muhyiddin.

Speaking to reporters, he said he was pleased by the huge turnout and accused the Government of being "cowardly" for trying to stop the rally. He stopped short of comparing it to the time when he was prime minister when he would have done the same. He knew how to push the right buttons to get back into the game.

I was at Bersih 5 with tens of thousands of others. I took the LRT to the Bangsar station in the morning. The train was jam-packed with many people wearing Bersih T-shirts or just anything in yellow, the trademark colour of the movement.

When we arrived at Bangsar, the station was overly crowded as this was one of the several meeting points for rally participants before we were to march to Dataran Merdeka, the designated gathering place.

Unfortunately, the march could not be completed because the police blockaded all the routes to Dataran Merdeka. We were stopped along Jalan Bangsar by a phalanx of riot squad police with standby water cannons. Negotiations with the police to let us pass were futile.

Then word came from the rally organisers of a change of plans. The new gathering place would now be the Kuala Lumpur City Centre where the iconic Twin Towers, built during Mahathir's premiership, were located. So we moved there.

I took the LRT to the KLCC station. On arriving there, I saw DAP MP Tony Pua being swarmed by fans clamouring to take photos with him. He willingly obliged. I told him in jest, "You're becoming a rock star." He chuckled and proceeded to pose with his next batch of fans.

The rally proceeded peacefully, with activists and Opposition politicians, Pua included, running down Najib and his government in speech after speech. Mahathir and Muhyiddin also spoke, from the cargo bay of a four-wheel-drive truck. The crowd chanted, "*Tangkap MO1!*" (Arrest MO1!) and "*Tangkap KBAB!*" (Arrest KBAB, referring to IGP Khalid Abu Bakar, suspected to be the snitch who saved Najib from being charged by the attorney-general who was eventually removed).

The rally turned out to be essentially a *ceramah* with an attendance of about 40,000 people. It ended when rain started to fall before 6pm. The participants then sang the national anthem and dispersed.

A notable absentee at the rally was Bersih chairperson Maria Chin Abdullah, who was arrested the night before together with Bersih secretariat member Mandeep Singh.

Also arrested was Jamal Md Yunos, leader of the Red Shirts, a right-wing group said to be secretly endorsed by Najib which was formed in 2015 to counter the yellow shirts of Bersih. After the Bersih 4 rally that year, the Red Shirts held one of their own a month later retaliating against Bersih 4 as well as championing the special position of the Malays and showing support for Najib and his government.

The rally was marked by clashes between the rally participants and the Federal Reserve Unit (FRU) when the latter prevented them from charging into the Petaling Street area where Chinese traders did business. The Red Shirts threw plastic bottles and hurled verbal abuses at the law enforcement unit, calling them "*barua Cina*" (pimps of the Chinese). The FRU unleashed water cannons on them.

It was more of a racial rally than anything else. The Red Shirts carried provocative banners containing racial slurs, the speakers used words like "*Cina babi*" (Chinese pigs, a derogatory term used against the community), and the protestors wanted to force their way into Petaling Street.

And yet Najib sent them his thanks afterwards and congratulated them for having held a peaceful rally.

Jamal led the pack then, and was going to do the same against Bersih 5. He even threatened before the event, "We will not hesitate to do anything to stop the Bersih rally. For me, our struggle will continue even if we are bathed in blood."

The police feared that a clash between the Red Shirts and Bersih rallygoers might end in disaster, so they arrested him and Maria.

However, while Bersih 5 proceeded and drew the numbers, the Red Shirts' supposed counter-rally was a lame affair. Only 250 Red Shirts showed up. The crucial difference between the two groups was that Bersih had a creditable cause and its supporters were committed. The Red Shirts were just *lalang* (weed) without a cause.

Maria held under SOSMA

After the rally, Jamal was released, but Maria was sinisterly held under SOSMA. It came as a shock to Bersih supporters and fair-minded Malaysians. She was wrongly and unjustly being treated like a terrorist. I wrote an article for *Malaysiakini* calling Najib a liar and demanded that Maria be released at once.

The authorities waffled when asked why they used SOSMA on her. Deputy minister Nur Jazlan tried to pin her to threatening parliamentary democracy, but IGP Khalid said she was being held for committing an offence related to national security because of a document the police had found in Bersih's office.

Umno information chief Annuar Musa chipped in by alleging outrageously that she had links with America's Central Intelligence Agency (CIA).

Maria was held in solitary confinement in a windowless cell and made to sleep on a wooden plank without a mattress. The Human Rights Commission of Malaysia (Suhakam) found out about this and released a statement, "She indicated that she would like a mattress at the very least to cushion the discomfort of the wooden bed." She also requested a copy of the Quran and reading materials, as well as access to her children and family.

Recounting her experience to *Free Malaysia Today* in December, Maria said eight different Special Branch officers took turns to interrogate her from 9am to 6pm. She was also not allowed to wear undergarments, "and this made me feel extremely vulnerable especially when all the interrogators were men".

She had no idea where she was, and she was not allowed to use her name. "I was referred to only as 378."

From the line of questioning she was subjected to, it seemed as though the police were trying to form a conspiracy theory about Bersih having received funding of RM3.2 billion from a foundation linked to billionaire George Soros.

"From 2010 to 2011, we did take funding from Soros but we had declared it. In 2012, we filed a suit against *New Straits Times* for falsely reporting that we got US$20 million. The newspaper had to apologise to us. It didn't work then, it wasn't going to work now," she said.

During her detention, candlelight vigils were held nightly at Dataran Merdeka at which the people showed their moral support and called for her release. On some nights, as many as a thousand sympathisers came. Then suddenly, the mayor of Kuala Lumpur closed down the area without giving any reasons.

Bersih announced that the vigils would continue at a location nearby until Maria was released. Mahathir came to one of the vigils with his wife, Siti Hasmah, and told the crowd, "It is torture and against the law to put her in detention. I'm sad that she was put into that cell. So continue with this protest until Maria is released."

Maria's sons were also there. One of them, Aziman Yunus, said, "My mother is a very strong person. If you're trying to break her will, no, you won't."

On November 28, 10 days after Maria's arrest, the police suddenly released her. Former Bersih chairperson Ambiga tweeted: "Our dear friend Maria has been set free! Praise God! She is with me and is well!!!"

That night, supporters assembled at the usual venue for the candlelight vigils to greet Maria. It rained, but they were not deterred. Her arrival was met with loud cheers. She told the crowd, *"Hidup rakyat!* (Long live the people!) I was released because of all of you and your support. Thank you, thank you all. There's more work to be done."

Asked by the media to explain her release, IGP Khalid Abu Bakar said, "No comment." In all likelihood, they had no case against her. They were just out to intimidate, in a new round of scare tactics unleashed against critics of Najib and 1MDB.

Malaysiakini's Steven and Premesh targeted

One of the unfortunate targets was *Malaysiakini* editor-in-chief Steven Gan. Just the day before the Bersih 5 rally, he was called to face four charges under the Communications and Multimedia Act 1998.

Two of them were for airing a video on the *KiniTV* website allegedly containing offensive comments with the intention of annoying another person. The video was of a press conference held by Khairuddin Abu Hassan in which he called for attorney-general Apandi's resignation.

The other two charges were for Gan's being a director of *KiniTV*, which aired the video in Malay and English.

In May 2017, *Malaysiakini* CEO Premesh Chandran was also slapped with the same charges when he took a break from his sabbatical in London to face the court.

If convicted, Gan and Premesh faced a fine up to RM50,000 or one year's jail, or both.

In the video, Khairuddin criticised Apandi's handling of the 1MDB scandal, called him "*haprak*" (worthless) and demanded that he resign. What was the offence in criticising a government officer if he was deemed to have been remiss in carrying out his duties? And why go after the news website when it was just reporting the story?

Gan said it was "a case of harassment", and considered getting Apandi to testify at the trial. "He has to explain why reporting on someone who is describing a public official as worthless is a crime," he said.

"We will try to prove to the court that by covering a press conference, we did not commit any crime and that we were only doing our job as journalists."

On September 20, 2018, Gan and Premesh were to be vindicated when the charges against them were dropped.

Charged for insulting false democrat

Insulting Najib proved to be a chargeable offence in August 2017.

Nor Sabariah Abdul Kadir, a recruiter, got hauled to court for having posted a comment about him on the 'Otai Bersih' Facebook page in February.

Ng Thai Quen, a storekeeper, was charged for posting an edited image of Najib and Rosmah on his Facebook page in 2016.

Roti canai seller Mazlan Yusoff was accused of posting an article titled 'Zimbabwe Today is M'sia Tomorrow' with an edited photo of Najib and China's former leader Mao Zedong in 2016.

They each faced a maximum fine of RM50,000 or one year's imprisonment, or both, upon conviction.

Well, so much for Najib boasting in his blog on September 10 that his government was committed to defending freedom of speech and democracy in Malaysia.

Zunar and laughter as protest

Earlier in 2016, there was more persecution. On November 25, political cartoonist Zunar was attacked by 30 people at his exhibition in Penang. They were led by a Penang Umno youth chief.

They yelled obscenities at Zunar, called him names like "*haram jadah*" (bastard), and demanded that he remove cartoons of Najib that they considered insulting to the prime minister. Before Zunar could finish removing the cartoons, they began kicking down some of his works and threatened to burn his published books.

The next day, ironically enough, Zunar was arrested for sedition. This was the tenth time he had been arrested for sedition. He had already had nine outstanding sedition charges against him for his Twitter posts commenting on the sodomy trial of Anwar Ibrahim. If he were to be found guilty, he stood to face a cumulative 43 years of imprisonment.

As for the people who broke up his exhibition and vandalised his artworks, no action was taken against them. It looked like there were different sets of laws for people from Umno.

Zunar was a fearless critic of Najib and Rosmah. In many of his cartoons, he daringly lampooned them over issues ranging from Rosmah's famous diamond ring, her Birkin bags, her passion for shopping, the murder of

Altantuya Shaariibuu, the Scorpene submarine controversy, 1MDB and the RM2.6 billion and many more.

He even brought out a book solely on Rosmah called *ROS in Kangkung Land*, which he said in jest was "specially dedicated to her". He also said he would present her with an autographed copy "to show my gratitude". I wonder what Rosmah did with it.

"I cannot survive as a cartoonist if I depend on her husband alone," he further joked. But, seriously, "it is an open secret that she is more dominant and more powerful than the prime minister himself," he said. She is also "very cartoon-able".

But, again seriously, "What is more important is the subject matter of my work, which is the corruption plaguing the nation," he said.

After the book on Rosmah, he came up with one on Najib entitled *Sapuman – Man of Steal*. The title is self-explanatory.

Zunar was harassed countless times, banned from travelling overseas, but he never gave up. "Stop the import of ink into the country if you want me to stop drawing," he once said, cheekily.

He encouraged his readers to laugh because "laughter is a form of protest". He followed that up with, "These leaders, they cannot handle laughter. Perhaps, they might pass an anti-laughing law one day where people have to get a permit to laugh."

On his sedition charges, he said, "I am going to face the nine charges head-on. It's good for the authorities if I run away, but I will be staying put here. I will face the consequences. Someone has to cross the line of fear for you will not know what is beyond until you cross the line. But when you find out what it is, you will overcome the fear."

In July 2018, Zunar was justly vindicated. The court acquitted and discharged him of all the nine sedition charges. It was a joyous day for freedom of expression.

British political cartoonist Martin Rowson said of Zunar in 2015, "He's the bravest man I've ever met. As a cartoonist, he enables people to carry out this essential act of defiance to tyranny: laughing."

Fahmi makes Najib a clown

Another braveheart, Fahmi Reza, distinguished himself as a portrayer of Najib as a clown.

On January 30, 2016, the day Apandi cleared Najib of wrongdoing over the RM2.6 billion allegation, Fahmi released his first Najib clown sketch as a Twitter post, along with the caption: "In 2015, the Sedition Act was used 91 times. *Tapi dalam negara yang penuh dengan korupsi, kita semua penghasut* (But in a country full of corruption, we are all instigators)."

The Police Cyber Investigation Response Centre saw it and told Fahmi to use Twitter "responsibly and in accordance with the law". It, however, failed to intimidate Fahmi. He instead responded with a Facebook post saying, "In a country that uses the law to protect the corrupt and oppress those brave enough to speak out against it, the time has come for us to stop being polite and courteous when fighting against the Government's corruption."

This prompted fellow graphic artists to create their own versions of a clown-faced Najib, in solidarity with Fahmi. He was surprised by the outpouring of support from the graphic art community. It proved there were "others who share my outrage".

The satirical caricature went viral and spurred a protest movement online, with people using the hashtag #KitaSemuaPenghasut.

In March, Najib's clown face went outside cyberspace on to street signs, alley walls, even signboards on the expressway. Fahmi was literally making a clown of the prime minister!

T-shirts were printed, and they were snapped up. In June, while Fahmi was selling the T-shirts at the KL Alternative Bookfest, he got arrested. Event organiser Pang Khee Teik, community activist Lew Pik-Svonn and comic artist Arif Rafhan Othman were also arrested.

All four were released the next day, and Fahmi, instead of being cowed by the arrest, wrote on Facebook immediately, "If you think your actions will scare me and break my determination to fight corruption by authorities using art as a weapon, then you are wrong."

On June 6, he was charged under the Communications and Multimedia Act 1988 for posting Najib's clown face on his Instagram account "with the intention to hurt other people's feelings".

Out on bail, Fahmi read to the media a statement he had written: "In a country where a graphic designer can be censored, investigated, and prosecuted for his art, it is important that ... using parody and satire as a form of political protest continues to be practised and defended at all costs. As a design activist, I will continue to use my graphics as a tool to raise awareness, to wake people up, as a medium of protest, and as a tool to push for change in Malaysia."

He was, however, to be acquitted and discharged in October 2018 after the Attorney-General's Chambers agreed to withdraw the charge.

Fahmi faced another charge on June 10, 2016, at the Ipoh Sessions Court of posting on Facebook a poster depicting Najib in clown face accompanied by the Malaysian Communications and Multimedia Commission (MCMC) logo.

In February 2018, he was found guilty of this second charge and sentenced by the Sessions Court to a month's jail and fined RM30,000. The court allowed a stay of the sentence pending an appeal to the High Court, and Fahmi was allowed bail of RM10,000 with one surety.

Nonetheless, Fahmi turned to crowdfunding to raise the RM30,000. Within three days, to his surprise, he had collected the money he needed. "I'm speechless, I don't know what to say except *terima kasih* (thank you)," he wrote on Facebook.

He promised that if he was eventually acquitted, the money would be used to support other persons charged under the same law for political satire or dissent who did not have the means to pay for their bail or fine.

Of his experience of persecution, he wrote, "This guilty verdict is an affront to all artists and persons exercising our democratic rights and freedom of expression enshrined under Article 10 of our Federal Constitution. People holding positions of power in this country should be ready to accept criticisms, no matter how unpopular or dissenting. If they cannot respect these democratic values, then it is our duty to continuously remind them we will not be cowed by such authoritarian tactics. The only lesson I have learnt is the power of protest art in mobilising resistance against corruption and repression."

Oh, why did Fahmi make a clown of Najib? His answer: "The whole country has become the butt of a joke."

It had. Thanks to the clown and his stooges for violating the law and imposing it in laughable ways.

GAME FOR POWER

The recharged Opposition got down to serious business.

Mahathir officially launched his party, PPBM, on January 14, 2017, at a stadium in Shah Alam, Selangor, packed with 10,000 people.

He promised to abolish GST if the Opposition were to win GE14, and replace it with a sales tax. The crowd greeted that with thunderous applause and hoots of delight. This was, however, not the first time he had mentioned abolishing GST. As far as back as April 2015, he had advocated it at a forum in Kuala Lumpur, a few days before the May Day Anti-GST Rally.

In March 2017, Mahathir announced that PPBM would be officially joining PH. The coalition would need to ensure straight fights with BN, and come up with a common manifesto, a new logo and perhaps even a new name.

For the new name, Mukhriz had earlier proposed 'Barisan Rakyat'. He said it was originally suggested by netizens. Now Muhyiddin was suggesting the same. "Maybe we can name the new coalition Barisan Rakyat – Barisan Rakyat to fight against Barisan Nasional," he said.

That did not sound very smart. 'Barisan' in the name would just remind voters of the hated coalition that had ruled for six decades and given them enough bad memories they would rather forget. What was wrong with Pakatan Harapan, anyway?

The next day, Mahathir appeared to have changed his mind about coming up with a new name. "People are familiar with Pakatan Harapan, and that must be taken into consideration when deciding what we should call ourselves," he said. "We will wait for the decision by the technical committee which will be studying the proposal."

Good sense prevailed in the end and the name Pakatan Harapan was retained. The next thing to do was to get the new coalition registered with the RoS.

Previous attempts to register Pakatan Rakyat, the predecessor to PH, had not been approved by the RoS. Would this new one get lucky?

Royal pardon for Anwar?

In April, the issue of Anwar came up before Mahathir. Political scientist Wong Chin Huat pointedly asked him at a forum what he felt about PH seeking a royal pardon for Anwar in the event it formed the next government.

He had been noncommittal when activist Ambiga Sreenevasan advocated adding Anwar's release as one of the demands of the Citizen's Declaration the year before. This time, he said, "If the people want Anwar, who am I to reject their wishes?" He also said he held no grudges.

On May 4, PH announced its leadership line-up, drawn up to fulfil the requirements of the RoS for the registration application. Wan Azizah would chair the Presidential Council with three vice-chairmen, namely, Muhyiddin, Mat Sabu and Lim Guan Eng.

Mahathir was named adviser. He would have no executive powers. Which was surprising.

Each component party would have three representatives in the council. Mukhriz was one of the three from PPBM.

According to PPBM strategist Rais Hussin, the list was not final, and that "three or four people", probably meaning the chairman and vice-chairmen, were too many to determine the direction of the coalition. There should ideally be two, hinting that one of the two could be Mahathir. He said the final list was expected to be out in two weeks.

But after two weeks, there was still no final list.

On May 13, Mahathir was again confronted with a question on Anwar when he was interviewed by the Australian broadcast agency SBS. He was asked if he had apologised to his former deputy for sending him to jail 18 years earlier.

"No, no, no. I didn't apologise for anything," he said. "That was something in the past. We can't be apologising for what happens in the past. We have all said nasty things about each other. I don't ask people to apologise for calling me all kinds of names and accusing me of all kinds of wrongdoing."

'The placard stunt'

Then the PKR general assembly came around. And the party demonstrated whom they wanted to take over as prime minister if BN were to lose in GE14. After Wan Azizah delivered her policy speech, party leaders and 1,000-odd delegates held up placards declaring 'Anwar for 7th Prime Minister'.

Mahathir was on stage between Kit Siang and Azmin when the placards went up. He did not hold one up. Kit Siang did. Mat Sabu did.

Muhyiddin, who was also present, did not hold it up either.

However, Mahathir did sign the Free Anwar Campaign, relaunched at the general assembly. But when he was asked by the media afterwards whether he would support Anwar as the next prime minister, he typically gave an oblique reply: "That's up to anyone." It gelled with his not holding up the placard.

His party's youth chief, Syed Saddiq Syed Abdul Rahman, took umbrage against what he called "the placard stunt" and questioned the motive behind it.

He felt that Mahathir and Muhyiddin were "humiliated" by it because prior to the event, there had been no discussion on who would be the next prime minister. By holding up the placard, was PKR trying to "trap" the PPBM leaders into endorsing Anwar for that position?

"Do they think the people's support, especially from the Malays, will be with them with this kind of attitude which could damage the strength of PH? Do they not want to work with PPBM anymore? How sincere are they in accepting PPBM?" a rather irate Syed Saddiq asked.

If asked, would Mahathir be PM?

Things were not looking good. They got worse when the issue of the next prime minister came up again on June 1, this time in a live question-and-answer session hosted on Mahathir's official Facebook page.

One of the questions was: If the *rakyat* were to ask Mahathir to take on the role of prime minister, would he accept it?

The master politician gave a startling answer: "I cannot ignore my friends in Pakatan Harapan. If they have such a suggestion and it is agreed upon, then I might be forced to consider. At this time, I don't agree to be prime minister … at this time."

Reacting to it, Anwar said it was not for Mahathir to decide who would be prime minister, that there must be consensus among PH members in naming the candidate.

"People don't volunteer to be prime minister, there has to be a consensus," he stressed.

Two days later, Mahathir said it again, in an interview with *Nikkei Asian Review*, but this time he appeared to have taken note of what Anwar had said, "If there is no candidate … I might try, only on condition that everybody agrees."

And as if to justify his eligibility for the premiership, he also said he had "a lot of experience in winning elections". Which was true, as he had led BN to five electoral victories before, but his statement about trying for the position certainly underscored his interest in becoming PM 2.0.

No consensus on who will be chairman

On May 31 and June 9, PH leaders met to discuss the final Presidential Council line-up, but both times they could not come to a consensus.

There was disagreement over Wan Azizah being given the chairmanship because earlier, on May 12, she had told *Al-Jazeera* she did not mind being a "seat warmer" for Anwar until he was released from jail because "he is a better leader". That could negatively affect public perception of PH.

Muhyiddin proposed that Mahathir be the chairman instead while Wan

Azizah take the president's post. But at the June 9 meeting, discussions came to a halt after three hours when a letter came from Anwar saying he wanted the original line-up agreed to on May 4 to remain.

On June 13, however, after Mat Sabu and Amanah vice-president Husam Musa met with Anwar, the latter agreed to leave the final decision to his party.

Four days later, Anwar did even better. He made a statement from prison saying, "In order to call for a focus on the general election, I am choosing not to offer myself as the candidate for prime minister."

He also said, "In hopes of amassing all strengths in a team to go against Umno-BN, it is fair to ensure the participation of all leaders effectively. This includes benefitting from the position and role of Mahathir."

PKR faction says no to Mahathir as PM

This gracious concession from Anwar should have removed any obstacles to Mahathir being made chairman and resolved the crisis. Besides, Mahathir had the support of the DAP, Amanah and PPBM. But a faction within PKR objected. They did not trust Mahathir. They feared he might not relinquish his power after becoming prime minister. They also feared he might usurp Anwar's legacy.

On June 20, Mahathir told Channel NewsAsia that the formal registration of the coalition was being held up because party leaders could not decide on who would head it.

"Unfortunately in the informal meetings … the question of calling the head person 'chairman' or some other name cropped up. Some people are against the word 'chairman' being given if I hold that position. If somebody else holds it, it's all right, but not me," he said.

"There was some ridiculous suggestion it should be called executive adviser. It is a contradiction in terms. You can't be an executive and an adviser. I think some of them worry, they distrust. They feel I'm stealing the show, hijacking the party. I offered to back down. I said I will have no role at all except when you ask me to give talks."

Mahathir also touched on the subject of becoming prime minister. He said he personally did not want the position, but if "in the end, nobody comes forward, nobody agrees to any candidate and they point to me, it'll be churlish of me, just because I want to retire and rest and all that, not to respond to them".

He said, rather assuredly, "If there are no more candidates and if all the parties in the coalition agree I should be a part-time, interim prime minister, I'll come back."

He was, however, careful to add, "We'll sit down and find out who is most eligible. It is not for me to dictate."

Mahathir asks to pull PPBM out

And yet for all that, he must have been peeved by the resistance to his becoming PH's chairman. Or maybe he felt he had to pull a stunt to jolt the other leaders in the coalition. Because in late June, as he was about to leave for London for the Hari Raya holidays, he did something drastic. He wrote a letter to Muhyiddin asking him to pull PPBM out of the coalition.

That rattled the coalition leaders. If PPBM pulled out, the Opposition might as well forget about getting near Putrajaya. They would not capture enough Malay-majority seats. They had come this far, it would be a shame to lose the best opportunity they had ever had of winning. So Nurul Izzah was sent to London to meet with Mahathir.

She was to recall to *Malay Mail* in 2018, "I think my mission at the time, my purpose was to ensure the coalition remained intact, and to do so we needed to ensure there were compromises, and several degrees of engagement."

When she met him, she reminded Mahathir that "Malaysians were looking to us to unseat the BN government", and assured him that "we could work together on a possible agreement".

"I told him I felt that a Mahathir outside the coalition just wouldn't work," she said, "and the rest, as they say, is history."

Leadership line-up decided

She saved the day. And on July 14, 2017, Mahathir himself announced the new leadership line-up, after a four-hour meeting, at a press conference held past midnight.

He was now the chairman. Anwar was named *de facto* leader. Wan Azizah became president. Her deputies were Muhyiddin, Mat Sabu and Guan Eng.

Mukhriz was moved up to vice-president, among three others.

So, did Mahathir threaten to pull out because he desired to be chairman and potential prime minister? What about his son? Did Mahathir negotiate for him to be vice-president, having a higher status than before? Was there truth, after all, in the talk that had been going around for years that he had aspirations for Mukhriz to be prime minister one day?

Well, Mahathir was famous for having things his way. It looked this was another instance of that.

Some tough compromises were made, all right. The DAP, despite being one of the two senior partners in the coalition, was not represented among the top three, whereas the other senior partner managed to get a *de facto* leader and a president. And the PKR faction that distrusted Mahathir had to accept his becoming the head honcho.

That night, Mahathir also announced PH's commitment to apply for Anwar to be pardoned and released, a process that would be initiated within a week after the coalition formed the Government.

He declared that within the first 100 days of forming the government, PH would abolish GST, stabilise the price of petrol, focus on efforts to ease the people's burden, start a comprehensive process of institutional reform, fight corruption, form a Royal Commission of Inquiry into the 1MDB scandal, and restore Felda, the Federal Land Development Authority that was currently embroiled in a scandal involving dubious sales of its land and other shady business dealings.

The turning point

DAP strategist Liew Chin Tong wrote of that night with jubilation: "When the dust settles after the next general election, especially if a Pakatan Harapan government is installed, history is likely to mark July 14, 2017, as the turning point that made the difference. ... There is a sudden surge of hope that Prime Minister Najib Razak, Umno and Barisan Nasional can now be defeated. And visibly, the Najib government did panic. Ministers were still sticking to the old script that the DAP calls the shots in PH in order to put fear into Malay voters ... Such claims won't stick now that it is the joint Mahathir-Anwar leadership team that they are facing."

Yes, it was Mahathir and Anwar together again. After all these years. And Anwar, as Mahathir made it a point to highlight, would be the eighth prime minister, not the seventh, because he needed to be released from jail first. "Well, there has to be an interim prime minister. There is no way he can become PM from jail because he cannot compete in elections," he rightly explained.

But who would be the seventh prime minister? "We did not discuss who will be interim PM," Mahathir said. That would foreseeably be another drama for another day.

For now, Mahathir had outwardly accepted the idea of Anwar becoming prime minister. When he was asked if he had any regrets about his treatment of Anwar in 1998, he said he was merely "responding to the situation at hand" then.

"But now, it is different," he attested. "If we keep on raking up the past, you can never work with anybody. You will always be fighting against your enemies, and that is bad. I'm not angry over the past, he is not angry over the past also."

He even told the U.K. newspaper *The Guardian* that Anwar should be released from jail if he was a victim of a political vendetta.

"We can make a case that he was unfairly treated. The decision of the court was obviously influenced by the Government and I think the incoming government would be able to persuade the King to give a full pardon for Anwar," he said. "In which case, he would be able to participate in politics and become PM. I can have no objection to that."

That sounded more magnanimous about his old nemesis than he had ever been before.

Old foes now friends

He had favourable things to say about Kit Siang as well, remarking that the DAP adviser was "not as bad" as he had made him out to be in the past. He admitted it was all part of a strategy to portray political enemies in a negative light.

A year before, Kit Siang had said he "never hated Mahathir, never hated anyone" because "in politics, you cannot be personal".

Old foes were now friends. They seemed to have been united by the axiom "the enemy of my enemy is my friend". PH was now on track to face the elections. The question on everyone's mind was when it would be called. Would Najib be as indecisive as he was before he called GE13?

For GE14, Chin Tong opined, "Had Najib called for snap elections in the second half of 2016, or even early 2017, the chances of a handsome victory for BN would have been high."

That was when the Opposition was in tatters. But now the scenario had changed, the Opposition was united.

Najib would have to think of new ways to stop it in its tracks. Even if it involved playing dirty.

NOUVEAU NONAGENARIAN

As Najib waited for some shaman or guru or numerologist or whatever to inspire him with the perfect date for GE14, PH started getting ready regardless.

In August 2017, the coalition had given up talking to PAS and decided that there would be no cooperation between both sides. So now it was going ahead to make preparations in order to be ready for the elections should it be called anytime.

The two crucial tasks they had to accomplish were the allocation of parliamentary seats in Peninsular Malaysia among the component parties, and the nomination of the coalition's candidate for prime minister.

On the first two days of December 2017, PH held a retreat in Putrajaya attended by virtually all the parties' bigwigs to discuss the pressing matters.

Out of it came the decision to nominate Mahathir as prime minister candidate and Wan Azizah as his deputy. It was supported by top leaders Guan Eng, Mat Sabu and Muhyiddin.

But, as before, a faction within PKR did not agree with the decision. PKR vice-president Tian Chua refused to accept it as being final. This would lead to a meeting of the party's political bureau to deal with it on December 19.

On December 14, Mat Sabu openly declared his support for Mahathir in an interview with *The Malaysian Insight*.

"I see that the support of Malays in rural areas is higher for Mahathir than for Anwar. Like from Langkawi and Felda schemes. I believe this is an added value to Mahathir leading PH," he said. "If PH has decided, there should be no problem for Mahathir to be the prime minister candidate."

On December 28, Nurul Izzah said the matter was still being discussed and that priority was being given more to the finalisation of seats, which was almost completed.

Three conditions for Mahathir

That day, PKR set three conditions for the acceptance of Mahathir as interim prime minister.

One, Anwar be immediately released from jail and installed as the prime minister within a year of the Opposition coming into power. Two, PKR be allotted the most number of parliamentary seats to contest in GE14. Three, Mahathir to agree to reform the country's institutions.

It seemed that PKR wanted the most number of seats because it was afraid that Umno leaders would cross over in droves to join PPBM after GE14 and make it the strongest party in PH. This was a genuine fear because for all Mahathir's protestations of not going back to Umno, he still had strong ties with its party leaders some of whom were old friends, so the reverse flow could happen. In a big way, too.

On December 29, Anwar weighed in and asked for further discussions within the party and also with community organisations in order to come up with a decision that would reflect what the *rakyat* wanted.

Muhyiddin, however, said PH must name the candidate ahead of the elections. "Everywhere I have gone and through the feedback from the ground, we know voters want to know what they are getting into … what's important is what the people want," he said.

He stressed that the announcement should not be delayed.

On January 4, 2018, another Presidential Council meeting was held to finally decide the matter. But a letter came from Anwar asking PH to continue its tradition of consulting civil society groups and activists to get their feedback on the candidate. This caused another delay.

The media was then told that the final decision would be announced on January 7 at PH's annual convention.

On January 6, PKR Wanita chief Zuraida Kamaruddin told reporters that Mahathir should not be prime minister again as he would be better off as a senior minister because of his "track record as a statesman".

She proposed that Azmin be prime minister instead with Mukhriz as his deputy, because their selection would be in keeping with the trend of younger leaders becoming heads of government in other countries.

Who will be PM-designate?

The next day was the day of the convention. It was filled with anxiety and apprehension. Who would be the person to lead the country if PH won GE14? Would it be a nonagenarian who had come in from the cold just a little over a year ago, who had said in March 2017 that he would not be contesting in GE14 and then changed his mind in October?

It would, and Wan Azizah would be his deputy.

When the announcement was made, the crowd at the convention roared with approval and chanted, "*Hidup Tun! Hidup Tun!*" Mahathir stood up, turned and bowed. His wife, Siti Hasmah, burst into tears. She later said it was a sad moment for her.

Nurul Izzah read out a speech written by her father saying, "In the spirit of cooperation and working together, we accept the decisions of the leadership."

In a blog post written a few days later, Mahathir revealed that PKR agreed to his nomination only at the eleventh hour. But he also wrote, "I believe the agreement was due to Anwar being able to overcome his feelings and putting the country's importance first."

He did not say it but there was also an agreement that the leaders of all the component parties had to sign, stating that Mahathir must give up the premiership to Anwar once the latter was released from prison and given a royal pardon. This was in deference to a demand made by PKR.

'Malay tsunami'

At the convention, the finalised seat distribution was also announced.

This greatly impressed political observers because the Opposition had never looked so organised before. Its ability to agree on seat distribution this early, even before the elections had been called, also reflected a united front.

PPBM would contest in the most number of seats with 52, followed by PKR with 51, the DAP 35 and Amanah 27.

PKR did not get what it asked for, after all, but although PPBM had the lion's share of seats, most of them were in areas where Malays made up over 60% of the voters. These were the seats PH greatly needed to wrest from Umno.

The plan seemed to accord with what Liew Chin Tong had been urging. That for PH to "win resoundingly, with a very convincing margin", in order to ensure a stable government with more than 130 seats in the 222-seat Parliament, the coalition could not depend on just the kind of support it had been getting the past two general elections.

It still needed the very strong support it had been getting from non-Malays, but it also needed a substantial increase in Malay support.

Better still, it needed a groundswell of Malay support, especially from power bases that traditionally voted for Umno or PAS.

A "Malay tsunami".

Liew first coined the term "Malay tsunami" in 2015 when he analysed that the Opposition was capable of winning GE14 if it could defeat Umno in about 35 to 40 marginal seats which were "mostly semi-urban mixed-race seats in the West Coast of the peninsula". Seats that PAS minus its progressive faction would find very hard to win.

He advocated building trust and solidarity especially among Malay youths in the semi-urban areas, and finding ways to help them overcome their economic difficulties.

They were the hardest-hit economically because they had to compete with the myriad foreign workers that were being brought into the country. They earned wages that were not sufficient to cope with the rising cost of living and GST. While they suffered, Umno cronies were the ones who benefitted.

Chin Tong argued that if the Opposition could convince the people that it was Umno's cronyism that deprived Malay youths of decent jobs and adequate pay, not the Chinese, the DAP or any other bogeyman, it might generate "an anti-establishment wave or even a tsunami that will sweep Umno away for good".

Now in 2018, on top of the economic hardship, there was the 1MDB scandal. And the Felda scandal. These had caused a further loss of faith in the Umno leadership under Najib. A credible alternative to Umno was needed. PPBM could be the answer. With ex-Umno leaders Mahathir and Muhyiddin leading it, Malay voters would be more willing to put their faith in the party because both men could be depended upon to look after Malay interests and assuage their fear of change.

Besides, Mahathir was a leader still revered by the Malay masses. He could attract huge crowds at PH gatherings in semi-urban and rural areas.

So, it looked like a "Malay tsunami" could be waiting to happen.

But more importantly, according to Chin Tong, PH needed to articulate "a new vision" that built trust among supporters, across ethnic groups, and with Sabah and Sarawak, "so that eventually a Malay tsunami meets with a general Malaysian tsunami".

'A pipe dream'

BN, as expected, poured scorn on Chin Tong's prediction.

MCA publicity spokesman Ti Lian Ker called it a "pipe dream" and a "myth" because when PAS left Pakatan Rakyat, it took away 25% of Malay support which, he said, Amanah could be hard put to regain.

He also said PH miscalculated in backing Mahathir, and that PPBM was not gaining enough ground.

Najib said that from the results of recent by-elections that would have served as an assessment of Malay sentiment on the ground, "I don't see a Malay tsunami".

Khairy Jamaluddin said in-depth studies done by Umno and BN had found that the majority of Malay voters were still with the party and coalition. The "Malay tsunami" idea was just propaganda drummed up by the Opposition. In reality, it did not exist

Meanwhile, Mahathir's confirmation as PH's prime minister-designate sparked off another round of heated debate among Malaysians.

Political analyst Jeniri Amir said PH would be perceived negatively by the people. "Can't they propose more dynamic leaders or are they so desperate that they feel that he is the only viable candidate?" he asked, and predicted a GE14 victory for BN but with a reduced majority.

However, political scientist Wong Chin Huat demurred. "Ultimately, as in many party states, it will take someone from Umno to defeat Umno," he said. And Mahathir provided the continuity in change that could make it easier for hardcore Umno and BN supporters to accept.

Fellow political scientist James Chin said almost the same thing in another way, "Naming Dr Mahathir is a smart move as they are telling the Umno Malay voters, if you vote PH, you get the original Umno, not Najib's Umno."

The Mahathir dilemma

Ubah supporters, however, felt torn. Social media featured posts by many casting aspersions at Mahathir and expressing uncertainty over how they would now vote.

Lawyer Art Harun, who was also a blogger with a big online following, addressed their dilemma and suggested a rational approach to it.

He said when Mahathir was prime minister in the past, he possessed "unbridled power". But this time round, he would "not have a compliant Cabinet, MPs and minions like before". He would be surrounded by people who would have been voted in "based on their promises to make Malaysia a better place".

He would have "to live with Muhyiddin Yassin, Tony Pua, Lim Kit Siang, Khalid Samad, Azmin Ali, Rafizi Ramli and a slew of strong-headed bedfellows who are not about to be yes-men like those who existed when he was the PM before".

Art said if PH were to win, it would mean "the people have KICKED ASS!" And Mahathir would know that "if the people have kicked ass once, there is nothing stopping the people from kicking ass again, including his ass".

"So, think about it," he urged those who did not want BN to continue to rule. "You want to continue to wallow in self pity … or do you want to take a calculated risk and make an unemotional and rational choice?"

A 92-year-old for PM? Seriously?

What about Umno? How did it react?

With sarcasm and derision.

Minister Nazri Aziz described the decision as "a joke" and said it was ridiculous, stupid and regressive.

"In Zimbabwe, they kicked out their 93-year-old president (Robert Mugabe). But an advanced country like Malaysia is fielding a 92-year-old man to be the next prime minister," he said.

Deputy Prime Minister Zahid sneered, "This recycling of past mistakes is very much awaited by Malaysians. There is no other leader more qualified than Mahathir to bring about damage and ruin to the country."

Minister Rahman Dahlan said it was "laughable" for PH to appoint someone they once called the most corrupt man in Malaysia as the next prime minister and expect him to implement reforms. He called it "a tragedy to their own cause".

"Anyway I thank PH for making it even easier for BN to win the upcoming general election," he said.

BN could win two-thirds

Speaking of that, on the same day as PH's announcement, Merdeka Centre released its findings of a survey it had conducted in December 2017 on the possible outcome of GE14.

It revealed that BN would win the elections. But more than that, a combination of three-cornered fights and redelineation, which was currently in progress, could even enable it to regain a two-thirds majority in Parliament.

This was a shocker for many people, especially the bit about the two-thirds.

The survey also observed that the Opposition's prospects ranged "from slim to zero" as only 21% of its respondents said they were "happy" with PH. Furthermore, PAS leaders appeared keen to prevent a PH victory. Its refusal to work with PH would effectively split the Malay vote for the Opposition and that would benefit Umno.

As for Najib's integrity and the 1MDB scandal, they emerged as the respondents' least concerns, at 3% and 2%, respectively.

Could all the findings be true? But then they came from Merdeka Centre. Surely, they must be reliable?

Merdeka Centre's Ibrahim Suffian had this to say, "While the survey currently indicates the situation as being uphill for Pakatan, we still have perhaps two to three months to the elections, which is at least half a lifetime in politics."

Was he hinting that there was still hope?

Why long wait for registration?

Anyway, preparations for the elections continued for PH. Its next important concern was getting the coalition registered by the RoS.

Submission for this had been made in June 2017 but seven months later, the coalition had still not been registered. PH had written letters of enquiry to the RoS but the registrar had not replied.

Mahathir was upset. "Not approving our application or approving it late will only weaken us, and benefit BN and Umno. There are elements of *mala fide*, ill intentions in RoS' move to not reply us over our registration application," he wrote in his blog.

During two meetings between the RoS and PH, the reasons for the delay were made clear. The RoS clarified that the registration was being held back because it had issues with the DAP and PPBM that had not yet been resolved.

The RoS did not recognise the DAP's central executive committee (CEC) elections held about four years ago. And, based on more than 400 complaints received by the RoS from members, PPBM had not held its annual general meeting in accordance with the party's constitution. The RoS threatened to deregister the party.

Following up on this, the DAP set about to appease the RoS. It held fresh elections for its CEC. By February, the RoS was satisfied by it and declared the party's issue resolved. It, however, could not do the same for the PPBM issue, so PH's registration remained unapproved.

Anxious that the elections might be called soon, PH leaders filed a civil suit on February 22 to seek a response from the RoS to the coalition's registration application.

The next day, PPBM also filed a suit against the RoS. It sought a declaration on the status of the party's registration.

At the same time, a group of PPBM members staged a demonstration in Putrajaya to press the RoS to investigate the 400-over complaints it had submitted. Among them was a former PPBM vice-president.

Suspecting sabotage from within the party and realising that PH would have to resort to a new plan quickly if the coalition did not get registered on time, Mahathir announced on February 27 that all the four component parties would now stand in the elections using a common logo chosen from one of theirs.

He had stressed the importance of a common identity from long before and was hoping it would be the PH one, but since it was not yet registered, a logo from one of the parties would have to stand for all. As to which party's logo it would be, that had not yet been decided.

RoS partial to Umno

On March 1, Muhyiddin noticed a transgression committed by Umno that the RoS had chosen to overlook.

Umno was supposed to hold its party elections on October 19, 2016, but it sought to postpone it. The RoS gave its approval. The elections would then have to be completed by April 19, 2018, as the maximum period of postponement allowed by the party's own constitution was 18 months.

However, when the date drew near, Umno applied for a further extension of a year to 2019. This already contravened its party constitution, yet even so, the RoS approved it

Muhyiddin therefore pointed out that instead of granting that extension, the RoS should instead have deregistered Umno if the party did not hold its elections by April 19, 2018.

He accused the RoS of practising double standards for going easy on Umno while applying intense pressure on PPBM.

"The RoS should treat everybody equally. This issue is not about political parties but about the party constitution and being fair," he said.

He also asked, since Umno had gone against its own constitution, "What is the status of Umno's president, his deputy and the Supreme Council members? Do they still hold the positions?"

Responding to this, 16 disgruntled Umno members from several states filed an application in the Kuala Lumpur High Court on April 20 to challenge the party's legal status. They sought a court order to nullify the decision by the RoS to grant the party a further extension to postpone its elections.

A week later, the High Court threw out the case.

Back to the case concerning PPBM, the RoS decided to get tough with the party on March 9. RoS director-general Surayati Ibrahim gave it an ultimatum to submit the minutes of its AGM and those of meetings of its divisions and branches, as well as its financial statement, by March 29. Or face dissolution.

PPBM crippled

The party failed to meet the deadline. So on April 5, the RoS lived up to its threat. It temporarily deregistered PPBM.

RoS Director-General Surayati Ibrahim said the temporary deregistration would take effect for 30 days during which PPBM would not be allowed to conduct any activities or use its logo and name.

PPBM was crippled. It would not be able to campaign using its name and logo or solicit funds. It was effectively written out of contention.

Minister Nazri Aziz was asked if the temporary deregistration would benefit BN. He arrogantly replied, "No, not at all, no. How do you feel about mosquito bites? I think you just scratch it off. You will scratch it and still enjoy it."

He said, "Suspended or not, or whether or not it's good for us, I think voters have decided and they know whom to vote for."

Mahathir called the RoS order an act of "tyranny". He said, "There is no fair election. There is no rule of law. And Najib is cheating to win the elections by terrorising his opponents. Whatever happens to us, we are going to contest ... no way are they going to stop us from contesting."

He called on the people to vote for the Opposition. "We are in a critical time now, facing a situation which we have not experienced before," he said.

That would have struck a chord with many people, including fence-sitters, who felt incensed by the unfair action that Surayati had taken. It looked like what was intended to be a move to favour BN had turned out to be a mistake. BN tried to cut out the competition but ended up cutting itself.

Game-changing move

Then on April 6, Mahathir announced at a press conference, "It is my pleasure to announce to all of you, and all of Malaysia, and the whole world that we will be contesting under one symbol, the PKR symbol."

This was a brilliant move, but it understandably caused much unease among the leaders and grassroots of a long-established party like the DAP, which had been contesting under its own iconic rocket symbol since the 1969 general election.

Founding member and former chairman Chen Man Hin was not happy with taking on another party's symbol because he felt the DAP's older supporters might be confused. Kit Siang was also upset. So were other leaders.

But in the end, they had to make a "painful and heart-wrenching" decision to go along with the plan. They realised it was more important to make the required sacrifice in order to project coalition unity and "save Malaysia from the fate of a failed, rogue and kleptocratic state".

However, in Sabah and Sarawak, the DAP and Amanah would continue to use their own logos because the PH Presidential Council agreed that as there were so many parties there, it would be confusing to adopt the same strategy. Besides, the parties' chapters in both states were autonomous and they felt more comfortable using their own logos and flags.

The news of the common logo was received with apprehension by PH supporters. They agreed that the issue of voter confusion was real. What needed to be done next was to make it clear to voters that PKR now stood for PH. And they had only about a month to accomplish that.

The people helped to propagate the idea by relaying the information to everyone they knew. There was no end to sending through WhatsApp countless images carrying the PKR logo with the voting mark 'X' next to it. Or photos of DAP, PPBM and Amanah leaders tagged with the PKR logo. They looked out of place at first associated with another party, but after a while, people got used to it.

The shared logo move turned out to be a game-changer. It gave the people confidence in PH because they could now see it as a united coalition. It also served as a compelling symbol of Mahathir embracing Anwar and the spirit of reformasi that Anwar's party stood for.

Malay voters were better able to accept the DAP now because with the party having shown its willingness to give up its own symbol, they realised it might not be true what BN had been saying, that the DAP was dominating the Opposition.

When Najib was told about Mahathir's announcement, he dismissed it as poppycock. He thought the person telling him that was joking. But when he realised it was true, that the four parties were indeed standing under PKR's symbol, his face turned pale.

EC chief told to '*podah*'

The next day, Election Commission (EC) chief Mohd Hashim tried to be funny. He said PH needed to get the EC's permission to use the logo it was going to adopt in GE14. "The EC will approve the use of the logo if it does not contravene the regulations," he said.

Mahathir reacted to this with the Tamil word, "*Podah!*" (Get lost!)

He was right to react that way. As *Malaysiakini* explained, all that was required for PH candidates from other parties to use the PKR logo was an authorisation letter from PKR signed by a high-ranking leader, typically the party president. That was the procedure in GE13 when PKR fielded Parti Sosialis Malaysia candidates under its logo. There was no need to seek approval from anyone else, certainly not the EC chairman.

Well, Mohd Hashim asked for it, and he got it.

But that was not all. Mahathir was not in a forgiving mood. The RoS had given him and his party grief, and now the EC fella, "*apanama*" (whatsisname), was trying to be cute. He had had enough. He asked for Mohd Hashim and RoS chief Surayati to be shamed in newspapers and on social media. He wanted the world to know they had been doing Najib's "dirty" work for him.

"Let the whole world know that because of *dedak* (euphemism for "bribe"), or more than that, they are willing to deny Malaysians their rights," he said.

Mahathir's followers heard him and the next thing you knew, the photos of Surayati and Mohd Hashim were on Facebook, Instagram and Twitter accompanied by outrageous captions and expletives.

Parliament dissolved

The next day, April 7, 2018, Parliament was dissolved, paving the way for GE14.

Najib had announced its dissolution the day before, and so the EC would meet in a few days to fix the dates for nomination and polling.

Realising what a titanic contest GE14 would be and how high the stakes were, Najib called it "the mother of all elections".

Political blogger Mariam Mokhtar called it "the general election in which Malaysians will experience the mother of all riggings, to stop the mother of all defeats".

The people prayed for the mother of all victories.

HOW TO STEAL AN ELECTION

Before Najib dissolved Parliament to pave the way for the general election, he made sure that other measures were taken first to ensure that BN would win.

The big one was redelineation.

This was so important that Najib had to wait till the final redelineation report was submitted to him to be tabled in Parliament before he called the elections. It took a longer time than expected because of legal challenges that arose along the way, but it did eventually arrive on Najib's desk on March 9, 2018.

The report was then tabled in Parliament on March 22 and approved on March 28.

For the redelineation, the Election Commission (EC) saw to it that electoral boundaries were redrawn supposedly to ensure the convenience of voters and elected representatives, and address the demographic changes that had taken place in the country since the last exercise was conducted in 2003.

But what it came up with drew severe criticism from Bersih, Opposition parties and citizens who were knowledgeable about the process.

In many cases, the new proposals did not comply with the principles enumerated under the Thirteenth Schedule of the Federal Constitution. The most glaring was not ensuring that the number of voters within each constituency in a state was approximately equal.

Worse cases of malapportionment

In fact, the new proposals gave rise to worse cases of malapportionment covering nearly a quarter of the total parliamentary and state seats in Peninsular Malaysia.

Bersih drew attention to the creation of super-sized constituencies. The top 10 largest parliamentary constituencies had sizes ranging from 108,156 voters to 150,439 voters, much larger than their state average.

"These constituencies are created by packing in predominantly Opposition voters into already large constituencies," Bersih observed.

Such a move greatly devalued the worth of the votes in the super-sized constituencies compared to that of those in smaller-sized ones. For example, in Selangor, Sabak Bernam had 37,126 voters whereas Kapar had a phenomenal 127,012. And yet each had only one representative in Parliament. This glaringly violated the principle of "one man, one vote" central to parliamentary democracy.

In Selangor, seven parliamentary seats held by the Opposition had the numbers of their voters drastically increased. On the other hand, the total number of voters in BN's seats was only a quarter of the Opposition's.

Such malapportionment was what caused the Opposition to lose GE13 despite winning the popular vote. Because the constituencies won by BN were markedly smaller, the 47% of the popular vote it managed to secure was enough to cover 60% of parliamentary seats.

Bersih noted that based on given electorate figures and the constituencies won by BN and the Opposition in 2013, BN could be returned to power again if it lost the popular vote in GE14.

It added, alarmingly, "Given that the smallest 112 parliamentary constituencies contain only 33% of total electorate, a simple parliamentary majority could theoretically be won with just 16.5% of the popular vote. This figure may go lower if votes are effectively split in multi-cornered contests."

Another criticism of the new proposals involved the obvious shifting of voters of a particular ethnic group from one seat to another to favour BN.

The 2003 exercise showed how the EC applied gerrymandering and malapportionment to help BN by breaking up Malay-majority seats, which were then seen as pro-Opposition during the 1999 general election.

However, the following general elections, GE12 and GE13, then showed that mixed and Chinese-majority seats were the ones that had become pro-Opposition instead. So for the current exercise, the EC was prompted to transform 15 previously mixed parliamentary constituencies into eight Malay-majority and seven Chinese-majority constituencies.

In Selangor, the number of state seats with 60 to 80% Malay voters increased from 13 to 27, while those with 60 to 80% Chinese voters increased from three to eight.

Danesh Prakash Chacko, mapping adviser of electoral NGO Tindak Malaysia, expressed concern that this would bring about increased ethnic segregation.

He gave as an example the state of Perak where Malay voters were moved into BN seats while Chinese voters were packed into PH seats and Indian voters into those that marginally favoured BN. He observed that the Indian voters were being used to swing the tide towards BN.

In Kedah, the number of Malay voters had been increased in nine seats while in Selangor, Chinese voters had been packed into Opposition areas.

Despite this, Danesh said the way the political landscape had evolved, with PPBM having joined PH, the redelineation might not work for GE14 as intended because the exercise started in 2016. Political preferences would have changed since then.

The executive director of independent research company Ilham Centre, Hisomuddin Bakar, agreed. "To combat PPBM and Mahathir, BN needs a 'handicap', the redelineation. But this could end up being more disastrous for BN if there is a Malay swing," he said.

No less than 15 legal challenges were made against the redelineation proposals, starting in 2016. The most dogged plaintiff was the Selangor Government, which pursued the matter as far as it could go. But ultimately, all the cases were thrown out.

EC plays out Selangorians
The EC played out Selangor residents when it submitted to Najib in March

its first redelineation proposal for the state instead of the revised second one, which was drawn up after receiving 800 objections from voters and hearing some of them out in December and January. In the final report, the EC reverted to the first proposal without giving any reasons.

That was not only sneaky, it totally disregarded the time and effort the Selangor residents had spent preparing for the objections and hearings. Even more inexcusable, it betrayed the hopes of hundreds of thousands of Selangor voters affected by its reversal.

It also showed that EC chairman Mohd Hashim Abdullah had dishonoured the assurance he gave in his earlier interview with Bernama, "Every eligible party has the right to protest, and the protest is heard in local investigative sessions held. The EC will take into account any relevant proposal for change in its recommendation."

Rise up and stop the cheating

The report was pushed through Parliament by Najib and passed on March 28. Attempts by Opposition MPs to delay it were unsuccessful. After the vote, PH MPs held up placards of protest that urged the *rakyat* to rise up and stop the cheating.

PKR MP Wong Chen said the redelineation threatened to make the country "an electoral one-party state where a kleptocrat survives".

Former Bersih chairperson Maria Abdullah Chin, who by now had quit Bersih to stand as a candidate in the elections, called it the "biggest cheating to ever happen".

Almost as if to affirm that, deputy prime minister Zahid said the new electoral map could have a positive effect on BN's chances of wresting back Selangor.

"In fact, we believe we can even increase the vote majority in the seats we won in the last general election," he said. A bit too ingenuous, wasn't he?

I was incensed that my parliamentary constituency in Selangor was changed from Subang in the past general elections to Damansara, which used to be Petaling Jaya Utara with a voter population of 85,401. Now renamed and re-engineered, it had a voter population of a whopping 164,322! How would the elected representative be able to serve so many people?

If the EC had not played us out, I would still be voting in Subang.

The DAP candidate, Tony Pua, knowing that Damansara was overrun by Opposition supporters, joked at a PKR fund-raising dinner that he would probably end up winning with the largest majority ever recorded.

Sure enough, he was to do that on May 9. His winning margin of 106,903 votes would create history by turning out to be the highest majority nationwide.

A scary law

After redelineation, the next measure Najib had to take was to get the Anti-Fake News Bill passed.

Despite being heavily criticised, it was tabled on March 26. Opposition MPs and civil society groups feared it would be another instrument to crush dissent ahead of the general election.

The law was aimed at anyone who was found "maliciously creating, offering, publishing, printing, distributing, circulating or disseminating" any fake news or publication containing it.

Fake news was defined as "any news, information, data and reports, which is or are wholly or partly false, whether in the form of features, visuals or audio recordings or in any other form capable of suggesting words or ideas". It sounded too general and vague.

The punishment proposed was severe, with imprisonment of up to six years and a maximum fine of RM500,000. The original proposal was maximum jail time of 10 years, but was reduced as a compromise.

I surmised the Government wanted to keep the definition of fake news vague so that the law, when passed, could be applied arbitrarily.

Just the week before, deputy minister Jailani Johari said something telling although it sounded stupid. He said any information on the 1MDB issue other than that verified by the Government was fake news! How ridiculous was that?

But it was telling because it unwittingly revealed that one of the reasons the Government wanted to introduce the anti-fake news law might have been to prevent anyone from further disseminating news about 1MDB, including the Malaysian media.

And if the Government could say that news reports about 1MDB from established publications like *WSJ* or *The Economist* were fake, then it could virtually say that other news reports by them or other publications were fake as well. If it chose to.

By the same token, the Government could, if it chose to, haul someone to court by just arbitrarily declaring that they had created or disseminated fake news even if the news was real.

As a hypothetical example, if in the near future, the foreign media published a report about the U.S. DoJ declaring that MO1 was indeed Najib Razak and provided evidence of that, and a Malaysian netizen posted the report on social media, the Government could arbitrarily call the report fake news and arrest the netizen for having disseminated it.

That was how scary such a law could be.

But it got passed, anyway, on April 2. The next day, it was ratified by the upper house, Dewan Negara (Senate). And on April 11, it had already got the King's consent and been gazetted as law. All in nine days. That was superfast. Was it expedited to be employed in the coming general election?

Free Malaysia Today interviewed me about the new law on April 4 and I said it was "an attempt to shut people up". I also warned that BN would go all out to win big in GE14 so as to ensure its perpetual hold on power.

"People had better be aware of that," I said. "If BN gets its two-thirds majority, that's the end of Malaysia. It will bulldoze through anything it wants and the only reforms we're going to see are reforms that will make the system work to BN's benefit."

Polling day in middle of the week

On April 10, four days after Najib called the elections, the EC made the announcement that everyone had been waiting eagerly for – the polling date.

Expectations were high that it would be on a weekend as in the past few general elections so that voters could return to their registered constituencies if they were currently domiciled elsewhere. It would be especially helpful for those returning from Singapore or to and from the East Malaysian states of Sabah and Sarawak.

But a weekend it was not to be. Mohd Hashim announced that election day would be on May 9, a Wednesday.

This caused mayhem on social media. Netizens yelled bias, and Mohd Hashim became an object of contempt also in coffeeshop talk and private conversations. Because not only had he chosen a weekday, he had chosen a day right in the middle of the week.

This would cause untold inconvenience to voters. It could deter some from making the effort to go back to where they were registered to vote, especially if it was in another state. And those who could not get extended leave to make the journey would be deprived of their right to vote.

Straight away, people accused the EC and the caretaker BN government of conspiring to bring about a lower voter turnout that would disadvantage the Opposition. They screamed blue murder at the dirty trick.

Political scientist Wong Chin Huat observed, "By deliberately choosing a weekday for polling, after deregistering PPBM, it confirms that Najib strongly believes in a Malay tsunami, which would be a Malaysian tsunami if the non-Malay turnout stays high."

Anger, helplessness, despair, feeling of defeat. This was the spectrum of emotions people experienced at that moment.

It was getting too much. First, there was the BN-favouring redelineation, thanks as well to the EC. Then the Anti-Fake News Act. After that, the temporary deregistration of PPBM. Now this. One dirty trick after another to make it increasingly difficult for the Opposition to fight on a level battlefield.

Najib proclaimed himself a "Bugis warrior" not too long ago, but he was approaching the fight for Putrajaya like a coward, putting obstacles in his opponent's way. How would he attain a real and honourable victory this way? How would he be able to feel proud of himself if he won by foul means? How could he claim to be a legitimate prime minister?

He would only continue to be the most hated Malaysian prime minister ever. Even more hated than he was now.

He should be stopped from becoming PM again. BN should be dumped into the dirt for playing dirty. Malaysians should come out in overwhelming numbers on May 9 and vote bloody BN out. Those working away from home seats must take leave and go home and vote bloody BN out. Those working in Singapore must return to their own country and save it by voting bloody BN out. Those living outside of the country, even as far away as the U.S. or Latin America or Antarctica must come home and do their national service of voting bloody BN out.

Malaysians must do it!

Malaysians mobilise

And then the people put aside their rage, came together and mobilised.

Within hours of the EC's announcement, Marble Emporium, a construction material company based in Shah Alam, Selangor, posted on its Facebook page that it would give its Sabahan and Sarawakian workers three days' paid leave plus air ticket and RM300 allowance each to fly back and vote in GE14.

Its proprietor, Sim Yen Peng, when contacted by *The Star*, said he was doing this because "voting is a responsibility".

Facebook user Choon Hoe posted on the page, "Really salute your company. You have set a very good example to many big firms out there."

Indeed, other firms announced promptly that they would give their employees leave to go and vote.

Among them were H2S Consulting; non-profit organisation Happy Bank; GRIM FILM; public relations firm Shekinah PR which decided to close its office for two days and also pay for its employees' petrol and toll charges; online florist Happy Bunch; The Edge Media Group; Seksan

Design which offered its staff paid holidays from May 8 to May 10; publishing group Karangkraf; and creative agency Forefront International which announced days off and travel allowances for its staff.

Even IKEA Singapore chipped in and offered its 80 Malaysian employees a paid day of leave to return home to fulfil their electoral duty. Also helpful was the owner of a Singapore-based jewellery store, Ngo Hea Ong, who gave his Malaysian staff members the day off.

Airlines such as national carrier Malaysia Airlines, Cathay Pacific, AirAsia and Malindo Air announced they would waive their flight change fees for Malaysians with existing bookings so they could be in Malaysia on election day.

Declare a public holiday!

Meanwhile, Bersih criticised the choice of Wednesday for polling because it also caused inconvenience to polling agents and volunteer observers.

It called on the caretaker federal government to announce polling day as a public holiday and on the caretaker state governments to do the same on the day before or after polling day.

However, caretaker deputy minister Nur Jazlan tweeted, "No need to declare May 9 a public holiday to allow people to vote. Under the Election Commission Act (Election Offences Act 1954), employers are compelled to let their employees go and vote. Neither are they allowed to intimidate and prevent their employees from voting. Punishment for an offence is RM5,000."

How unsympathetic coming from a government man. This was going to lose BN votes!

Student Arveent Kathirtchelvan then took the initiative to start a petition addressed to the King asking for at least May 9 to be declared a public holiday. One was never sure of how effective such petitions were or whether the addressee would even get it, but in less than 24 hours, more than 100,000 people had signed it.

The next day, the caretaker government decided to do the right thing. The Prime Minister's Office issued a statement declaring May 9 a holiday.

Home tweet home

Even so, for many Malaysians, logistics and cost remained hurdles.

Malay Mail reported the case of Iggy Amabel who tweeted that she was unable to afford a return ticket from Kuala Lumpur to Sabah to vote, and how from there Malaysian generosity surfaced spontaneously to offer her help, leading to the creation of the #PulangMengundi (Return to vote) hashtag which connected angel donors to those needing help.

It was created by *Malay Mail* staffer Joe Lee at 2.39pm on April 10. By 10pm, Lee proudly reported to the online newspaper that #PulangMengundi had helped "at least a few dozen" Malaysians to return home.

"It shows that Malaysians do take their responsibility and privilege to vote seriously," Lee said.

"#PulangMengundi is not backed by any party or NGO, it is made up entirely of the Malaysian Twitter-verse. Who says social media is toxic?" he added, taking a dig at what minister Khairy Jamaluddin had said some months before.

That night, the hashtag became Malaysia's number one trending topic.

The hashtag was soon developed into a website, *pulangmengundi.com*, to connect donors and recipients. It was jointly created by Timothy Teoh, Sue Ling Gan and Wong You Jing. These were young people who would not have been spurred to get involved if polling day had not been set for a Wednesday.

Carpooling groups also sprouted.

'Jom Balik Undi' (Let's go back and vote) was actually started two weeks earlier by Twitter user Sandra Tang to facilitate those who wanted to offer rides home to those in need of them. By now, it had amassed nearly 11,000 members.

On Facebook, there were a few 'Jom Balik Undi' groups too. One group had a membership of 43,000. It clarified, "We do not represent any political party ... any posts in support of any party will be deleted."

On April 10, writer Nizam Bakeri started #CarpoolGE14, and Izzah Azura set up a crowdfunding platform on Facebook to help those who needed financial aid to travel home and vote.

A group called 'UndiRabu', started by lawyers, accountants and others like Alzari Mahshar and Tengku Elida Bustaman, turned to crowdfunding as well and within two days, it told *Malay Mail* it had collected RM65,461 and received requests for financial help amounting to RM47,750.

Most of the requests for aid came from first-time voters, many of whom were students of public and private institutions of higher learning.

Dian Lee, a good Samaritan, posted on Facebook her offer to help student voters studying in the Peninsula to fly back to Sabah and Sarawak to vote. She would pay 80% of the flight tickets ranging from RM550 to RM800 each.

Touched by what was going on, @Ashwene_THINA tweeted, "Malaysians are definitely one of a kind, because I just saw tweets about how everyone is helping one another with #CarPoolGE14 & then I saw another tweet where this girl can't even vote yet but was willing to spend some money on bus tickets for those in need."

In Singapore, Malaysians were also making plans for the big day. *The Straits Times* reported, "A check with four coach companies that operate buses from Singapore to Malaysia revealed that tickets for the weekend of May 5 are running out or fully sold for destinations such as Kuala Lumpur, Taiping, Ipoh and Penang."

A bus company which had 50 buses going to Malaysia every day was considering doubling the number to 100 a day for the May 5 weekend. It said demand this time around was higher compared with that for the 2008 general election.

Better still, volunteers sponsored free return bus services to ferry voters from Singapore to Melaka, Kuala Lumpur and Ipoh on May 8 and back on May 9.

In January, Nur Jazlan had said he did not expect Malaysian voters living in Singapore to return in droves this time because they had done so in 2008 and 2013 but felt "cheated" by the Opposition because it did not succeed in forming the government.

"I think they might not even bother to come back to vote," he said. How wrong he was.

'Nur Jazlan, we are coming back'

Free Malaysia Today captured the attitude of Malaysians working in Singapore towards GE14 effectively when it interviewed a few of them on it.

Anita Hassan said she and her friends had been anticipating polling day to be in early May, so they had planned their schedules around that month. Now they knew the date, they would be buying their tickets to go home.

"So, Nur Jazlan, we are coming back," she said.

Shatir Baha had already bought his flight ticket home. And Lim Thian Yi said he and his colleagues had already applied for two days' leave, one paid and one unpaid.

"For the first time, I am witnessing so much unity after the last general election. I feel Malaysians are even more united this time around," he said.

As for Loo Xian, she declared defiantly that "the more they try to make it difficult for us to go back to vote, the more I want to prove them wrong". She would have been riled to hear what deputy prime minister Zahid had to say on April 13.

"In my view, the Government neither encourages nor discourages people to return to vote as that is an individual right," he told *Malaysiakini*. "But if the employer from Singapore does not permit their Malaysian workers to take leave, then I think the best thing to do is to not come back to vote."

What a thing to say! His remark set off a buzz on social media. Many felt this was a sure sign that BN was scared of a big turnout.

Trinna Leong was spot-on when she tweeted, "Dear great Malaysian leader aka deputy prime minister Zahid Hamidi, why shouldn't Malaysians go home to vote if leave not approved? Can you please explain ah?"

Darsh Kanda urged Malaysians not to listen to Zahid. "If you're Malaysian & you care about the direction the country is taking, vote. Those short on funds/need a ride can refer to #PulangMengundi #CarpoolGE14 #undirabu," he tweeted.

Even farther away, Tham Pei Thing bought her flight ticket home from Australia within half an hour of the polling date announcement. She would volunteer to be a polling agent on May 9 as well. "I want to take action to get the change that I hope for," she said.

Syed Naufal Syed Ahmad Alhabshi was flying back from the U.S. He solicited funds through his Facebook page and managed to get enough from "generous Malaysians" to buy his ticket.

Jagjit Singh could have opted for postal voting but he would rather travel back from Doha and vote. He said his friends were not surprised because they knew he loved his country.

It was truly heartwarming. Adversity had brought out the best in Malaysians. Another of BN's dirty tricks to make victory impossible for PH had backfired.

From this point on, it looked hopeful that BN would be given a hard run at the polls. Because – and BN knew this – voters who were keen to make the effort to go home and vote were usually those who would vote for the Opposition. Including the domestic ones.

Yet even so, with the gerrymandering that had been done and all the other dirty tricks that BN had pulled, would the elections still not be stacked in favour of the incumbent?

And might there not be further obstacles put in the Opposition's way when the campaign period started?

The people were about to find out.

READY TO MAKE HISTORY?

Sure enough, on April 25, the EC suddenly came up with a surprise restriction.

Only images of party presidents and deputy presidents – or their equivalents – were allowed to be used on campaign materials.

This was obviously aimed at cutting down Mahathir's public exposure. He was neither a president nor deputy president of any contesting party. So he was banned from appearing on PH flyers, posters, banners, billboards.

Only exception for him was in Langkawi, Kedah, where he was contesting the parliamentary seat.

Bersih questioned why the guideline was being introduced in this GE. There was no need for it in the past. Furthermore, stakeholders were not consulted. And the guideline was announced at the last minute. The materials had already been printed.

Disregarding the ruling, PH put up some materials carrying Mahathir's image. But enforcement officers came and cut out Mahathir's face. The result looked hilariously odd, especially if the image was a half body shot. There would be a gaping hole where his face used to be, which made the rest of his body look headless.

A giant billboard in Yong Peng, Johor, made the news. Photos of it before the excision and after went viral. One minute, Mahathir was seen flanked by candidates Liew Chin Tong and Chew Peck Choo. But the next minute, he was gone. The enforcement officers were efficient at their job.

Chin Tong complained that the new ruling was nonsensical. "Why can't we put up Mahathir's picture? He is the prime ministerial candidate for Harapan."

Enforcement officers also removed another billboard in the area. It said a vote for MCA's Ayer Hitam candidate, Wee Ka Siong, was a vote for Najib and his wife, Rosmah.

Earlier, the EC had asked the DAP to remove the billboard. The EC said Rosmah was not an election candidate. But the DAP just cut out her image. That was not enough. Enforcement officers came and took the whole billboard away.

You can bet when it came to Rosmah, there was no compromise.

Anyway, the unfair ruling turned out to be another EC boo-boo. Something Mohd Hashim would not live down. Twitter was abuzz with condemnation of it and the cutting-out of Mahathir's image.

Myriam tweeted, "What backhanded gifts they give. Banning the image only reinforces the 'missing' personality in the public's hearts & minds & even more sympathy votes. Wow, thanks are in order!"

Singabola warned, "There is a universal law which says: 'For every action there is an equal and opposite reaction.' Expect a backlash from the *rakyat*."

Peoples Power was pithy: "Making voters more angry."

Six PH candidates rejected

More problems came for PH on nomination day, April 28. Six of its candidates got rejected.

The most prominent case was that of PKR vice-president Tian Chua. A RM2,000 fine had been imposed on him the month before. The amount was actually within the threshold of acceptance of election candidates. But the returning officer disagreed. And disqualified him.

Tian Chua argued that he was allowed to contest in GE13 although he was fined RM2,000 in 2010. The returning officer couldn't care less. Tian Chua alleged the action against him was an underhanded tactic.

Another unfortunate incident happened in Negeri Sembilan. PKR candidate Streram Sinnasamy was denied entry into the nomination centre. He didn't have a pass issued by the EC. So he failed to file his nomination papers. The state seat of Rantau was therefore won unopposed by BN's Mohamad Hasan. He happened to be the caretaker *menteri besar* of the state.

Actually, there was no law saying candidates must have passes to enter nomination centres. So the returning officer's decision smelt fishy.

On the whole, almost half of the 222 parliamentary seats and 505 state seats would see three-cornered fights. Most of them would involve Umno, PAS and PPBM or Amanah.

Right! Now that the gladiators were confirmed for "the mother of all elections", let the revels begin!

Ceramahs were held every night. The PH ones drew record attendances. Shouts of *"Ubah!"* rang out loud again like in 2013. And, unlike 2013, there were now shouts of *"Hidup Tun!"*

The biggest turnout was in Penang. PH held simultaneous gatherings there. On the island and the mainland. Once on April 28 and again on May 2.

The one that was held at the Esplanade and Butterworth was stupendous. Attendance was an awesome 120,000. So said caretaker chief minister Guan Eng. His coalition was going all out to win Penang for the third consecutive term.

'Malay tsunami will sink you forever'

With Mahathir at the helm of PH, the crowds came. There were 10,000 in Putrajaya, a BN stronghold. Where the majority of voters were civil servants.

Mahathir told the crowd, cheekily, "I thought people from Putrajaya were cowards. I am truly shocked to see such a huge crowd. I thought the people of Putrajaya were scared but I am wrong. I hope all of you are here to save Putrajaya."

He scolded the authorities for tearing down posters and banners with pictures of him. "They are so scared of a picture that would not have done any harm. It's not like my picture is going to swallow someone, is it?"

Temerloh, Pahang, drew a crowd of 20,000, mostly Malay. It was the biggest turnout for an Opposition *ceramah* in the town. Was a Malay tsunami taking shape?

Mahathir said, "They say there won't be a Malay tsunami. Wait. You will see. The Malay tsunami will sink you forever."

He added, "There will also be a Chinese tsunami and an Indian tsunami."

PH managed to penetrate the normally Opposition-averse Felda settlements. In GE13, Pakatan Rakyat *ceramahs* were attended by only a handful. And by crickets, someone said. Sometimes, the politicians even got chased away. But now, to everyone's amazement, thousands came.

In GE13, the Opposition won only six Felda seats, three of them by PAS. Now it looked like the number would increase.

In Johor, BN's fortress, Malay support for PH in GE13 was only 13%. Now the sentiment was different.

Muhyiddin was confident. As early as May 6, he announced at a *ceramah* in Pagoh, "In Johor, I believe we have won." It was greeted with a thunderous roar. "Because more Malays have abandoned BN. They are fed up."

Manifesto delights

PH told the people that if it won GE14, it would abolish GST. In the first 100 days of its coming to power. This was promised in its manifesto.

The manifesto also promised that the posts of PM, CM and MB would be limited to two terms. And the PM would not be allowed to be finance minister.

Draconian laws would also be repealed. Sedition Act. Universities and University Colleges Act. Printing Presses and Publications Act. Anti-Fake New Act. *Merdeka*! (Liberation!)

Malaysian institutions would also be reformed. The MACC and the EC would be placed under the authority of Parliament to give them independence. The roles of attorney-general and public prosecutor would be separated. The voting age would be lowered from 21 to 18. Voter registration would be made automatic.

All very good. But, as Suaram (Suara Rakyat Malaysia, or Voice of the People) adviser Kua Kia Soong pointed out, the manifesto lacked a race-free agenda to unify the nation. There was also no mention of an end to the New Economic Policy (NEP).

Fund-raising dinners organised by PH parties were fully subscribed. Especially the DAP ones. Extra tables had to be opened on the spot. People who had not booked earlier kept coming.

People came not so much for the food but to listen to the speakers. They made the crowd feel good. They sent out positive vibes. They assured they would win. Did they have more conviction when they said it this time?

The crowd also gave generously when the donation box came around. Towards the end of the dinner, someone would announce the total amount collected. It was usually a lot.

This was so different from attending a BN event. There, you'd get free food, you didn't need to donate. Someone might donate money to you instead!

Like the one in the fishing village of Sekinchan, Selangor, on May 1. About 1,500 people came for the lavish buffet. And to see a hologram of Najib talking about promises from the BN manifesto.

Jamal Md Yunos was the emcee. The leader of the right-wing Red Shirts. Also Sungai Besar Umno division chief.

The main event was the lucky draw. Top prize RM25,000 and a brand new motorcycle.

Jamal said the sponsor was local businesspeople, not BN. He also said a "donor" was offering RM2,000 to Sekinchan residents as an "incentive" to vote for the BN candidate.

'We all make mistakes'

The campaign period also saw countless videos being made and viralled. Not only by politicians but also concerned citizens.

The most notable one was a 10-minute short film entitled *Harapan*. It features Mahathir and two young children. One of them, Aisyah, bumps into Mahathir in his office. When he first appears, he looks like an aged version of Robert DeNiro. The camera shoots upwards to give him physical stature.

Aisyah asks why he is still working at his age. He replies, "It is because I have to do some work with regard to rebuilding our country, perhaps because of mistakes I myself have made in the past and because of the current situation."

Aisyah's brother, Adam, joins in the conversation. He apologises to Mahathir for not having been listening to his grandfather whenever the latter talked about Mahathir. "It's all right, Adam, we all make mistakes," Mahathir assures him.

Then he starts to get emotional when he says, "I am already old, I don't have much time left, but within my means" ... he starts choking back tears ... "I will do my best to work with all my friends to rebuild our nation, Malaysia."

The music builds up. Mahathir is in tears. Aisyah then leaps to hug him. In slow motion. At that point, the viewer would also be shedding tears.

It was a masterstroke. The film conveyed viscerally and effectively what Mahathir wanted Malaysians to know. That he had made mistakes in the past and was now trying to rectify them. He should be forgiven because it was all right to make mistakes.

Most people watching that film would have given him their vote there and then.

'Our ONLY chance to win' so shut up!

That was fine with me, but I had to warn against lionising Mahathir even though he was now with the Opposition. I posted on Facebook, "We must not get carried away just because he is leading the fight to kick out Najib. Let us not forget his past misdeeds. Besides, the ending of this video promotes idol worshipping."

I got slammed for that by netizens. They said this was not the right time to say something like that. They told me to stop harping on the old issues and look at the bigger picture. They said this was "our ONLY chance to win" so don't rock the boat.

Praveen Sankaranarayanan wrote, "Mahathir is deserving of idolisation or lionisation. He's putting everything on the line at 92, when he could just be sitting at home in silence. If you're voting for PH, well and good, but we don't require these mood dampeners now. Period."

Angel Fernz was more gentle: "Whatever his past misdeeds, they are already done. We can't change that. Many people have been hurt by his single-mindedness and arrogance, look at Anwar, Kit Siang, Tian Chua, Mat Sabu, Guan Eng and a host of others. Indirectly you and me. But if all these wonderful men can put aside old heartaches and pains for a greater cause, surely we can too. Take heart, forgiveness is the key."

Guat Hee Tan underscored the importance of choosing Mahathir in mythic terms: "Caught between the Dracken and Medusa, we will just have to choose Medusa for without Medusa, we can't turn Dracken into stone and defeat it."

Ha Lee was straight-to-the-point: "We need a devil to remove a bigger devil."

Askiah Adam was, however, more circumspect: "Bring down the devil only to resurrect his mentor? Doesn't sound good. But let's see how it goes."

Well, I wasn't saying don't vote for PH, just don't lionise Mahathir, but that fine point didn't matter to the people then. The general sentiment was in favour of supporting him regardless of anything else so that we could "bury BN for good".

It was now or never. And Mahathir, as Khoo Hock Aun wrote, "represents the best chance to tip the scales in our favour".

Make the two-party system a reality

I also made my own appeal to voters, speaking directly to them in a video.

In my own small way. I sent it out through WhatsApp and posted it on Facebook. Two days before election day.

I said if PH won, we'd be able to see "big drama" in the form of the 1MDB investigation. "Wouldn't you want to see that show?" I asked. On the other hand, if BN won, 1MDB would be covered up. In a few years, it would be forgotten, like the Altantuya murder.

I pointed out that Mahathir had been calling Najib a thief. By several names. *Pencuri, penyamun, perompak, penyangak.* Yet strangely, Najib had not taken any action against him. Not even a defamation suit.

I said the most important thing to consider was that if PH were voted in as the new government, "we would be making history". Because "we would be making the two-party system a reality".

"This has to happen, because Malaysians have to see that it can happen before they'll believe it. And when it does, we will then have two viable parties contesting for our support. They will be struggling hard to give us the best options. We will experience what it means to be a democracy. No more one-party rule. And of course we can begin to believe that Malaysia will not die if BN is not in government."

I said GE14 provided "the best chance for change". And it could be the last one for a long time to come. Because if BN were to win again, it would probably change the rules in order to stay in power "perhaps forever".

I ended by asking my fellow Malaysians to "make history" and look forward to "a better Malaysia".

Who will win?

Predictions of the election results.

Merdeka Centre – BN 100, Harapan 83, PAS 2, another 37 too close to call. But on the whole, "we anticipate BN will prevail in the elections".

Ilham Centre – PH could win 100 out of 165 parliamentary seats in Peninsular Malaysia. Johor likely to go to PH, close fight for Kedah and Perak. Penang and Selangor assured for PH.

Rafizi Ramli's INVOKE Malaysia – PH would win 111 out of 165 parliamentary seats in Peninsular Malaysia, with BN securing the other 54 seats. PAS would get zero Parliament and state seats.

PH would win the majority of the votes in Kedah, Penang, Perak, Selangor, Federal Territory, Negeri Sembilan, Melaka and Johor. States expected to be won by BN were Kelantan, Terengganu, Perlis and Pahang.

PH would make a clean sweep of all the 22 parliamentary and 56 state seats in Selangor.

Netizens responded to INVOKE's findings.

"Rafizi must be daydreaming!" said Mathew Kong

"Would be glad if he could share what he's smoking," quipped Zaidy bin Ahmad.

"Denying PAS of any seat in Parliament and state constituencies is a ridiculous prediction," said Mohari Tamin. I had to agree with that.

Universiti Sains Malaysia political scientist Sivamurugan Pandian and political analyst Jeniri Amir both predicted that BN would win.

On April 26, Najib himself told Bloomberg he was expecting a "better result" in GE14.

"We are reasonably confident of a good result," he said in a one-hour interview. "There is no movement for changing the Government, I don't see that. That's not saying we will win with a huge majority, no I am not going to predict that, but I am going to say that we are reasonably sanguine about the result."

No movement to change the Government? What had he been smoking the last five years?

Memes made in Malaysia

Memes flew all over cyberspace reminding people to vote, some hilarious.

One had a photo of deputy minister Ahmad Maslan, the guy Malaysians loved to laugh at, juxtaposed with the words: "If you don't go out to vote, one day people like me will become prime minister." That should frighten people into voting!

Another had education minister Mahdzir Khalid threatening teachers they would lose their jobs if they voted for the Opposition, which he actually did four months earlier, and a sweet-looking female teacher retorting, "If we vote for the Opposition, it is you who will lose your job."

One that took the cake for being numerically witty went: "April 28 (nomination day) is 4+2+8=14, May 9 is 5+9=14, this GE is 14th GE. All these coincidentally point to 14, and '14' in Cantonese sounds like 'sure die'. It seems Najib has unwittingly chosen to 'die'. Bye bye the PIRATE REGIME. We shall bury you!"

Dignity vs Cash

On the night of May 8, both Mahathir and Najib gave their final messages.

Najib spoke from a family home in Pekan, Pahang. It was transmitted live on TV and Facebook.

Mahathir spoke from Dewan Ho Ping in Langkawi, Kedah. His speech was transmitted live on Facebook and also to PH *ceramahs* all over the country that were happening at the same time.

Najib continued pork barrelling in flamboyant fashion. Down to the last minute! Now he was trying to buy the young over. He said if BN won, all youths aged 26 and below would get full tax exemption, from 2017 onwards, with immediate effect.

Actually, how many youths of those ages would make enough taxable income to benefit from that, eh?

Then Najib promised a special holiday for two days if BN won. On May 14 and 15. To let the people spend time with their family and prepare for Ramadhan.

He was following Mahathir's lead, announced two weeks before. Those would be on May 10 and 11. They would bridge May 9 and the weekend to result in a five-day break.

But in the PH case, the holidays were not meant for leisure. The idea was thought up by Dzulkefly Ahmad, strategy director of Amanah. To forestall international investors reacting adversely to the regime change and allay their fear of unpredictable changes.

The two-day break would be useful for reassuring players in the financial markets that all was well and that political stability was assured. The new government would also have time to prepare for business to proceed as usual on Monday, May 14, and restore confidence. It was brilliant.

Back to Najib. Now into his "third announcement". If BN won, he would declare that for Hari Raya Aidilfitri, "there will be no highway tolls throughout the country for five days".

I actually felt quite embarrassed for him watching him grovel for support. It was like he had no dignity left. Like he was a child abandoned by everyone and the only way he could try and win people back was offer them goodies.

Mahathir, on the other hand, talked about regaining dignity. The country was once one of the economic "tigers" of Asia, and would have become a developed country by 2020 if not for Najib. Now it was known as one of the top 10 corrupt countries in the world.

"We can only restore our dignity if we change the government, replacing it with a party with limited power to prevent abuse," he said.

He called on the people to come out in force and vote for PH "to save Malaysia from kleptocracy, restore democracy and the rule of law". He asked them not to "pawn the future of our country for that little bit of money which will not last".

He drew attention to his age which had been a much-talked-about issue, "I know I am old. There is not much time left for me. Many are of the view I should just rest. I wish I could rest, but many have met me and urged me to do something to stop the rot in the country. This will be the last time I will get to contribute whatever little I can to the struggle for my beloved country."

And there we had it, the contrasting styles of the two men. The different visions. In fact, what was Najib's vision? He had been so busy fighting for his survival, thinking of ways to destroy his enemies and covering up 1MDB's dirt, he had lost track of a vision for the country.

His speech was hollow and all he could do was lie towards the end of it that "the country is doing well". If it were, the people would not have been so unhappy with him.

And that was why they couldn't wait till the next day to take him out.

They didn't succeed in 2013. Would they succeed this time?

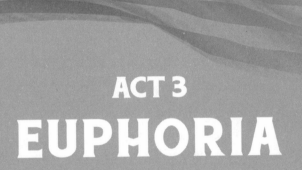

ACT 3
EUPHORIA

LIKE WATCHING A B-MOVIE WESTERN

May 9 for a lot of people is a do-or-die day. In a manner of speaking. If they don't manage to "do" it, how will they tolerate living for another five years under Jibby and Umno and BN?

This means May 9 is going to be a long day. A day full of apprehension. Are enough people turning up to vote? Mahathir has said 85% turnout is the minimum PH will need to win. A low turnout favours BN. Are voters heeding Mahathir's call? Are there long queues like in 2013? Will the weather be fine the whole day or will it rain in the afternoon? If it rains, will it deter people from coming out to do their all-important duty?

But there is a sense of goodwill and festivity too. Some eateries and restaurant chains are offering free meals, free desserts, free drinks to voters. In the true Malaysian spirit. What they are actually doing is, they are encouraging people to vote. Because there's so much at stake. The country's future. The future of our children and grandchildren.

A noodles chain, cafes in malls, a *bak kut teh* restaurant, an economy rice stall, an ice cream parlour, bistros. These are just a few of the civic-minded enterprises that show they care for what happens to the country.

To get a free meal, all a voter needs to do is show their finger. Er … coated with indelible ink, that is. As proof that they have voted. No such thing as a free lunch, you say? Not true. There is no catch to it. It's heartwarming altruism. And it unifies people through food. Just look around, the restaurant is filled with eaters with stained fingers. Are they fellow conspirators who have done their part to topple the Government? Ask and they'll tell you.

I go to cast my vote with my wife and daughter at the nearby school. It's around 11.30am. We, too, are worried it might rain later.

I'm a bit downhearted that there doesn't seem to be such a lot of people there as I had hoped. Or is it my imagination? Anyway, it still takes quite a while waiting in the queue. I happen to have been designated a *saluran* that moves slowly. Just my luck. Or maybe there are more people in my *saluran* than in any of the other ones.

My wife and daughter are done in less than an hour and I'm still waiting. After a while, I'm wondering if the EC loaded some *salurans* with more people so that the *salurans* will move more slowly and by the end of the day not all the people in them will get to the polling booth in time and therefore lose their chance to vote. Is this part of a conspiracy to favour BN? If not, why hasn't the EC worked out beforehand a way of distributing voters equally among all the *salurans*? Oh well, apprehension brings out all kinds of crazy thoughts.

As I'm reaching nearer the voting room I've been assigned to, I peek inside the one before it to observe the process going on. I recognise my friend Fawzia seated at one of the tables. I smile and wave to her. She smiles back. She asks me to take a photo of her doing her job. I oblige and WhatsApp the image to her instantly. I guess she's serving as polling agent for the DAP candidate since she's a DAP member. Well, it's nice to see someone I know helping out.

I'm feeling guilty myself that for this general election I didn't sign up to be a polling agent because I've been swamped with work. So now if PH were to win, I won't be able to say I helped to make it happen as a polling agent. My loss.

After one-and-a-half hours, I'm done. I look up at the sky as I'm leaving the polling centre. Ominous clouds are forming. The dreaded rain might come in the afternoon.

I find out later that a wait of one-and-a-half hours is not that bad. There are a lot of people who have to wait for three hours.

Elsewhere, 22-year-old law student P. Prabakaran casts his vote. This is the first time he is voting after coming of age the year before. He also happens to be a candidate for the Batu parliamentary seat.

He started out as an independent, which was both courageous and foolhardy, but after Tian Chua, the PKR incumbent, was disqualified by the returning officer on nomination day, the party decided to cut Prabakaran a deal to stand under the PKR ticket.

The youngest candidate in the elections agreed. Now, because Batu is a sure win for PKR, his chances of becoming a member of the august Dewan Rakyat are almost assured, when before, as an independent, they were virtually zero. Talk about being at the right place at the right time!

In the news, Umno vice-president Hishammuddin Hussein, Najib's cousin, is disparaging INVOKE's prediction that BN big guns are going to lose three parliamentary seats in Johor, including his in Sembrong.

The other two are new Felda chairman Shahrir Samad in Johor Bahru, a seat he has held for several terms, and caretaker Johor *menteri besar* Mohamed Khaled Nordin in Pasir Gudang.

No one can blame Hishammuddin for pooh-poohing the prediction. All three are stalwarts. And Johor is Umno's fortress. How can they lose? He calls the prediction a lie concocted by Rafizi, INVOKE's founder. Let's see who will get the last laugh.

Maybe they'll be saved by postal and advance votes. According to Merdeka Centre, studies show that in GE13, BN was saved by such votes in 22 parliamentary seats.

For GE14, the EC announced that 278,590 voters, comprising mostly security forces personnel and their spouses, would take part in advance voting on May 5, while another 21,665 would cast their votes by post. The latter batch would be kept in police lock-ups and counted only on May 9 at 4pm.

Is this cause for apprehension?

Meanwhile, Malaysians overseas are anxious that they might miss out having a say in the elections. Many received the ballot papers sent to them by the EC late. And they have to mark their vote and send the ballots back to their respective constituencies in Malaysia by 5pm today. Will they reach in time?

On May 7, two days before the deadline, Malaysians in London took part in a protest organised by Bersih UK at Trafalgar Square. They had still not received their ballot papers, which therefore means that when they do, it will be too late anyway for them to send their votes home in time.

Global Bersih complained, "Malaysian voters in Germany and Netherlands are receiving confirmation e-mails from the courier service stating that the ballots will arrive at their addresses as late as May 8. So how does the EC expect these voters to return the ballot papers to their returning officer before 5pm on May 9? It is simply impossible."

"If this was done on purpose, then they're sabotaging the elections," says student Hor Ying Jie, based in Finland. "If they didn't foresee that coming, then Malaysia has really incompetent people making important decisions."

Asked for his take on this fiasco on May 7, caretaker deputy home minister Nur Jazlan tweeted cavalierly that Malaysians voting overseas did not even make up 0.1% of the population. "It won't change any result. Don't get excited about it."

That simply confirms that the BN government is made up of goons. He totally disregards the paramount principle of voting being a constitutional right of all citizens and is even telling the overseas voters that their votes don't count! He should have instead apologised for the delay in the delivery of the ballot papers and promptly investigated the reason for it.

But trust Malaysians not to be defeated by the EC's inefficiency. Some have decided to fly home to vote when they realised the situation had become impossible. In doing so, they are able to collect other ballots from Malaysians in their area and bring them home before the deadline.

Facebook group 'GE14: Postal Voters Discussion', led by Alex Yap and a few others, coordinates the distribution of the ballots to the respective constituencies throughout the country after receiving them from the overseas returnees. It calls for painstaking planning. And help from other volunteer groups like UndiRabu and PulangMengundi.

Runners have to be ready to receive the ballots from the returnees at the Kuala Lumpur International Airport, and what happens from there has to be worked out ahead because some of the ballots received have to be redirected to other parts of the country. Volunteers have to be found to help with the distribution. Friends have to be approached for help. Friends of friends too. Even strangers. Engineering a cohesive chain is very complicated.

On the part of the Malaysians overseas, the extent they would go to in order to make their votes count is exemplary.

Take the case of the group in Houston who turned up at the airport there brandishing placards asking if anyone was headed for Kuala Lumpur. Just before the final check-ins were over, they managed to find someone who was on his way home to vote. The total stranger graciously agreed to take the ballots.

In the U.K., a few students got together and chipped in money to buy one of their friends a plane ticket so he could fly home to deliver their ballots. What dedication!

Eswari Kalugasalam, who is based in Omaha with no Malaysians living near her, received her ballot paper as late as May 7, but this did not deter her from couriering back her ballot for which she had to spend an exorbitant US$114, hoping against hope that it will arrive in her home state of Johor in time.

She originally thought of flying home to vote, but when news came that she could register as a postal voter, she did. She trusted the EC. But now she says, "I am angry and frustrated. Every vote counts. I am a Malaysian. I am not about political parties. I am about doing the right thing."

The best of the Malaysian spirit shines through again in this race to do the right thing. Seeing how determined and enterprising these young people are in upholding their democratic right for the betterment of the country, one cannot but feel proud to be Malaysian. They are the antithesis of the corrupt politicians of Umno and BN who obviously cannot claim to have any feelings for the country since they have had no qualms about stealing from it.

They should be kicked out, but can it be done when the odds are so heavily stacked against the Opposition? At 1pm, the voter turnout so far is reported to be only 55%. With only four hours left, can it reach the magical 85%? Doesn't look hopeful.

Moreover, the queues are long, and many people have been waiting but still not got to vote yet. It's partly because the proceedings are slow. Were the EC election officers instructed to slow things down? Ah, another conspiracy theory!

Bersih issues an appeal to the EC to allow those who arrive at polling stations before 5pm to cast their votes. Former Bersih chairperson Ambiga says the EC can exercise its discretion to extend the voting hours "and has done it before". But the EC is adamant that voting must stop at the gazetted time. This means at 5pm, if you are still in the queue, too bad for you. You won't get into the polling booth. All doors will be shut.

At 2.41pm, a Twitter user posts a photo of an elderly voter seated in a wheelbarrow as polling clerks check her details. "This breaks my heart," reads the caption. There have been many other images posted of elderly Malaysians going to exercise their constitutional right, but this one says it all.

In fact, the determination of the elderly to go out and vote, many of them arriving at polling centres in wheelchairs, proves to be inspiring.

As Chong Pooi Koon tweets, "Overheard at my polling station this morning: my grandma is 95 this year. She just voted. Another aunty said: ya, those young ones really have no excuse not to come. Don't complain if you give up your rights."

Nauwar Shukri tweets, "I've been in line for over three hours because I'm in the most populated constituency in the country. But a high turnout is good. To keep my mind off my legs going numb, I'm going to look at this photo of my grandma going out to vote."

Sheena tweets about her grandma who is in her 70s. "She usually stays home cause she can't walk easily but she headed out determined to make her country a better place this morning. If my grandma can do it, so can you."

At 3pm, the EC announces that the turnout is 69%. PPBM is prompted to post on Facebook a desperate call, "Guys! Please call all your friends who have not voted to come out and vote. We need 85% turnout to ensure BN is toppled. Please. Help us! SOS!"

At a little past 4pm, with less than an hour to go, Bersih sends out a message telling those who lined up before 5pm to stay and insist on their right to vote.

"Do not go away even if the EC says you are too late. If you are already there and in queue before 5pm, the EC must allow you to vote and cannot ask you to leave. It is not your fault that they are too slow."

At around 4.30pm, *Free Malaysia Today* reports that the turnout in Sabah is at its lowest in recent times with only 67.49% and only 30 minutes left for polling.

This may not look good for Shafie Apdal's party, Warisan. And PH as a whole. Because they both concluded an electoral pact in April. Warisan would contest only in Sabah and lead the pact there. If they managed to form the state government, PH would have ministers in it. In return, if PH formed the government in Putrajaya, Warisan would have ministers in the Federal Cabinet.

It's an astute arrangement. PH knows it will not make much headway in Sabah on its own, and that it will also need parliamentary seats coming from Sabah to boost its total to form the federal government. Warisan, on the other hand, may need the seats won by the DAP and PKR in Sabah to have enough to form the state government. Both need each other. So making the deal is a win-win for both.

However, if the turnout is so low, will Warisan do well?

In the Peninsula, PH leaders are beginning to feel frustrated, especially with the long lines of voters still not getting to vote as the clock ticks on to 5pm.

PKR's Azmin and Nurul Izzah and PPBM's Rais Hussin call for an extension of the closing time. But the EC will not budge.

"We will close at 5pm for those not in the voting room," EC chairman Mohd Hashim tells RTM1. This is because votes cast past that time can be challenged in court, and counting has to start at 5pm.

And so at that designated hour, voting does stop. No statistic is given immediately on the total turnout. But it's generally surmised that it's lower than the 84.8% in GE13. That's not good.

At the Taman Dato' Harun school, one of the polling centres for the Petaling Jaya parliamentary and Taman Medan state seats, a commotion breaks out.

Twenty-six voters queuing up outside the school are shut out and prevented from entering the compound. Inside the school, 26 others who failed to get to the voting rooms in time are told they can't vote. They, however, refuse to leave. They insist on voting. Some of them have been waiting since 2pm.

They are being encouraged to stand their ground by about 250 voters who are also gathered outside the school gate. They have already voted but decide to stay back to provide moral support to their fellow voters.

At 6pm, a team of 13 Federal Reserve Unit personnel and 20 police officers are deployed to stand guard inside the school gates.

Maria Chin Abdullah, who is PH's candidate for the Petaling Jaya seat, tries to negotiate with the returning officer to extend voting for half an hour. The officer declines.

There is a stand-off and no sight of resolution. Maria and Syamsul Firdaus Mohamed Supri, PH's candidate for Taman Medan, finally get the voters to disperse after assuring them that they will lodge a police report and challenge the EC in court.

That evening, I decide to stay at home to wait for the election results because I have work to do. But I keep an eye out for the latest updates from *Malaysiakini*'s live reports and WhatsApp messages from friends.

The first result, but an unofficial one, comes out at 6.30pm. The victory goes to BN. For the parliamentary seat of Kalabakan which Abdul Ghapur Salleh has won for a fourth term,

PH's first victory, also unofficial, is DAP's in the state seat of Skudai in Johor.

At 7.10pm, Shafie Apdal has unofficially won the Semporna parliamentary seat. The victory, however, is expected.

Close to 8pm, after unofficial results establish that BN has lost five parliamentary seats in Sarawak, political scientist James Chin declares that the state is no longer considered BN's "fixed deposit".

"At the end of the day, vote-buying did not work simply because the Umno brand was too toxic. Sarawak BN made a mistake by saying 1MDB is an Umno problem and has nothing to do with Sarawak," he tells *Malaysiakini*.

Is this a prelude to more good news?

At 8.10pm, MCA's first top gun falls. Vice-president Chua Tee Yong has lost in the Labis parliamentary seat contest. Labis is in Johor.

This is followed by news that Prabakaran has won Batu. Good for him! He smashes Najib's 40-year-old record for youngest MP ever. Najib was 23 when he won the Pekan seat in 1978.

At 8.30pm, PAS has succeeded in capturing the Jengka state seat in Pahang. This is official as it comes from the EC. There goes INVOKE's prediction of PAS winning zero seats in the whole general election!

Good news at 8.35pm. The MIC's head honcho, S. Subramaniam, has lost the Segamat parliamentary seat in Johor after having held it for four terms.

It comes as a shock. He is the first minister in Najib's Cabinet to fall. And he is defeated by someone who is contesting for the first time in an election, PKR's Edmund Santhara Kumar Ramanaidu.

What's more, just two days earlier, Subramaniam had given out a replanting incentive of RM4,000 each to 250 settlers in two Felda settlements in Johor. Looks like the pork barrelling didn't help.

Although Subramaniam is my former classmate in school, I am elated.

Because if a top gun like him has been rejected, it could mean that more top heads are going to roll!

True enough, two deputy ministers lose in Muar and Ledang. And a BN state executive councillor also loses in Sekijang. All three seats are in Johor. Does this show that PH might just win Johor after all?

In Sarawak, another unexpected victory comes up. Sarawak PKR chief Baru Bian has captured Selangau, a BN stronghold.

It's getting exciting. At 8.48pm, I post on Facebook: "It looks to me from the voting pattern that the Malays are indeed split three ways. This is encouraging for Pakatan Harapan which also enjoys massive non-Malay support. Will we see a new government installed, my friends? Will we see a new dawn for Malaysia? Have Malaysians finally woken up? Will we see the birth of the two-party system? Did we do our part?"

At 9pm, PAS wins its first parliamentary seat after capturing Setiu in Terengganu. INVOKE is wrong again!

Shortly after comes another big blow for BN. MCA president Liow Tiong Lai has been defeated in the parliamentary seat of Bentong in Pahang after having held it for four terms. Is the MCA falling apart?

In Baling, Kedah, BN's Abdul Azeez Abdul Rahim, chairman of Lembaga Tabung Haji, or the Hajj Pilgrims Fund Board, surprisingly loses to a PAS candidate. Or is it that surprising after all?

Najib, however, is successful in defending his Pekan parliamentary seat in Pahang. But with a majority less than what he got in 2013. Then, he obtained a 35,613-vote majority. Now it's 24,859.

Mahathir is also successful in Langkawi. This makes him eligible to be prime minister if PH forms the government. One of the candidates he has defeated is BN's Nawawi Ahmad, the guy who once stupidly wrote on Facebook that MO1 was the King.

More revealing results. PKR has snatched the Tanjung Malim parliamentary seat from BN. This is the first time ever that the Opposition has won in the biggest Felda area in Perak, with 10 Felda settlements.

Is there a "Malay tsunami" against BN after all?

And speaking of Felda, its chairman, Shahrir Samad, has indeed lost Johor Bahru as predicted by INVOKE! By an unexpectedly huge majority too!

At 10pm, the PH chief for Negeri Sembilan, Aminuddin Harun, declares that a "*tsunami rakyat*" has swept through the state and PH will form the state government.

DAP's Charles Santiago warns PH supporters to refrain from celebrating if PH forms the new government. And PKR's R. Sivarasa cautions against doing anything impulsive. They advise supporters to wait for directions from PH leaders.

The fear is strong that Najib might not accept the election results if BN were to lose and the outbreak of a violent incident could give him the opportunity to invoke the National Security Council Act 2016, which could lead to a state of emergency.

On May 4, Mahathir had said, "There is a rumour I have heard … that Umno will create trouble. They have thugs who will create trouble and there will be a state of emergency or a state of national security, then Parliament will not be called, and the rule of law will be suspended." Ah, but that's just a rumour, right?

At around 10.30pm, *Free Malaysia Today* reports that in a WhatsApp text made available to it, the press secretary of Kedah caretaker *menteri besar* Ahmad Bashah Md Hanipah "has conceded that BN could possibly lose Kedah".

Wow! The "Malay tsunami" has happened, eh?

In Pulai, Johor, Nur Jazlan gets his just dessert when he is defeated by Amanah's Salahuddin Ayub.

Just five months before, he had disputed a study by the ISEAS-Yusof Ishak Institute of Singapore saying that his constituency would fall to the Opposition. He had said it would not be easy. But now he has lost by a whopping majority of nearly 29,000!

Perhaps one or two of the votes came from overseas.

Sad news, however, comes after 11pm. PH's brilliant strategist Liew

Chin Tong has been defeated by Wee Ka Siong in Ayer Hitam. Even more sad, Wee has won by a razor-thin majority of only 303 votes.

Chin Tong knew it would be an uphill battle against the MCA's deputy president, but he sacrificed himself nonetheless for "a battle that is nationally symbolic, in which we present a choice between the new government and the old government".

Close to midnight, Mahathir announces that according to unofficial results, PH has won six states, namely, Penang, Melaka, Selangor, Negeri Sembilan, Johor and Kedah.

He also claims that the coalition has won more than the 112 parliamentary seats required to form the federal government. And he's waiting for the parliamentary seats won by Warisan in Sabah to add to the total.

The EC, however, has not confirmed Mahathir's claim. It has been slow in announcing official results.

The situation is getting tense. I must be feeling like millions of others who are dying for change, holding back exultation. We know that nothing is for certain until the EC declares it, but it seems to be delaying.

Twitter user Guo Zhang tweets a message that brings some comic relief, "Come on, man. We're Asians. We do NOT take that long to count."

At 12.30am, Nurul Izzah says she's confident that PH has already secured the mandate to form the next federal government. "I hope Malaysians will experience a smooth, safe and peaceful transition for a better Malaysia," she says.

At 1.10am, Mohd Hashim announces the results for five states. Finally. But they are for Penang, Perlis, Kelantan, Terengganu and Pahang. Only the first is won by PH. Kelantan and Terengganu go to PAS, and the remaining two to BN.

"*Yang lain belum lagi* (the rest not yet)," he tells reporters. He also denies that anything suspicious is going on.

No? Then why is he holding back announcing the other states won by

PH, if Mahathir's claim is to be believed? Is the EC employing the same tactic as it did for GE13?

It's getting frustrating waiting for answers that are not forthcoming. I can imagine what Mahathir and PH leaders and MPs gathered at the Sheraton Hotel in Petaling Jaya, Selangor, are feeling.

At 1.30am, BN's Khaled Nordin is officially declared to have lost both the Pasir Gudang parliamentary and Permas state seats. INVOKE has got this one right as well!

More cheer as another two ministers are beaten. One is Ahmad Shabery Cheek and the other is Rahman Dahlan, who has been much reviled for his steadfast defence of Najib.

This is capped by the EC's official announcement of PH winning Negeri Sembilan.

The EC also confirms that PH has so far won 91 parliamentary seats, BN 67 and PAS 14. Independent candidates have won three while Parti Solidariti Tanah Airku in Sabah has won one.

This leaves a remainder of 46 seats yet to be announced. PH needs another 21 to win, but it can also rely on Warisan to add more.

But speaking of Warisan, the EC has so far been announcing only a few results from Sabah. Ironically, though, it has almost finished announcing those of the bigger state of Sarawak. What is going on?

At 2.30am, I whoop with delight to note that minister and Najib champion Salleh Said Keruak has also lost. That is sweet.

Next is Perak caretaker *menteri besar* Zambry Abd Kadir, defeated in Lumut.

I'm reminded of what I wrote in my book *March 8: The Day Malaysia Woke Up* about my response to the exhilarating results of GE12 confirming the defeats of BN top guns in 2008: "It was like watching a B-movie western in which the bad guys bit the dust one by one."

The same thing is happening now but even more "bad guys" are biting the dust, and the feeling I'm getting is many times more exhilarating! After 10 years since of struggling to get here, I'd say the reward is supergratifying!

Meanwhile, as the long night's journey goes into morning, the EC confirms that Johor, the birthplace of Umno, has fallen to PH. It won 36 seats, BN won 19, and PAS won one. A decisive victory. This is the icing on the cake.

Selangor remains with PH with a thumping two-thirds majority. PH won 51 seats, BN four, and PAS, which had won 15 in GE13 when it was part of Pakatan Rakyat, now is left with only one.

The assembly in Perak is hung. Of the 59 seats, PH has 29, BN 27, and PAS three. As 30 state seats are required to form a simple majority, PAS is in a position to be the kingmaker.

In Kedah, there is also no clear majority although PH has 18 seats. PAS has 15 and BN three. If BN and PAS join forces, this will result in a hung assembly. Then it will be up to the Sultan of Kedah to decide who becomes *menteri besar*. By convention, the Sultan will choose a representative from the party with the highest number of seats.

At 2.30am, Najib's press aide announces to the media that Najib is expected to hold a press conference at 11am.

Why then? Why not now? If he has realised that BN has lost, why doesn't he just concede defeat and pledge a smooth transition of power? Does he have something up his sleeve?

It turns out he is in "a state of shock", "traumatised". These are words he would use when he is to speak to the media nearly two months later about his reaction to the results. He does not give a press conference because: "It is not easy to meet the press the same night, for I had to gather my thoughts and get the final results."

He does, however, call Anwar twice, Reuters is to report a week later. Anwar is to tell the news agency that Najib was thinking of what he could do and whom he could consult, but did not approach him for a deal to shift allegiance in any "serious manner".

"After the second call he was totally shattered," Anwar would say. "He was just very evasive ... he refused to concede early. ... I advised him as a friend to concede and move on."

Asked about this later, Najib would say, "I think that conversation should be best left on a private basis."

That night, he is also probably busy planning the transfer of cash and valuable items in his and Rosmah's possession to safe havens. Because on May 12, police raiding six residences linked to Najib are to seize cash in 26 currencies amounting to RM116.7 million as well as 12,000 pieces of jewellery, 284 designer handbags, 423 luxury watches and 234 pairs of sunglasses.

Police are to estimate the total value of the seizure at as much as RM1.1 billion.

Meanwhile, back to GE14, at 2.30am, *Malaysiakini* calls a victory for PH. The online news website's unofficial tally has PH leading with 114 seats, slightly more than half the total of 222.

The EC has still not confirmed this, but at 2.50am, Mahathir tells the media that the new prime minister will be sworn in later today.

He says the king has summoned to the palace the leader of PKR, since this is the party whose logo PH used in the elections.

Mahathir also pledges that the new government will work on getting Anwar a royal pardon. "Once he is pardoned, he will be eligible to stand for elections to be an MP. Because in our country, a person has to be an MP or senator first before he can be prime minister."

When asked whether action will be taken against Najib over the scandals he is alleged to be involved in, Mahathir says, "We are not seeking revenge. We are seeking to restore the rule of law. If anybody breaks the law, they will be brought before the court."

He says he has asked the chief secretary to the Government to announce today and tomorrow as public holidays, as promised by the coalition.

"But there is no holiday for the victors," he quips.

At 3am, too ecstatic to sleep, I write on Facebook:

"WE HAVE WON! WE HAVE WON! ... We will have a new government! ... We have also brought to reality the two-party system. From now on, the political system should be improved. Let us all keep a close watch on the new government to ensure that it delivers. In the days to come, may we have a better Malaysia.

"Well done, my fellow Malaysians. We the *rakyat* won on May 9. We made history. And we showed we had the power to bring down the mighty BN. We came of age. Let us never forget the power we have as we move forward towards a brighter future."

After I've hit the 'Post' button to send out my thoughts to the public, it finally sinks in.

PH has won! Umno-BN is kicked out at last. After 61 years! We are liberated at last. I never thought I would live to see this day! I weep with joy uncontrollably.

And in my heart I say, "This is the real Merdeka!"

'WE DID IT!'

Our nation is reborn! It's a new day. We have been given a second chance.

— **Dennis Ignatius**
(political commentator and former ambassador)

This shows that no matter how strong and powerful a government is, ultimately its own arrogance and perception of invincibility would be its Achilles heel ... This general election is proof that there is a limit that is drawn and defined by the collective conscience of the people in any democracy.

— **Art Harun**
(lawyer and political commentator, appointed new Election Commission chairman in September 2018)

We, the Malaysian public, have regained our pride and our faith in ourselves and each other. Now we can look forward to ushering in an era of change or *ubah*! So congratulate yourselves, Malaysians, and pat yourselves on your backs – you bloody well deserve it.

— **P. Gunasegaram**
(business journalist and author of 1MDB:
The Scandal that Brought Down a Government)

Despite clumsy and desperate attempts by the compromised
Malaysian Communications and Multimedia Commission to block
the GE14 results being reported by *Malaysiakini* and equally pathetic
and annoying attempts by the EC to delay confirming the results,
and despite delays in the swearing-in of the new PH government, the
Malaysian public patiently waited. And the rest, as they say, is history.

– Zaharom Nain

(media studies professor at Nottingham University Malaysia
and political commentator)

Malaysia's political landscape has been transformed by the ouster
of Prime Minister Najib Razak and the ruling United Malays
National Organisation.

– Wong Chin Huat

(political scientist and activist)

What we have seen in Malaysia is what history has shown in
countries with authoritarian rule: when political elites feud, regime
change can occur … As for the Malaysian electorate, who should
be congratulated for instituting this long-overdue regime change,
they are now well aware that they do have the power to discipline
politicians who do not govern in the interest of the nation.

– Terence Gomez

(professor of political economy and author of Minister of Finance
Incorporated: Ownership and Control of Corporate Malaysia*)*

On May 10, Malaysians wake up to a day like no other.

My friend Azmi Sharom writes, "This morning, after a mere three hours'
sleep, I woke up. And like so many of us blessed and cursed by smartphones,
I reached for my device to check my messages. There was one from an older
colleague. There were no words, just a video. I touched the screen and the

first few notes of my national anthem started to play. I couldn't help myself. The tears rolled down my face and I cried like a newborn baby … which in a way, I suppose I was."

Like Azmi, many feel reborn in a country that's been given a second chance. A second chance to restore the rule of law, repair the sullied institutions, unite the different races, work towards prosperity, inculcate positive values, and make Malaysia a great and respectable country.

Looking very much forward to that, many people express their heartfelt gratitude on social media to Mahathir.

Twitter user @viveksharmaaa pours out his heart, "Thank you, Tun, you're truly a living legend. Thank you for saving us, this is as good as a modern MERDEKA."

Wan Azizah is not forgotten.

Nuha Jes Izman tweets, "Can we take some time to acknowledge the fact that Wan Azizah supported her husband through YEARS of political ambush, raised her kids while he was locked up and is now the FIRST ever female deputy PM of Malaysia!!! She is the kind of ROCK this country deserves."

Aysha Ridzuan feels "damn good" to know she made a change. "WE DID IT!"

Roshen Maghhan echoes that. "We did it. We've finally made history. For years, we've been the victims of self-centred and ignorant politicians. Hopefully, it ends here today. Welcome back, Malaysia, I've missed you."

Some netizens credit PH's success to Rafizi Ramli who founded INVOKE. Justin Lim tweets, "Everyone thanking Mahathir but it is Rafizi who engineered this win from behind."

William Lee says Rafizi "has done and sacrificed so much for this to happen". He says there are more people to thank "but I want to start with Rafizi".

Rafizi tweets back to say he has just dropped by INVOKE and thanked his staff who took two years off their careers to help. "These are the unsung heroes."

A Twitter user with the handle @JustinTWJ articulates succinctly a central factor of the GE14 victory: "Let us never forget this day. We made it happen. We made sure our voices were heard. Whether you're 15 or 95, you played a part in it as long as you opened your mouth. Even if you just tweeted once, you still played a part. This is the power of the people."

Journalist A. Kathirasen writes on *Free Malaysia Today* that when he watched the television commentary on the election results the night before, he was amazed at how the mainstream media had allowed thoughts to be expressed openly on issues such as 1MDB that used to be considered off-limits.

"It appeared as if the dam had been broken, and the water was gushing out. … And it was due to the fact that BN had been defeated; that Najib no longer held power," he writes. Because prior to that, most Malaysians had been living "in a climate of fear" and "did not have the guts to fight back".

"Yesterday, it was not just those guys on TV who were talking about it openly and honestly," he notes. "Even ordinary people were posting stuff or sending WhatsApp messages with candour, even abandon."

He says the real winner of GE14 is "the ordinary Malaysian", and that "the most important outcome" is that finally, the Malaysian voter realises that they wield the real power. "They now know that if the PH government forgets its pledges or begins to stifle their freedoms, or oppresses them or disregards their rights and needs, they can rise up again. They have got back their guts."

A new meme that goes viral sums up that point concisely and precisely: "Politicians can no longer frighten us with May 13. We can now frighten them with May 9!" Well said!

The GE14 result hits the headlines. *Sinar Harian* has a compelling one: '*Tsunami Rakyat*'. But *Kosmo!* does one better with '*Tsunami rakyat tenggelamkan BN*' (People's tsunami sinks BN).

Of the international headlines, *The Guardian* runs with 'Malaysia's former leader set to become world's oldest PM at 92'. It sounds rather funny, but it's a fact.

But the best is *The New York Times*' 'A stunning, sudden fall for Najib Razak, Malaysia's "Man of Steal"'.

Zunar must have felt honoured and vindicated by the reference to the title of his book of cartoons. It is a fitting tribute truly deserved.

So, it's out everywhere now. There's no mistaking the fact that PH has won GE14. The official result has even been confirmed by the EC, albeit only at 3.50am, four hours later than when Mahathir called it at 11.50pm the night before.

The voter turnout was 82.32%.

The Malay swing was not quite a tsunami, but it was a major wave. However, PH got only 25 to 30% of the Malay vote. PAS did better with 30-33%. The remaining 35 to 40% voted for BN.

But 19 out of 52 constituencies with Felda settlements were won by PH, thus the coalition did manage to erode BN's traditional power base.

PH was supported overwhelmingly by 95% of the Chinese electorate, an increase of 10% from 2013, and 70 to 75% of the Indian voters.

So, yes, it was a *tsunami rakyat*.

The Government to be formed will include PH's 113 MPs, Warisan's eight and the independent from Batu, P. Prabakaran. All these add up to 122.

Among PH's component parties, PKR won the most seats with 47. The DAP bagged 42, PPBM 13, and Amanah 11.

BN won 79 seats, which is a big drop from the 133 it won in GE13.

PAS ends up with 18 seats, three fewer than in GE13, which is, however, better than expected. INVOKE had predicted it would not get a single parliamentary or state seat.

The MCA won only one parliamentary seat, down from seven in GE13. This is its worst showing ever.

The MIC won two. And Gerakan lost its sole seat when its president, Mah Siew Keong, was defeated in Teluk Intan. The MCA and MIC presidents were also defeated.

On the whole, BN's eight ministers and 19 deputy ministers were rejected by the voters. I have long maintained that Najib's administration was a kakistocracy, i.e. a government made up of the least suitable or competent, and written a few books showing up their stupid utterings and laughable deeds. I'm chuffed that the people agree they're just not the right stuff and booted them out.

PH got 47.33% of the popular vote with 5.51 million votes. BN scored the lowest in its history with 36.42% (4.24 million votes). And PAS got 14.04% (1.63 million votes).

PH overcame BN in the states of Negeri Sembilan, Johor and Melaka while retaining Penang and Selangor.

BN lost Terengganu to PAS, which retains Kelantan.

BN is left with only three states, namely, Pahang, Perlis and Sarawak.

The formation of state governments in Perak, Kedah and Sabah is still hanging in the balance as there is no party with a simple majority in all three states.

Maria Chin Abdullah goes to Parliament after winning Petaling Jaya, on her first outing as a politician after switching from being a Bersih activist.

Hishammuddin Hussein won Sembrong. INVOKE got that one wrong. Still, two out of three ain't bad since INVOKE got the defeats of Shahrir Samad and Khaled Nordin correct.

Jokes start going round. One of the best is:

"Malaysian politics:

The 4th PM [meaning Mahathir] put the 8th PM [meaning Anwar] in jail 20 years ago, but returned as the 7th PM to release the 8th PM and put the 6th PM [meaning Najib] in jail after the 6th PM put the 8th PM in jail.

Wahseh! Even Bollywood and Hollywood are impressed!"

But there is no 7th prime minister yet. The swearing-in will take place only at 9.30am today. The media is already waiting at Istana Negara (National Palace) on Jalan Duta, Kuala Lumpur.

But the ceremony does not take place. It has suddenly been postponed, and no one is sure why. It is understood that an announcement will be made later.

Responding to this, lawyer Brian Jit Singh starts an online petition calling on the Conference of Rulers to endorse the PH government and promptly "declare a Government for Malaysia". In just three hours, it garners a phenomenal 220,000 signatures.

Meanwhile, the focus switches to the Umno headquarters in the Putra World Trade Centre, Kuala Lumpur, as Najib is set to give his post-election address at 11am.

The question on everyone's mind is, will he concede defeat graciously and hand over power smoothly and peaceably?

He starts off saying he "accepts the verdict of the people". Well and good. But he also points out that no party has won enough seats to form a federal government and so it is up to the King to decide who will be the 7th prime minister of Malaysia.

"It will be based on who commands support from the majority of members of Parliament," he says.

This is not quite conceding power. In fact, in saying that there is no party with enough seats to form the government he is trying to create confusion by not recognising PH as a coalition. Sneaky fella.

He has known all along that the PH that contested against his BN is a coalition at least in spirit if not in registered form and yet he is now splitting hairs. Did not the component parties discard their own logos to embrace a common one, thus behaving like a coalition? Besides, is the speculation wrong that the RoS refused to register PH as a coalition because of his say-so?

After Najib's address, Mahathir calls a press conference at the Sheraton Hotel in Petaling Jaya, Selangor, at around midday.

He says, "We want to make it clear that there is an urgency here to form the government today, because currently, there is no Government of Malaysia." As such, he hopes the King will swear him in at 5pm.

According to *The Straits Times*, however, a source close to the palace has informed the Singapore newspaper that "the palace would prefer not to hold a swearing-in this week". OMG! What are they thinking in there?

Why do they want to delay it? Come next week, Malaysia would be facing huge uncalled-for problems!

Mahathir is right in wanting to form the government as soon as possible. The longer this swearing-in delay drags out, the more it is going to be perceived by the world that a political crisis is looming. And that can prove to be financially damaging for the country because investor confidence will slump. The value of the ringgit and other things will be under threat. It cannot wait. And certainly not till next week!

Besides, Mahathir already has the support of enough parliamentarians to be sworn in as prime minister. The Federal Constitution says that as long as there is someone who enjoys such support, the King is obliged to appoint that person for the post.

"It doesn't say that he should have the support of any party," Mahathir rightly says. "Just majority of support from members of Parliament, that's all."

He also says that all PH MPs have signed a letter to support him as the prime minister and this will be presented to the King. "We will deliver this even though it is not the requirement for the naming of a prime minister."

He again stresses, "We need to have this government today without delay. There is a lot of work that needs to be done. There is a lot of mess in the country and we need to attend to this mess as soon as possible."

Mahathir also speaks about what happened in the morning. Instead of asking to see him, the King had asked to see Wan Azizah instead, because she is the leader of the party whose logo all the four parties used in the elections.

However, he assures the media that the "matter is being cleared up" because the leaders of the four parties are writing to the palace to support him for prime minister.

All right then. We shall wait and see what happens at 5pm.

Meanwhile, at around 1.30pm, the letter of support from PH leaders is delivered to and received by the palace.

At 2.45pm, the palace receives the official results of GE14 from the EC.

At 4.40pm, Mahathir and Siti Hasmah arrive at the palace in a Proton Perdana limousine with the number plate 'Proton 2020'. They are warmly cheered by hundreds of people already gathered outside the palace since 3pm or even earlier.

Mahathir is wearing a *songkok* (headgear) and traditional black *baju Melayu* (Malay outfit). He is met by Wan Azizah, Muhyiddin, Guan Eng and Mat Sabu.

Anticipation and excitement are building up among the well-wishers outside the palace. The crowd reacts every time a vehicle goes in or out of the palace.

The Star reports that veterinarian Calvin Cheah is waiting with four family members and friends, waving the Malaysian and PKR flags. "I think this is the moment every Malaysian is eager to see. I want to witness history being made," he says.

Oil and gas technician R. Ramachandran is there to show his support for Mahathir. "There is a change and I want to celebrate it," he says as he holds high a big PKR flag.

Amin Ashaari tweets to say the atmosphere is "awesome".

But the wait continues and at 5.30pm comes this disturbing tweet from Channel NewsAsia correspondent Sumisha Naidu: "JUST IN: Palace says not confirmed that Dr Mahathir will be sworn in today after all."

Then at 6.17pm, PKR MP Sivarasa tweets, "This is an audience – not a swearing-in. Purpose – to satisfy Agong that Tun M commands the confidence of the majority of MPs."

What? The King is still not satisfied? So when will he be satisfied enough to swear Mahathir in?

Anxiety builds up. Is PH going to be deprived of becoming the Government? Is there going to be a hitch in the process? Is something sinister hatching in some meeting room somewhere?

If the saga of GE14 were a three-act drama or a movie, the uncertainty of the swearing-in would have to be its second climax. After the first climax of Election Day on May 9.

Actually, something did happen this morning when Wan Azizah met with the King but Mahathir ignored to tell the media about this at his subsequent midday press conference.

What happened was, the King asked Wan Azizah to become prime minister instead.

To her great credit, Wan Azizah declined. She told the King she would honour the promise made by the coalition to appoint Mahathir for the position.

Wan Azizah then asked the King to pardon Anwar and release him immediately. He agreed to it.

All this is to be publicly divulged only on May 17 by Anwar himself, a day after he is to be released from prison.

So why did the King offer the job to Wan Azizah when it was common knowledge that Mahathir was the chosen one? Is it because Mahathir is not liked by some of the country's royal houses?

Well, in 1993, when he was prime minister the first time, he did amend the Federal Constitution to take away the legal immunity of the royals.

And more recently in 2016 and 2017, he was engaged in spats with the Sultan of Johor.

One was over the Sultan's *bangsa Johor* (Johor race) concept which Mahathir criticised as a parochial idea that could divide the people of Malaysia.

The other was over the proliferation of building projects in Johor undertaken by mainland Chinese companies but backed by the Sultan which Mahathir said amounted to selling Malaysia's sovereignty and making the country look like a satellite state of Beijing.

He slammed the construction of the US$42 billion Forest City project, co-invested in by the Sultan, warning that it would undermine national sovereignty because Chinese nationals would be buying most of the properties there and moving in to stay.

He even said, rather nastily, "I hope Forest City will truly become a forest … and its residents will consist of baboons, monkeys and so on."

Both times, the Sultan was livid and shot back at Mahathir. Over the second issue, he accused Mahathir of "playing the politics of fear and race".

Then a month before GE14, Johor crown prince Tunku Ismail posted on Facebook a warning to the people of the state against being "fooled by a forked tongue individual" who was "not trying to save the country" but was "more worried about what will happen to his children in the future". He was referring to Mahathir without naming him.

Then he entered a zone that he was not allowed to. He said he was aware that people were "discouraged by the leadership of the country", but he urged them not to "change the boat if the engine is not broken, don't even change the skipper". Instead, they should allow him and his father, the Sultan, to work with the "skipper".

He was interfering in politics. He was telling the people of Johor how to vote. And he was suggesting that the royal household play a political role in working with Najib and Umno.

He was slammed for it on the blog *FinanceTwitter*: "What type of grass has the Johor crown prince been smoking? The boat isn't working because its engine has been stolen by none other than the skipper. That's the only reason why the people want to change the skipper. ... It appears that the prince's agenda is very different from that of the people. The Royal Household of Johor doesn't need to worry about putting food on the table. And they certainly do not need to worry about GST or fuel prices as they drive fleets of Ferrari and Lambo flanked by bodyguards."

Johoreans and other Malaysians reacted in more than 13,000 comments to the crown prince's post mostly to disagree with him and to tell him that as a privileged royal, he couldn't understand or empathise with their daily struggle with the rising cost of living which they blamed on BN. They said they were suffering and directly called for a change of federal government. They also reminded him that under the system of constitutional monarchy, he should not show political favouritism.

One commentor went further and addressed all the royal households in the land: "Where are the royal houses when the *rakyat* are being squeezed by GST? Where are the royal houses when more of the *rakyat* are becoming homeless and getting less food to eat? Not getting jobs? Parents have to beg to pay for their sick children's medicine? Where are the royal houses when the subsidies for health, education and daily needs are cut to pay debts incurred by Najib? Where are the royal houses when the judiciary is now defending corruption? Where are the royal houses?! Why shouldn't we choose HARAPAN and Tun M?"

A retired colonel wrote disagreeing with the idea of the Johor palace guiding the "skipper". This can only be interpreted as "the need to have a puppet skipper that the palace can control" for "its own personal gains". He called on the prince to renounce his royalty and contest as a politician to "lead the people as an ordinary man" and earn their trust. Until then, "I cannot trust you".

The Straits Times called the strong public pushback "remarkable" because many of the commenters didn't care about the risk of being hauled up under the Sedition Act for "insulting" royalty.

Mahathir's response was classic cool. He said the crown prince's criticism would only make PH "more popular". Judging by the eventual fall of Johor to PH, he might just have been right.

In 2017, the Selangor Sultan also had an axe to grind with Mahathir. He took umbrage against Mahathir's comment about Malaysia being led by a prime minister who was descended from "Bugis pirates". He must have felt insulted because the Selangor sultanate also came from Bugis ancestors.

He called Mahathir "a very dangerous man" and also "an angry man" who "will burn the whole country with his anger". He claimed that his sentiment was shared by all of the country's nine sultans.

Mahathir responded to that in his typical jokey, sarcastic way, "Yes, I am a very angry man, you can see how angry I am. I will burn you, I am always burning things."

Following that, Mahathir and his wife, Siti Hasmah, gave back to the palace the state royal awards they had been bestowed years before.

Those were just the sultans. Mahathir also had a stormy relationship with the Kelantan palace beginning in 1990, when the King's father was the state's sultan.

In the elections then, BN lost the state government to PAS and was wiped out in Kelantan. Tengku Razaleigh and his Semangat 46 party were collaborating with PAS and it seems their victory was helped by the Sultan's support.

BN under Mahathir reacted by punishing the state in several ways and launching attacks on the royal house to embarrass the Sultan. There was even talk of a plot masterminded by Umno to topple him.

The memory of that painful period must still have been strong for the King at the time of his installation in December 2016 because Mahathir was left out of the guest list for that event. An invitation letter was, however, inadvertently sent to him, but when the mistake was realised, a second letter was dispatched to retract the invitation. It was a big embarrassment for the former prime minister.

So now, is Mahathir's past relationship with the Kelantan palace a stumbling block to his own installation as prime minister?

Perhaps not. But even so, if it was, the old hand at the game knows that nothing like that can block him from his goal.

When asked earlier by the media whether the delay in his swearing-in was because the royalty did not like him, Mahathir said, partly in jest, "I don't know about not liking me. I'm a very nice person. I have the support of the majority of the members of Parliament. That is what the provision of the Constitution says. It doesn't say, 'I like you, I don't like you, I love you'."

It takes a person in control of the situation to talk like that. He knows that under the Federal Constitution, the King is obliged to appoint him. There is no alternative.

It is the *rakyat* who are more anxious than he is. They have waited years, decades to see a new government in place. Try denying them that and goodness knows what hell might break loose!

Lawyer and activist Ambiga Sreenevasan calms everyone with her tweet: "Chill, folks. No one can act contrary to the will of the people who have spoken loud and clear and in such overwhelming numbers. I am sure Tun M will be sworn in soon. Constitutionally, the King will appoint the person who enjoys the majority of the House."

Someone sends out this playful meme for comic relief: "We vote from AM to PM, wait for results from PM to AM, now wait from AM to PM, but still no PM."

Anyway, at 6.48pm, Bernama tweets the information that the leaders of the four component parties of PH have completed their audience with the King.

Ten minutes later, Bernama and *New Straits Times* report that the swearing-in ceremony will now be held at 9.30pm.

This is confirmed by Mahathir's son, Mukhriz, who writes on Facebook, "After much waiting, my father has got the approval to be sworn in as the Prime Minister of Malaysia at 9.30pm."

The crowd cheer. It should be for sure this time, right?

Emma Melissa, who is among those waiting outside the palace, tweets, "Drama at Istana Negara? Who knows? Not here to speculate. We will still wait for our next prime minister, however long it takes."

Atiqah Nazir is more positive in her tweet, "It's happening, guys!!! *Malaysia Boleh*! (Malaysia Can!) We're ready to have our new government!"

Istana Negara finally issues a statement to confirm that it's happening. It also "strongly refutes" any allegations suggesting that the King delayed Mahathir's appointment.

On hearing the news, overjoyed supporters outside the palace wave PKR and Malaysian flags and sing the national anthem 'Negaraku' (My Country). Cars passing by honk their support.

"We are so happy, such a proud day for Malaysia," says David Thaiga.

Valerene Matthews enthuses, "Malaysia's full potential has yet to be tapped and now there's a greater possibility that it will be realised with better governance! I am full of hope for a better future."

And so at 10.05pm on the 10th of May, Mahathir Mohamad is finally sworn in as Malaysia's seventh prime minister. For the second term. At the age of 92. He sets a new record by becoming the oldest elected leader in the world.

New jokes make the rounds: "The retirement age has just been revised to 95" … "Malaysia is an environmentally friendly nation, we even recycled our PM" … "The man whose face they cut away from election billboards is now the man whose portrait will be hung in their offices … karma."

Well, love him or hate him, the man who once described himself as a political genius in an interview with *The Asian Wall Street Journal* has done it. The PH government is in business. The nation breathes a huge sigh of relief.

Amin Ashaari proudly tweets, "We got to escort our newly minted prime minister from Istana Negara all the way to Sheraton PJ. It was an honour. He waved at us!"

At his first press conference as prime minister at Sheraton Hotel, Mahathir shows gratitude for the people's support.

"What amazed us was the number of people who waited from 5pm until we came out of the palace. Their enthusiasm was fantastic. The reception I received when my car was driving here to Sheraton Hotel was amazing," he says.

"We want to thank the people. Nobody has seen the kind of support that we have seen for Pakatan Harapan." I'm sure he means it.

I suppose the support he has seen as an underdog Opposition figure is different from the support he saw when he was a BN Establishment figure. The difference in sincerity and genuinity would have been appreciable. Now I guess he knows what real support is, and how much more meaningful it truly feels. This one comes from years of guts, sweat and tears. He has now been on both sides of the fence; is it likely he will revert to his old self and his old ways?

Anwar Ibrahim will be pardoned in a few days. The state governments of

'WE DID IT!'

Kedah, Perak and Sabah will be formed after some political horse-trading, all in favour of PH.

After 20 years of fighting for *reformasi*, PKR is now in the Federal Government.

After five decades of struggle and sacrifice to uphold the principles of democracy, justice and equality, for which he suffered detention without trial twice, Lim Kit Siang finally sees his party, the DAP, in the Federal Government.

Mahathir did a sterling job of steering PH to victory. His experience in winning elections was a great asset, so was his stature as former prime minister and acceptability by some of the Malay voters. Frankly, without him, PH wouldn't have won. But he cannot be solely credited for the coalition's triumph either.

PKR had laid the groundwork with *reformasi*, which resonated especially with the young and the reform-minded.

The DAP had been working the Chinese ground for decades. It succeeded in attracting a phenomenal 95% of Chinese support by convincing the community that it would be a far better alternative to the MCA.

Guan Eng will be appointed finance minister, the first time a non-Malay fills this all-important portfolio in 44 years.

He will reveal that the national debt has exceeded a staggering RM1 trillion, not just RM685.1 billion as declared by Najib in June 2017. This is partly because Najib's government gave guarantees to companies, like 1MDB which now can't repay its debt.

Guan Eng will also reveal that Malaysian taxpayers are obliged to pay back that debt plus interest to the tune of RM50 billion right up till 2039.

How did this terrible burden come to fall on the people? How could anyone have been so irresponsible as to bring the country to such a massive financial catastrophe? Imagine what would have happened if BN had won GE14. What would that have done to the country ultimately?

My friend Sargunan Sockalingam, a doctor, calls the disaster 1MDEB (DEB standing for *Dasar Ekonomi Baru*, the Malay name for the NEP).

He says a monster like 1MDB could come about only because the NEP provided the "fertile ground" for it to grow. The NEP, by according special economic privileges to a particular race, entrenched the idea of "limitless entitlement" among the elite who then irresponsibly exploited money that they did not have to work hard for to feed their own greed.

Sargunan has a good point, and Malaysians must never let that happen again. However, I'd like to say that in all fairness to the artchitects of the NEP, they did not design it to last inordinately long. It was Mahathir who allowed it to carry on after 1990.

Malaysia's 2nd deputy prime minister, Ismail Abdul Rahman, who had a hand in creating the NEP, likened the policy to a handicap for the Malays that "will enable them to be good players, as in golf" but in time would be removed.

"The Malays must not think of these privileges as permanent: For then, they will not put effort into their tasks. In fact, it is an insult for the Malays to be getting these privileges," he said.

Ismail was a respected deputy at a more enlightened time to Abdul Razak Hussein, Najib's father. If Razak were alive today, it's likely he would be ashamed to see what his son has done.

By September 2018, Najib will have been slapped with 32 charges, ranging from receiving illegal monies to abuse of power to money laundering to criminal breach of trust.

Rosmah will have been charged in October 2018 with 17 counts of money laundering and tax evasion.

The couple will have made history, Najib by being the first Malaysian ex-prime minister ever to face criminal charges and Rosmah by being the first ex-premier's wife to do the same.

And it could only have happened because of the historic victory achieved on May 9. A victory considered improbable. A victory of underdogs against overwhelming favourites. Which makes it a hundred, a thousand, 2.6 billion times more precious!

But the victory would not have been possible without the desire, the help and the support of the people. They wanted it. And they helped in ways big and small. Members of civil society organisations, activists, cartoonists, artists, students, analysts, writers, bloggers, journalists, editors, lawyers, video creators, video producers, meme creators, political party volunteers, polling agents, data gatherers, researchers, fieldworkers, donors, carpoolers, anyone who ever attended *ceramahs* and political party fund-raising dinners, anyone who ever tweeted, WhatsApped, posted on Facebook anything that was political, anyone who ever took part in demonstrations and rallies … they all made it happen.

This was their victory. They took responsibility for their country. They took it back from the kleptocrats and the kakistocrats. They saved it from a party that cared more for being in power than for the country and its future. They saved it from heading towards ruin.

They worked for it. They rallied for it. They got arrested for it. They sweat in the hot sun, yelled for change with gusto, marched in the rain with dignity, faced tear gas with grit and nerve. When times were hard, they kept pressing on. When they felt despondent, they kept up their spirits. When they faced defeat, they did not give up. They tried and tried until they won.

So this was not just Mahathir's victory, or Anwar's, or Kit Siang's, or Mat Sabu's, or Guan Eng's. This was a victory of the people.

A victory of the Malaysian people.

ACKNOWLEDGEMENTS

Writing this book has been a massive undertaking for me because the subject is epic and I had to compel myself to finish writing it within three months in order to cater for the ongoing public interest in the unexpected and amazing event of Malaysians changing their government.

I would like to thank the following people for their help and support in making this book a reality:

Leslie Lim of Marshall Cavendish for broaching the idea to me of writing the book to be published by his company. We had worked together successfully on several titles previously so it sounded like a good idea to work together again. He was very enthusiastic about this book and about devising ways to promote it.

Lee Mei Lin for approving the project and participating in the early discussions, and providing encouragement throughout. We had worked on other books I wrote previously. It was great working with her yet again on this one.

Anita Teo, the editor assigned to manage the production of the book who had to tolerate my whims and eccentricities, and did so with genial conviviality and professional élan.

Benson Tan for designing the book and its arresting cover.

Other Marshall Cavendish staff members who have helped in one way or another, including Dennis Pook, Mindy Pang, She-reen Wong and Melvin Neo.

Lim Jack Kin for helping as my researcher. He was consistently prompt in answering my e-mails and WhatsApp messages, and ever willing to get

ACKNOWLEDGEMENTS

things done quickly whenever I asked. He often worked through the night, which made me wonder if he ever slept! Not once did he grumble when I pushed him hard.

My wife Choy Wan for putting up with my intensive schedule of work, work, work on the book from the time I woke up till I went to bed in the wee hours. I was most of the time a zombie in the house, but she was most understanding and accommodating about it. She calls the writing of this book my "labour of love" for my country. I couldn't have finished the work on time without her support and forbearance.

All my friends who had faith in me to say, "You can do it!"

ABOUT THE AUTHOR

KEE THUAN CHYE is an actor, playwright, stage director, journalist, political commentator and author who believes in the liberation of the Malaysian mind and looks forward to a better Malaysia. He advocates that a healthy disrespect for authority is always a good thing.

Photo by Lee Hock Aun

Also by Kee Thuan Chye:

No More Bullshit, Please, We're All Malaysians
Ask for No Bullshit, Get Some More!
The Elections Bullshit
Can We Save Malaysia, Please!
Unbelievably Stupid!
Unbelievably Stupid Too!
You Want This GOONvernment Ah?
March 8: The Day Malaysia Woke Up
March 8: Time for Real Change
1984 Here and Now (drama)
The Big Purge (drama)
*We Could **** You, Mr Birch* (drama)
Swordfish + Concubine (drama)
Old Doctors Never Fade Away (biography)
Just In So Many Words